AS I WAS SAYING

NYC
1/02

AS I WAS SAYING

Recollections and Miscellaneous Essays

V O L U M E   E   T H R E E   E

U R B A N I S T I C S

Colin Rowe

edited by Alexander Caragonne

The MIT Press   Cambridge, Massachusetts London, England

This book was set in Garamond 3 by Graphic Composition, Inc., and was printed and bound in the United States of America.

Library of Congress Cataloging-in-Publication Data

Rowe, Colin.
    As I was saying : recollections and miscellaneous essays / Colin
Rowe ; edited by Alexander Caragonne.
       p. cm.
    Includes bibliographical references and index.
    Contents: v. 1. Texas, pre-Texas, Cambridge. — v. 2. Cornelliana. — v. 3
Urbanistics
    ISBN 0-262-18167-3 (v. 1). — ISBN 0-262-18168-1 (v. 2.). — ISBN
0-262-18169-X   (v. 3)
    1. Architecture—Philosophy. 2. Architecture—Aesthetics. I. Caragonne,
Alexander. II. Title.
NA2500.R74 1995
720′.1—dc20   95-15191
                                                     CIP

Introduction   1

Cornell Studio Projects and Theses   5
  Center Binghamton
  Houston Satellite City
  Buffalo Waterfront
  Zurich Center
  South Amboy New Town
  The Figure/Grounds
  Bronx Development Project
  48th Street, West Side, Manhattan
  Manhattan Waterfront, West 14th Street
  South Baltimore Development
  Harvard/Charles River Design Project
  Upper Manhattan Development Strategy
  Marylebone District Development, London
  Providence: Capitol District Development Strategy
  Milwaukee Lakefront Design Competition
  Burlington, Vermont, Urbanization Strategy
  Turin: The Lingotto Site
  Warburg Institute, Pitigliano
  Boston Redevelopment
  Firenze: Fortezza da Basso, Stazione Santa Maria Novella,
    Cascine
  Three Projects for Rome: Largo Argentina, Quartiere dei Banchi,
    Piazza del Cinquecento
  Manhattan: Object/Fabric
  Chicago: A Plan for the Central Area

The New City: Architecture and Urban Renewal   87

Buffalo Waterfront   97

Nicollet Island, Minneapolis   121

Roma Interrotta   127

Rome: Piazza Augusto Imperatore   155

The Present Urban Predicament   165

Comments on the IBA Proposals   221

The Vanished City   243

A Student Project: Berlin   253

Urban Space   261

The Revolt of the Senses   271

"I Stood in Venice on the Bridge of Sighs"   285

Bibliotheca Alexandrina: An Also-Ran?   301

Interview: *Design Book Review*   319

Alvin Boyarsky: A Memory   331

Eulogy: Jim Stirling   341

Jim Stirling (1923–1992)   353

A Postscript on Alvin and Jim   359

Index of Names   361

AS I WAS SAYING

Introduction

It all began with John Reps. After observing the problems from which I was suffering with a group of bewildered graduate students whom I had inherited rather than selected and half of whom could scarcely speak English, it was he who said, one day early in 1963: "But why don't you forget about the title 'graduate architecture' and just call this outfit 'urban design'? You'd probably get a better quality of student that way."

Then, since in the general laissez-faire/laissez-aller of Cornell at that time—when graduate studies were regarded as something wholly extrinsic to undergraduate teaching—nobody seemed to mind very much, I felt compelled to make a highly positive response to this suggestion. I arranged that the outfit *should* be called urban design; and the first members of this new studio arrived in September 1963.

It was all very unpremeditated, very impromptu, and, slightly, desperate; but it was in this way that there was initiated a studio (*not* a workshop) which, with the usual vicissitudes and remarkably little financial support, survived until 1988, a studio whose members typically felt themselves to be representatives of an elite.

What may be imagined to be the content of this course is extensively written about in Colin Rowe and Fred Koetter, *Collage City,* and is presented in condensed form in the following pages as "The Present Urban Predicament"; but, perhaps, a little more should be said here. The studio was never tolerant of the urbanistic proposals of Le Corbusier and Ludwig Hiberseimer. It was never able seriously to regard either Townscape, as proposed by *The Architectural Review,* or Science Fiction as propounded by Archigram and others. If not conservative, its general tone was radical middle of the road. It believed in dialectic, in a dialectic between the present and the past, between the empirical and the ideal, between the contingent and the abstract. It believed in the virtues and the values of Synthetic Cubism. Simultaneously it was classical/anticlassical. It preferred what it called "Hadrianic disarray" to the classical set piece. In terms of specifics, presented with the plans of Vaux-le-Vicomte and Chantilly, invariably it opted for Chantilly. Its ideal was a mediation between the city of Modern architecture—a void with objects—and the historical city—a solid with voids. It also displayed some sort of passion, aided and guided by Wayne Copper, for the irregular and palatial megastructures of small princely German cities. And this is what, in its origins, it was all about.

It was never concerned with the dispossessed and the poor, nor with the affluent and the rich; but it presumed that all would benefit from a good gestalt. The word *contextualist,* so frequently used nowadays, probably first erupted in Cornell studio conversation—always very loud—between Tom Schumacher and Stuart Cohen in 1966.

In spite of hostility to Le Corbusier and Ludwig Hilberseimer, in its early years the studio was still accustomed to long skinny buildings; but this *Zeilenbau* fixation seems absolutely to have disappeared as a result of the revolutions of Paris 1968/Cornell 1969. But if Paris 1968 must be one of the most crucial twentieth-century dates and the Cornell scene a year later must be an entirely minor affair, I should still say that when, after a few months in Rome at the American Academy, I returned to Ithaca in January 1970, it was to an entirely different body of students. A great cultural event had occurred; but the students were not at all hostile. Simply they had become determined that *Zeilenbauen* were not their *thing;* and, from then on, it was to be trad city with trad city blocks.

A big *renversement?* But of course; and, of course, it wasn't all that traumatic. Although myself quite liked the *Zeilenbau* as presented by the Manica Lunga of the Quirinale and the Hofgarten of the Munich Residenz, there was no reason to remain excessively attached to these prototypes; and so we continued with some change of style and something of that attrition of quality which is always to be associated with a revolutionary aftermath.

In fact the early 1970s were far from happy years. Franz Oswald, who had been a member of the faculty from 1966 to 1968, left for Zurich and the ETH, and, in 1971, the U.D. Studio presumed to be a focus of formalist infection (?), there began a purge of those who might be associated with it: Alan Chimacoff and Roger Sherwood, who were "allowed to go" in 1972, Fred Koetter, who left in 1973, and Klaus Herdeg, who quit of his own accord in 1972. But, oh, those academic purges which are so divisive and which leave their survivors in an isolation far less than splendid! And this particular purge left me with a very small budget (for that matter a very small salary), no graduate assistant (previously I had had two), and only two effective faculty allies: Michael Dennis, new but tenacious, and Jerry Wells, who had himself been the victim of an attempted purge in 1970.

Thus, apart from the problem of post-revolutionary exhaustion, there is abundant reason for my lack of documentation for the early 1970s—no assistants, no money. However, towards 1980, things began to look better; and, from that time onwards, there ensued a phase of what, I think, was renewed brilliance.

In 1983, *The Cornell Journal of Architecture,* edited by Blake Middleton, published a highly perceptive issue (no. 2) on the U.D. Studio with an exceptional article, "Conjectures on Urban Form" by Steven Hurtt, which, I must confess, is a little too sophisticated for my complete understanding. But it is from that documentation of the U.D. Studio that a lot of what is written here is derived.

However, all this was almost too late for me. In my American moods I regard Upstate New York almost as much as I regard Texas; but, both by revolutions and purges, I had become disenchanted and disabused. I had come to spend increasingly less time at Cornell and more and more in Italy. More or less I had become *italianizzato:* Rome for half a year in '69, Rome in '77 and '78, Rome in '79, Rome in '80 to '81, Venice in '82, Florence for six months in both '86 and '87, Rome for six months in '88, Rome for the whole year in '89, and, as a result of all this, when I had almost forgotten about Upstate, there was begun the last phase of the U.D. Studio. This was mostly accomplished by Notre Dame graduates— those whom I had known in Rome in '80–'81 and who had followed me to Cornell.

There now follows, first, a display of studio projects and theses executed between 1963 and 1988.

Cornell Studio Projects and Theses

The remarks which follow are for the most part excerpted from Blake Middleton's publication in The Cornell Journal of Architecture, *no. 2 (1983), and these are signed D.B.M. After 1983 and where I have thought it desirable to introduce further remarks these are in italic type and signed C.R.*

The following design projects are from a collection of over 150 first-year projects and second-year theses completed in the graduate program of the Urban Design Studio. Dating from 1963, these examples represent different problem types and some basic design strategies; and the reader may note in this work some patterns in both the architectural elements used and the kinds of sites chosen for study. Most projects are not fully documented due to the limitations of space. The illustrations and accompanying descriptions should, however, give the reader a reasonable idea of the intent and scope of each design.

The first-year studio projects have a distinct pedagogic focus, often using a specific site condition as the basic parameter: waterfront sites or impacted grid collision areas are the most recurrent. But other problem types have been used, including large scale "mapping" problems (the formal relationships of whole city districts to each other), urban garden design (contour and spaces made from *verdure* instead of buildings), typology problems (such as tower versus perimeter block) and, more recently, design speculations and fantasies on historic city plans ("Roma Interrotta" and its spin-offs).

Contrary to the first-year projects, which are inspired by a professorial bias and curiosity, the second-year design theses often reflect the student's interest in a specific city. The site selected for the year-long thesis might be the "home town" or its emotional equivalent—a visual and experiential memory at once familiar to the student and yet, after the previous year of study, something different. The site under consideration would generally be seen as part of an urbanistic macrocosm (in both form and history); connections and relationships to other parts of the city are explored first, then a more detailed examination and its proposal are developed for a specific area.

D.B.M.

Center Binghamton
Erwin P. Nigg (1963–1964)

One of the earliest studio projects, this scheme demonstrates the initial concentration on Modern architectural building types and articulation. The program includes a mixed use residential building wrapping around a theater as part of a new civic center. The theater is oriented on axis to the old county courthouse and city offices, establishing a formal link with these civic structures. A complex section for the apartment building is proposed to facilitate connections to an urban square and parking below. The scheme retains many of the Modern architectural attributes of separation of pedestrian and

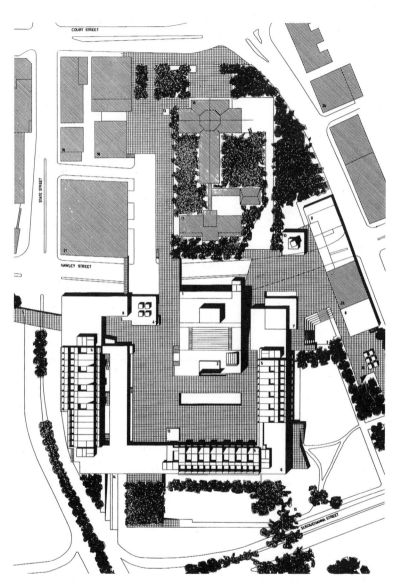

1. Center Binghamton, proposed site plan by Erwin P. Nigg.

vehicular movements, but at the same time focuses the apartments on a central space around public structures, much like European piazzas.

D.B.M.

Houston Satellite City
Irving Phillips (1965)

This design proposal for the development of a new "satellite city" outside of Houston, Texas on a large undeveloped forest site was submitted for consideration, along with a housing analysis, to the city of Houston in 1965. Situated next to a river that would be dammed to produce a small lakefront, the scheme envisions a new town developed perpendicularly between a highway connection to Houston and the waterfront. A gridded matrix of housing and streets is proposed: the housing ranges from high-density towers and row houses to low-density freestanding houses; the streets range from smaller access roads that wind through the forest to larger axial arterial connections to the major centers. All these elements are hierarchically arranged both in scale and use. The center of organizational gravity sits between the civic and shopping center along the highway and the clubs and the recreational center along the waterfront.

Although the scheme has many aspects of "ideal city" planning and certain English garden city precedents, it is provocative in both its composition and conception of the forest as *poché,* out of which streets and public park are carved, providing a conceptual infill of anonymous texture like that found in large cities.

D.B.M.

This project represented a major breakthrough. Not really a satellite city, it is rather a superior suburban subdivision located at an inconvenient distance from downtown Houston. In fact it represents the development of a piece of property in which its designer's family had substantial financial interests.

C.R.

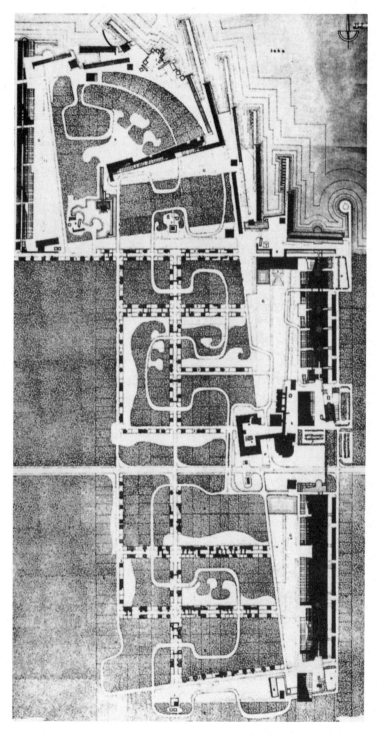

2. Houston: satellite city, proposed site plan by Irving Phillips.

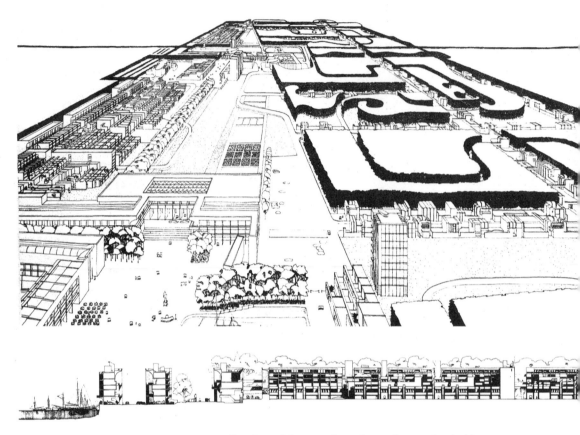

3. Houston: satellite city, aerial perspective and waterfront section, looking east.

Buffalo Waterfront
Group Project (1965–1966)

Buffalo Waterfront is the first of what the French would probably call the grands projets *to be associated with the U.D. Studio; and, to me, it still appears to be the best, the most extensive, the most conclusive. It represented an early super-climax for the studio. It was grand and its orchestration was beyond the capacities of that date (1966); and it is hence, and since it became an exhibition in 1969, that I have shifted it there from the category of studio projects.*

C.R.

Zurich Center
Franz Oswald (1966)

This thesis addresses a particular urban development problem in Zurich, Switzerland: the contradictory expansion tendencies along and across the river Limmat versus the lakefront. The center of Zurich has expanded continually from east to west, starting in the Middle Ages, shifting to the Bahnhofstrasse with the introduction of the railroad in the nineteenth century, and finally bridging the Sihl River in the present century. Recognizing the need for expansion in 1966, this scheme proposes a redevelopment within the center of the city on land currently public (old rail tracks and military barracks).

The primary design strategy is to reestablish the traditional urban links to the Limmat River and both sides of the Sihl River. A secondary and preexisting link along the fortification canal from the Sihl River to the lakefront is reinforced, enhancing the centralization of the medieval district. A new *Bahnhof* becomes the major linking device between the hill slope to the west and the Limmat River, consolidating the major transportation systems while enhancing the existing *Platz.* This "super-block" or composite form-building is the interface between highway, parking, and rail and tramway service for the city. The various spatial fields along the Sihl River are reconnected by means of reflexive spatial tactics, such as the apsidal building and the bridge and gate conditions.

D.B.M.

68

4. Zurich Center, existing plan (left) and proposed site plan by Franz Oswald.

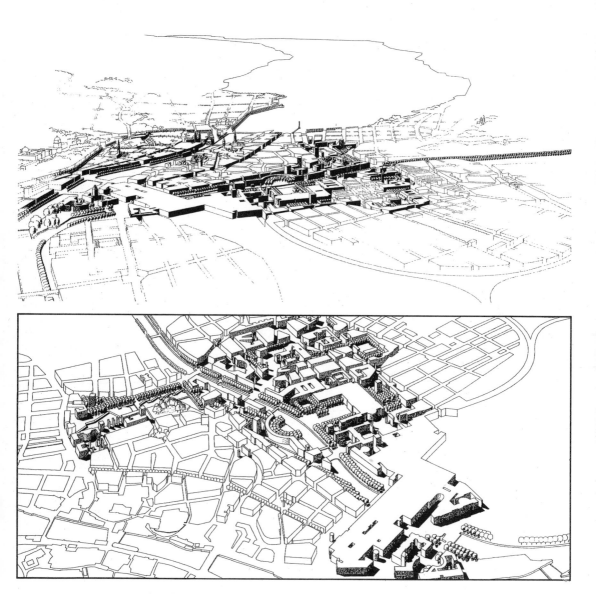

5. Zurich Center, aerial perspectives.

Cornell Studio Projects and Theses

Franz Oswald had come to the program after working for Oswald Matthias Ungers, who, at that time, displayed great intelligence and virtuosity. Particularly brilliant here, I think, is the capacity to cause a Zeilenbau *building in the process of development along the Sihl River to assume the form of the Royal Crescent at Bath. I regard this as a very Ungerian move; and, though I am sure that the volume of the extended* Bahnhof *must have become far too big, I have not seen planning of this sophistication associated with any of the work of IBA in Berlin.*

C.R.

South Amboy New Town
Tom Schumacher (1966)

Posited as a new town on a site in South Amboy, New Jersey, this thesis was one of the first to attempt a total fabrication of urban texture on an open site. The hierarchy of traditional open spaces— ordered squares and disordered fields—has been reversed in this scheme: the regularity of less important spaces is countered by the irregularity of more important ones. Civic structures and public functions occur in the larger irregular spaces. This is meant to sponsor great activity of spatial action in the specific spaces designed for such purposes. Housing systems have been invented to form a grid matrix, or field of blocks, with a hierarchy of public to private use. The housing blocks are also intended to be a modification of Corbusian *redents,* made denser and with a more elaborate section. The notion of transparency, or overlapping grids, is intended to minimize functional and regional edges and their separation from the centers of the overall site.

D.B.M.

Steven Hurtt, in "Conjectures on Urban Form" (The Cornell Journal of Architecture, no. 2 {1983}), publishes this plan alongside Le Corbusier's proposals for Antwerp; and I find this a very gratifying opposition to contemplate. Though much alike the two proposals are very different.

C.R.

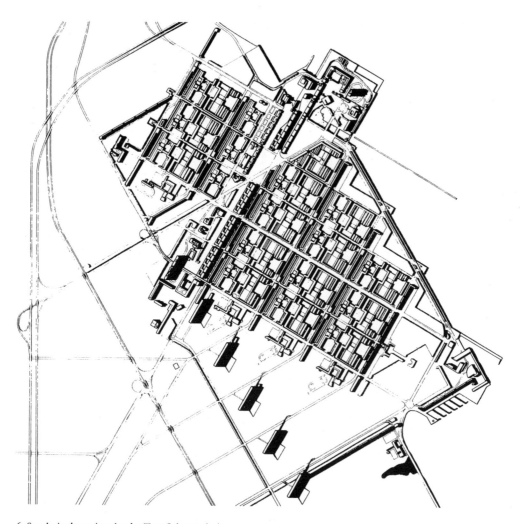

6. South Amboy, site plan by Tom Schumacher.

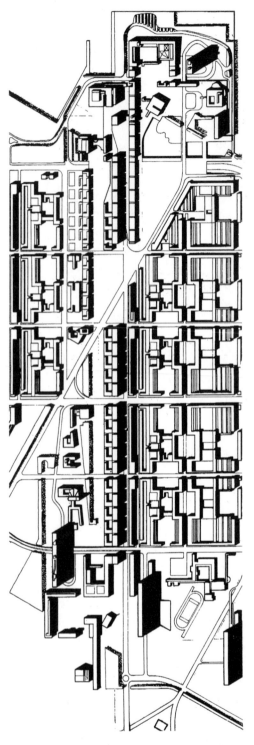

7. South Amboy, town center and housing. Detail.

The Figure/Grounds
Wayne Copper (Thesis, 1967)

Wayne Copper develops an argument for using figure/ground plans
as an abstract representational technique for urban form analysis
and design. Describing the conceptual reversal of buildings and
spaces, either of which can be highly defined or ambiguous, the
author demonstrates the interdependency of each, offering, through
these plans, a perception of the urbanistic whole. This method finds
certain antecedents and inspiration in gestalt images, the graphic hierarchy of Nolli's 1748 plan of Rome, and Sitte's plan analyses and
design proposals for Vienna.

  Copper's investigations in the form of drawn plates con-
firmed for the Cornell Urban Design Studio many of the formal
problems of Modern architecture in the traditional city context.
Written in 1967, often referred to yet never before published, this
graduate thesis had a tremendous impact on subsequent studio projects. Most of the drawings are of pre-Modern city plans. Drawn in
black and white, they illustrate the usual configuration of figural
spaces within a dense and randomly defined field of buildings. Modern city plans, such as Le Corbusier's Antwerp project, are included
in the study too, and they show the general modernist tendency to
polarize figural buildings in undefined voids.

                    D.B.M.

*Wayne Copper's thesis—a collection of highly idiosyncratic city plans with
comments—is of the same date (1967) as those of Franz Oswald and Tom
Schumacher; and, working with him, I discovered how lamentable is the defi-
ciency of city planning documentation in major libraries—at least in the
United States. He worked in the Cornell Library (not so bad), in the New
York Public Library (not so good), and in the Library of Congress (could be
better); but, extremely often, we had to rely on the plans—almost a subject
for romantic scrutiny—provided by Karl Baedeker.*

0   500 m.

Wiesbaden
The Cornell Journal of Architecture

8. Figure/ground drawings by Wayne Copper: Wiesbaden and Palais Royal (figure/ground reversal).

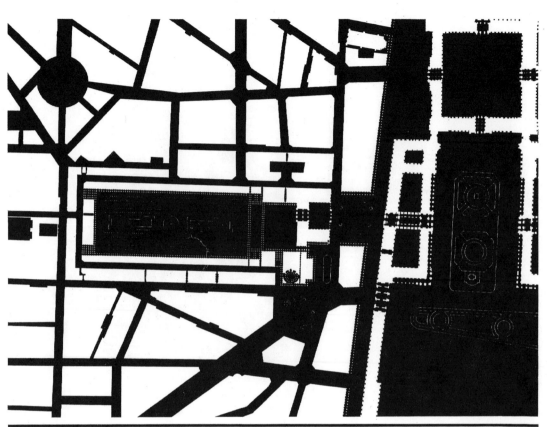

0   125 ft.

Palais Royale
The Cornell Journal of Architecture

Cornell Studio Projects and Theses

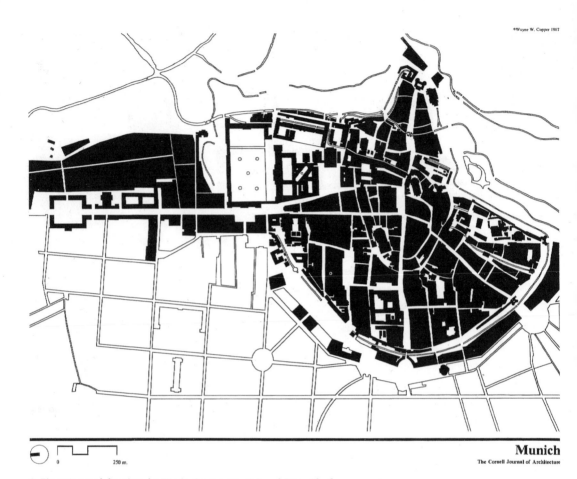

©Wayne W. Copper 1967

0   250 m.

Munich
The Cornell Journal of Architecture

9. Figure/ground drawings by Wayne Copper: Munich and Düsseldorf.

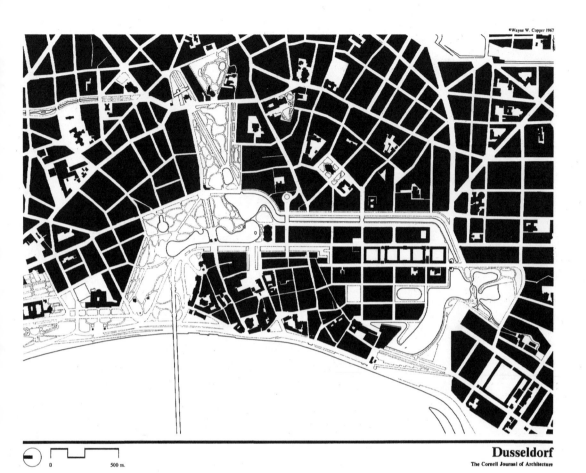

0   500 m.

Dusseldorf
The Cornell Journal of Architecture

Cornell Studio Projects and Theses

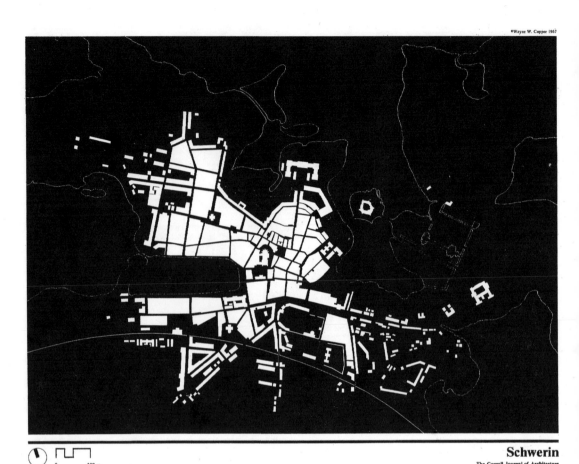

Schwerin
The Cornell Journal of Architecture

10. Figure/ground drawings by Wayne Copper: Schwerin (figure/ground reversal) and St.-Dié (1945).

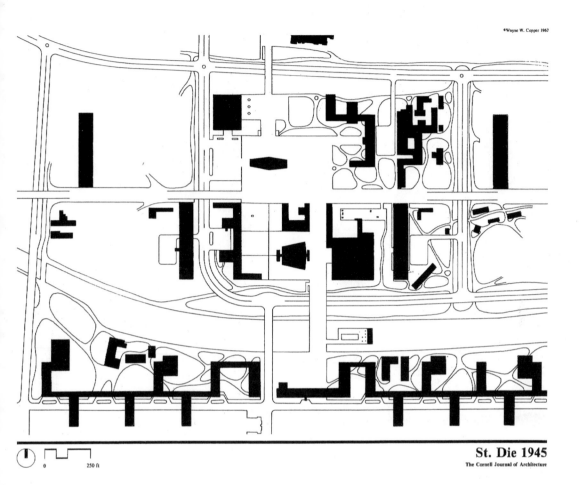

0   250 ft

St. Die 1945
The Cornell Journal of Architecture

Cornell Studio Projects and Theses

About Wayne Copper's plan of Wiesbaden Steven Hurtt writes:

Thinking of the city as a formal gestalt has been the most continuing underlying theme in studio procedure. Reducing the complex city to black and white (figure/ground) drawings which polarize mass and space, is the principal tool of analysis and design. Copper's figure/ground plan of Wiesbaden has become almost a symbol of the studio because inherent in the plan are the polar opposites of urban form. . . . Half the city is predominantly solid with spaces carved out of it; the other half continuous open space with a texture of object buildings; urbs, exurbs; thesis, anti-thesis; traditional city, modern city; here uniquely synthesized as a single duality.

But how well I know all this; and my own taste for gestalt confrontations must clearly derive from Robert Slutzky in Texas, meaning, before that, from Josef Albers at Yale and from Johannes Itten in the very early years of the Weimar Bauhaus. But how often I have been terribly bored by that eternal black and white which so much dazzles the eyes, and how often I have hoped for the pink and green of earlier, French interpretations. But this was scarcely to be of any avail. Simply my studio seemed to have compelled itself to the austerities of black and white.

Now the figure/ground technique will lend itself to the description of cities mostly on flat sites and, mostly, with a ceiling of about five stories; and, apart from that, it doesn't work.

Nevertheless I maintain a regret that Wayne, who is reclusive and shy, could never be persuaded to publish his book of plans.

C.R.

Bronx Development Project
Jon Michael Schwarting, Arthur Valk (1966)

This studio project is for a site on a hillslope near the Major Deegan Expressway in the upper Bronx, New York. Both schemes retain some buildings already on the site. New and higher density apartment buildings are proposed with open, semi-public spaces on the

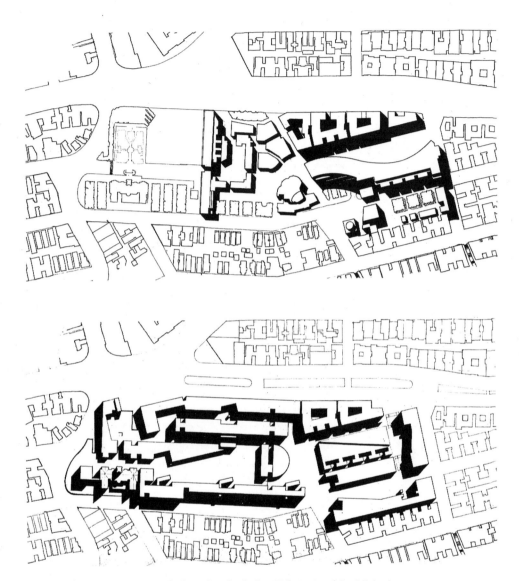

11. Bronx development project, shadow plans by Arthur Valk (top) and Jon Michael Schwarting (bottom).

interior of the block. Each design has a garden and terrace development with assorted parking facilities below grade. There is an attempt to create a higher density housing than what exists without destroying the immediate scale of the surrounding neighborhood. The Schwarting scheme proposes linear-type buildings, divided laterally like the row houses near the site; the Valk design envisions a larger, curvilinear apartment building to open up the land for terraces to the north. Both designs are inherently critical of the anonymous slab structures to the south of the site, which are aspatial and have no well-defined public realm.

D.B.M.

48th Street, West Side, Manhattan
Steven Peterson (1969)

The focus of this studio problem is on a new 48th Street spine, proposed by the city to revitalize the West Side, connecting Times Square and the theater district to the passenger ship terminals on the Hudson River. The solution envisaged an expanded site accommodating a new link to the West Side Highway, a diagrammatic extension to the south (the "pier" housing), and a new convention center just north of 42nd Street. The entire composition is a study of how the Manhattan grid might be translated from an orientation perpendicular to the river edge, into one parallel to it, while also accommodating the free forms of the highway, river edge, and convention center. Public spaces framed by repetitive rhythms of buildings and walls provide a contrast and setting for more fluid forms.

D.B.M.

Manhattan Waterfront, West 14th Street
Arthur McDonald (Thesis, 1973)

Because the harbor of Manhattan Island is no longer a great port where cargo ships unload, the docks of the waterfront and adjacent areas have great potential for development. The possibility of a phys-

12. Bronx development project, aerial views of models by Arthur Valk (top) and Jon Michael Schwarting (bottom).

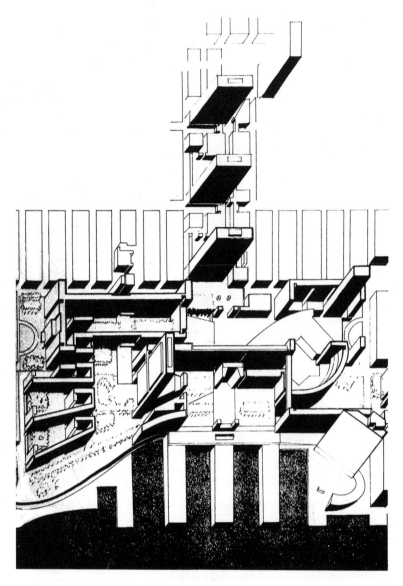

13. 48th Street, Manhattan, project by Steven Peterson: axonometric, model, and sketch.

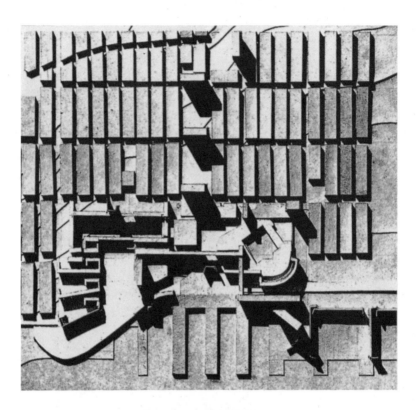

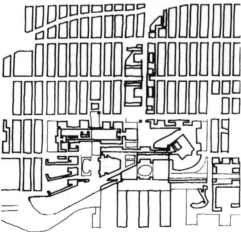

Cornell Studio Projects and Theses

14. Manhattan waterfront, existing site plan (top) and proposed site plan by Arthur McDonald.

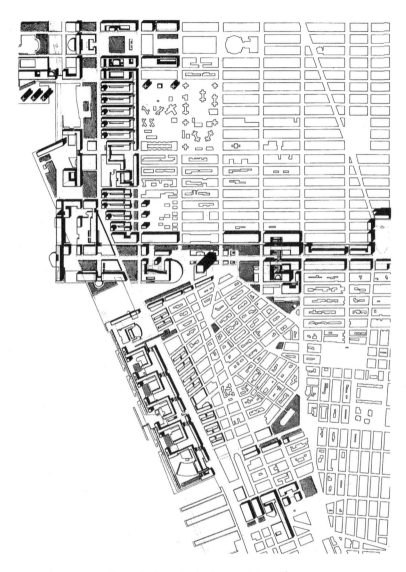

15. Manhattan waterfront, shadow plan by Arthur McDonald.

Cornell Studio Projects and Theses

ical link between the city's dense internal structure and its open waterfront edge is suggested at 14th and 23rd streets. The complex site conditions at the end of 14th Street become the inspiration in this thesis to (1) complete the major street grid of Manhattan, (2) accommodate the change in direction of the pier line edge (the approximate line of landfill), (3) provide a public transportation center with connections to the center of the city, and (4) open a direct sequence between the waterfront and the interior of the island.

The primary emphasis in this design is on the resolution of the grid shift on the west side of Manhattan, centered about 14th Street. The resolution is accomplished by proposing a large void that would provide a visual connection into the island center and at the same time establish a more appropriate southern terminus for Eighth Avenue. This scheme also proposes an extension of the island edge, continuing the landfill strategy for the new Battery Park City to the south. On this new fill a series of public park areas are located, varying from large landscaped spaces to linear promenades.

The gridded field of West Greenwich Village is currently disrupted by Seventh Avenue. Its proposed closure reinforces the current traffic circulation plan. Seventh Avenue terminates at Central Park at its northern end. It is not one of the through avenues of Manhattan. Therefore a southern terminus at 14th Street is feasible and might define Seventh Avenue as an internal link for local traffic, as well as allowing West Greenwich Village to reestablish its uniformity.

D.B.M.

South Baltimore Development
Kaya Arikoglu (Thesis, 1976)

The objectives of this design thesis for South Baltimore include developing a variety of waterfront conditions around the peninsula that would facilitate transportation links of rail, shipping, and highways to the center of Baltimore to the north, with a concomitant buildup of high-density, low-rise housing within the boundaries of

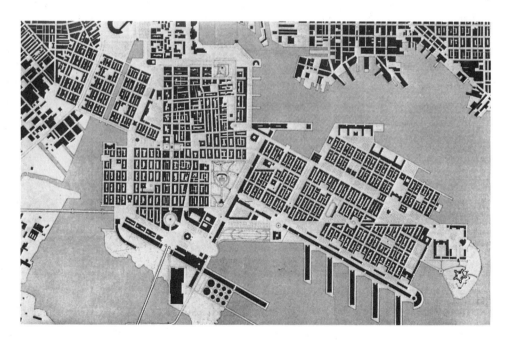

16. South Baltimore development, existing site plan (top) and proposed site plan by
Kaya Arikoglu.

Cornell Studio Projects and Theses

waterfront edges. The general design strategy has been to establish a ring-like boulevard about the center of the development (marked by the cruciform square) that sponsors extensions of streets and avenues to the east and to the west and a commercial waterfront zone to the south. A two-pronged street connection to Ft. McHenry is one of these extensions; the field of housing along a Middle Branch canal is another. The current rail yards are modified or removed to the commercial warehouses along the waterfront. The resultant open area is developed as an extension of the already existing housing. The new fields of the residential districts are polycentric, finding specific buildings and public spaces located at their edges or centers. Some of the primary north-south connections (Charles Center with South Baltimore) find specific termini along the waterfront on the southern edge.

D.B.M.

A hiatus or marking time in the studio. Zeilenbauen *remain persistent though reduced. However, city blocks have become decisive.*

C.R.

Harvard/Charles River Design Project
Douglas Bryant, David Griffin, Charles Graves (1977)

The open site by the Charles River in Cambridge is used as a problem for resolving the scale differentiation of surrounding building textures and connections from a major inner city space (Harvard Square) to the riverfront. Bounded by freestanding wood and brick structures to the west, Harvard dormitory quadrangles to the east, and four to five story commercial buildings to the north, the site is located in a dense and active part of the city. The John F. Kennedy Library is included as part of the condition, forcing each designer to accept and operate with it in his proposal.

The studio problem focused on more detailed resolutions for grid collisions and textural scale problems than some earlier projects. The schemes have an open space toward the river and some

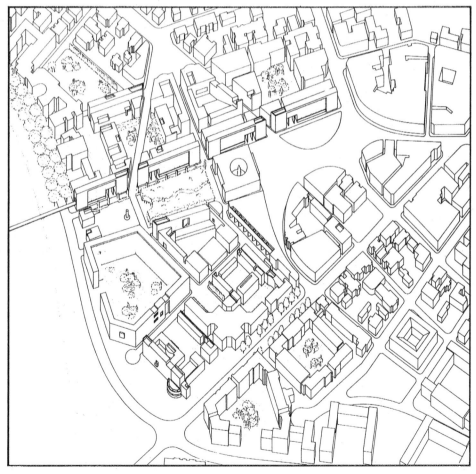

17. Harvard/Charles River design project, proposed site plan and axonometric by Douglas Bryant.

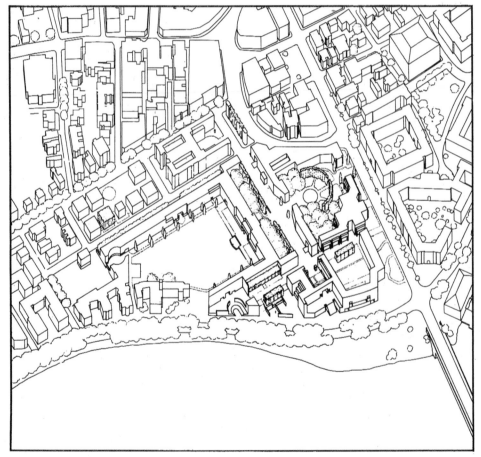

18. Harvard/Charles River design project, proposed site plan and axonometric by David Griffin.

semblance of a quadrangle organization. Each uses a variety of modern and traditional building types, as well as an emphasis on landscape elements for some of the difficult open-joint conditions.

D.B.M.

Upper Manhattan Development Strategy
Michael Manfredi (Thesis, 1978)

This study centers on a semi-vacant area currently owned by the City of New York and situated on the northwestern bank of the Harlem River. Two readings of the context prefaced the design solution:

A.   An attenuated development along the waterfront would make reference to Tenth Avenue as an important datum.

B.   The potential reading of Broadway as a spatially significant sequence tended to support a highly figural scheme.

The proposed solution has a centralized sequence and an orthogonal development along the waterfront. Included are the following components:

1.   The primary sequence links the Harlem River, Broadway, Isham Park, and Inwood Hill Park. This sequence varies perceptually from a clearly defined residential space on the Harlem River through a thick commercial zone at Broadway and on to the larger Isham Park. Finally, this sequence terminates in Inwood Hill.

2.   The gridded residential zone along the Harlem waterfront is intended as a foil for the complex topography of the region. It also reconstitutes a pattern along the waterfront suggested by existing buildings and streets.

3.   The scheme completes the curiously irresolute diagonal of 215th Street.

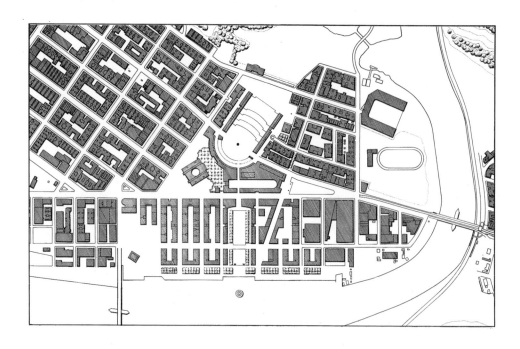

URBANISTICS

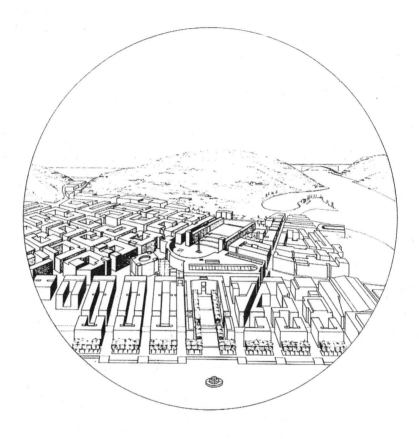

19. Upper Manhattan development strategy: proposed plan, site plan, and perspective by Michael Manfredi.

4.   The need to locate a highly identifiable community center
        led to the rotated positioning of a square freestanding build-
        ing on an axis with Sherman Avenue and to a raised garden
        connecting the center with the main commercial space off
        Broadway.

D.B.M.

This very succinct project seems to initiate a wholly new sequence.

C.R.

Marylebone District Development, London
Steven Fong (1979)

There are many residual pockets of land in London. The site selected for this thesis, a "backyard" to Regent's Park, is one of
these. The area is located over the rail yards at Marylebone Station,
bounded by a canal to the north and Regent's Park to the east. Pro-
ceeding from a study of the whole city of London, the eighteenth-
century estate, with its identity, centrality, and autonomy, was used
as a model for the new localized neighborhood. At the same time,
modern requirements of vehicular and public continuity were considered.
        The solution works from a centralized square of housing;
its grid alignment oscillates among the surrounding gridded fields
to establish its identity as a distinct development. At the same
time, different building types surround this centralized field to tie
it into the immediate context; terraces facing the canal (a modern
equivalent of the Nash prototypes across the park), a reflexive, composite building to the south, and anonymous block buildings to the
east reinforce these connections.

D.B.M.

*It is perhaps unfortunate that this extremely elegant thesis failed to incorpo-
rate more developed proposals along the line of the Regent's Canal.*

C.R.

20. Marylebone district development, London, proposed figure/ground and plan by Steven Fong.

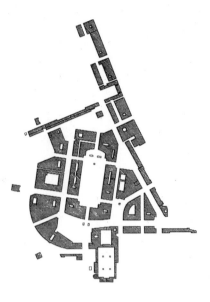

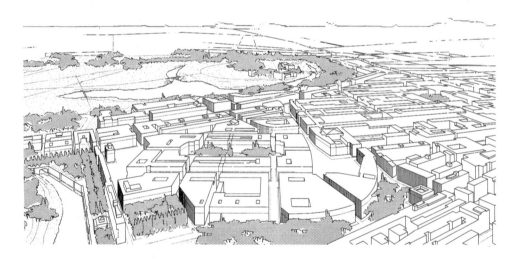

21. Marylebone district development, London, detail of plan and perspective.

43

Providence: Capitol District Development Strategy
D. B. Middleton (1980)

In a partially abandoned and totally non-honorific site fronting the Rhode Island State Capitol in Providence, this thesis proposes a restoration of appropriate landscape and architectural elements while simultaneously accommodating demands for new office and residential space. Conflicting problems of rail, watercourses, highways, and topographic edges all converge at this central location.

    The final design strategy for the site consists of three major, simultaneous, tactical operations:

1.   The isolation of the Capitol Hill area as a "citadel" with strongly defined edges and center. Buildings and *verdure* are used in a gridded field with alternating rhythms of orthogonal and irregular edges, the bulk of the Capitol dominating and controlling the entire arrangement of loose and ordered pieces. A proposal initiated in 1925 to extend the axis from the State House down to the central business district was used to visually and conceptually connect the city proper with the Capitol.

2.   The expansion of a waterway and park system as both binder and separator of the various gridded fields of College Hill, the central business district, and Capitol Hill. The park becomes the focus for the different districts as local edge conditions respond directly to it through the inclusion of a ring road and street embankment.

3.   The consolidation of existing fields by connections and in-fill. The lower edge of College Hill along Canal Street is strengthened with new housing and other structures; Kennedy Plaza is made a clearly orthogonal and impacted space, marking a center for the central business district field.

D.B.M.

Cornell Studio Projects and Theses

22. Providence, Rhode Island, Capitol District development strategy, existing figure/ground (left) and proposed figure/ground by Blake Middleton.

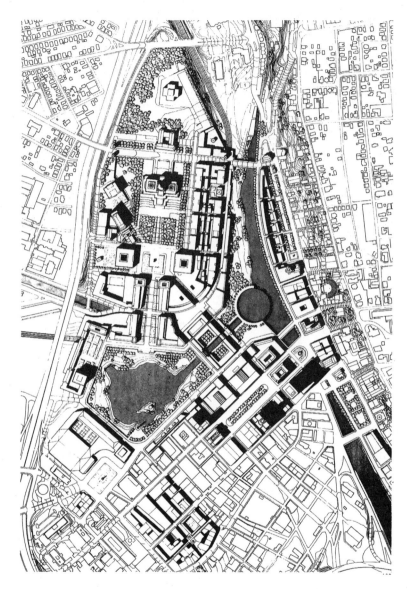

23. Providence Capitol District, site plan by Blake Middleton.

Cornell Studio Projects and Theses

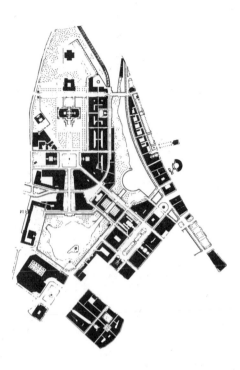

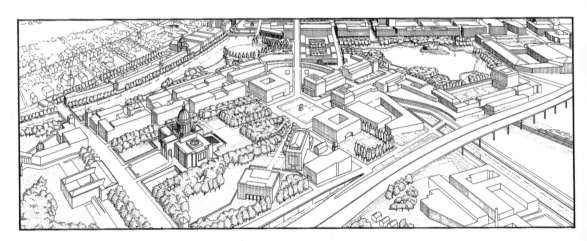

24. Providence Capitol District, infill plan and perspective by Blake Middleton.

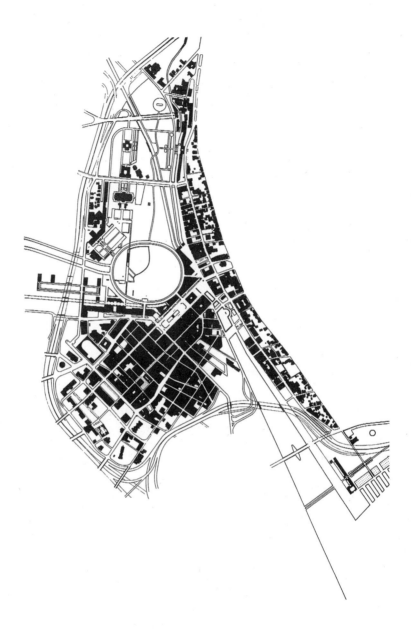

25. Providence Capitol District, earlier proposed site plan by Joel Bostick.

Cornell Studio Projects and Theses

This project should be compared with the much more perfunctory solution of the same site made by Joel Bostick in 1973 (fig. 25). Middleton's thesis appears to belong to the Manfredi-Fong sequence.

C.R.

Milwaukee Lakefront Design Competition
(1980)

This does not strictly belong to the category of studio projects, though it might well have done so. Instead it was a presentation sponsored by Lee Hodgden in which, apart from myself, two members of the studio, Douglas Fredericks and Derek Tynan, participated.

The site comprises 176 acres, divided by a bridge approach and freeway ramps. It consists mainly of a large landfill area along the lakeshore. As Milwaukee has a troubled economy and a declining population, there is proposed a modest amount of new construction in strategic places, combined with an extensive new waterfront park on most of the filled area.

At the lake end of the principal downtown street, a new city square is proposed. This arcaded square serves office and commercial purposes. An extensive terrace with parterres mediates between the commercial square and the lower level of the lakeside park. This terrace overlooks a new yacht basin and provides access to the War Memorial Art Museum. While the park contains many naturalistic areas and elements, its vast extent is stitched together by a formal axis parallel to the water. At one end of this axis is placed an artificial mound on which is to be built a "Bavarian Village" (something to do with ethnic origins and beer?), and this caprice is inspired by the reconstructed Spanish Village of the Barcelona Exposition of 1929.

A deteriorating commercial area is rehabilitated. A certain amount of luxury housing is added with a canal or basin supporting marina town houses.

The competition jury (professionals Garrett Eckbo, Rai Okomoto, Robert Venturi) characterized this design as influenced by the Beaux-Arts tradition; and we are happy that they recognized so much. For the indictment that we wish to revive the Beaux-Arts is correct in the sense that, while planning the pragmatic renewal of the city, we also wish to invoke the spirit and breadth of vision which once animated such great American urban planners as Daniel Burnham and Frederick Law Olmsted.

As I remember, the text is the product of Lee Hodgden, one of the most consistent of Alvar Aalto's devotees and equally devoted to the contributions made by Buckminster Fuller. But, then and incidentally—shades of the début de siècle *and the wildest of Wests—Lee also enjoys the distinction of being some sort of great-nephew of Buffalo Bill!*

C.R.

Burlington, Vermont, Urbanization Strategy
Craig Nealy (1981)

Burlington, Vermont is situated on a waterfront lying in ruins since the end of that phase of the industrial era that it served. The city has a central business district containing fragments of an Enlightenment-era gridded plan that contains a wide range of architectural building types, from single-family dwellings to perimeter block structures. The lack of connection and sequential 'dialogue' between center and waterfront was further exacerbated by the demolition of twenty-two acres in the city center and a partially completed zone of object-like buildings constructed in the 1970s. These buildings usurp the order of the area without providing a coherent replacement for it.

This design thesis plays on the contrapuntal relationship between open landscape and ordered urban development, a condition of great potential in cities like Burlington. The basic strategy for the inner city is the insertion of a series of new 'liner' buildings connecting the disparate modern office buildings and organizing them

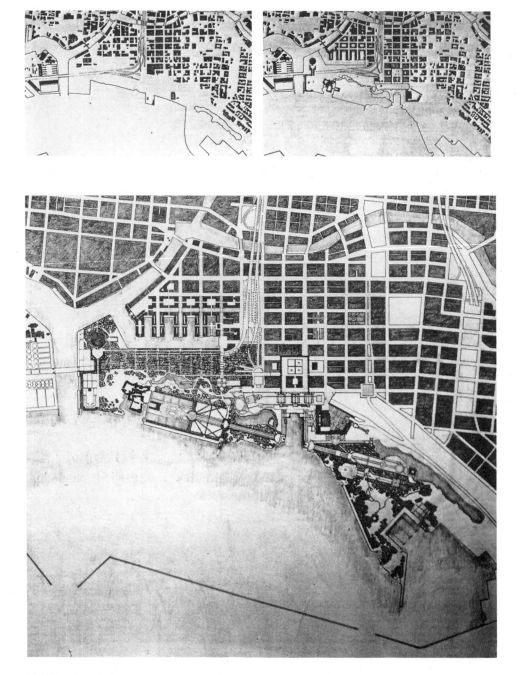

26. Milwaukee lakefront, existing figure/ground (top left) and proposed figure/ground (top right); site plan.

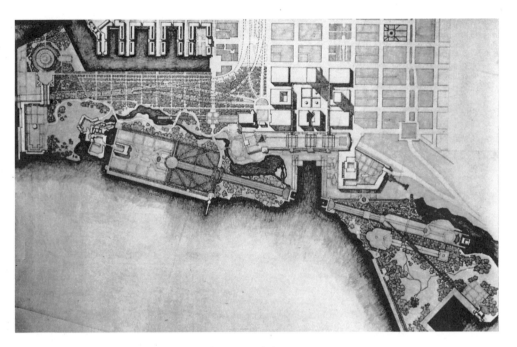

27. Milwaukee lakefront, extended context.

into a set of distinct spaces. These in turn are linked to the waterfront, where a new landscaped park with urban villas overlooking
the lakefront is proposed. This particular thesis from the Cornell
Studio places great emphasis on researching potential facade conditions for urban spaces, seeking to define succinct relationships between the 'old' Modern architecture and new structures.

D.B.M.

*This is a project for which, when it was produced, I had very little admira-
tion. Was this because of a skepticism about Vermont or because of the PoMo
quality of so many buildings? In any case I have long since relinquished
both inhibitions, and I have come to regard the sequence of apartment houses
(disguised as villas) along the lakefront to be a supremely intelligent, and
possible, proposition. By this time the former intellectual heat has left the studio; but, within its terms, an interesting and casual sensibility has taken its
place.*

C.R.

Cornell Studio Projects and Theses

28. Burlington, Vermont, urbanization strategy, existing figure/ground (top) and proposed figure/ground by Craig Nealy.

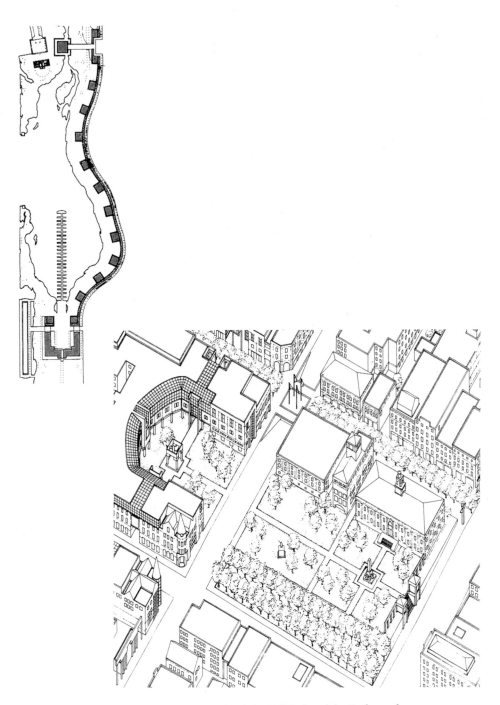

29. Burlingon, axonometric of City Hall Park and detail of waterfront.

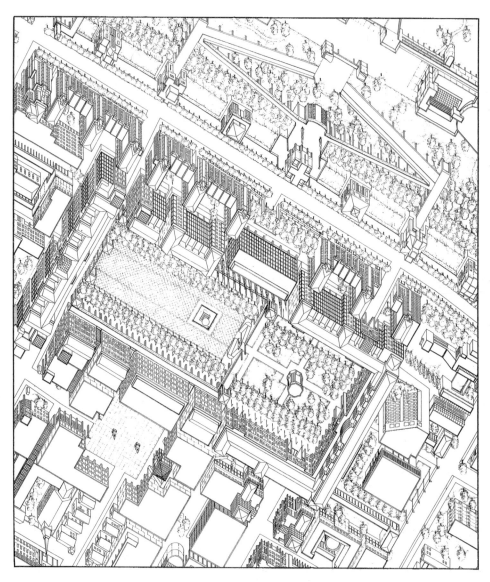

30. Burlington, axonometric of Chittenden Terrace and environs.

31. Facing page: Burlington, axonometric of Marina Square Housing and Club; perspective view, Battery Street South.

URBANISTICS

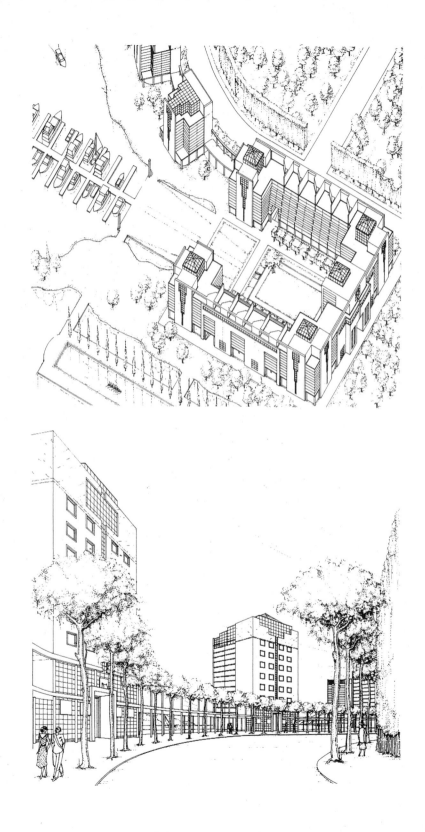

32. Turin, the Lingotto site, existing figure/ground.

Turin: The Lingotto Site
Jeffery Klug (1984)

The project for the Lingotto site in Turin dates from the fall of 1984 and may be considered a commentary upon the limited competition of the previous year. Most entries to this competition were concerned with only the FIAT factory and its very immediate vicinity; but it was an objective of the studio to address a more considered revision of the surrounding areas. Thus what emerged was the possibility of a direct relationship between the banks of the river and the site left by the existing railroad yards. Perhaps the better solutions, of which this is one, avoided preoccupations with an overall geometrical consistency and envisaged the area as a condition of overlapping or converging fields.

C.R.

Warburg Institute, Pitigliano
Paolo Berdini (Thesis, 1985)

Paolo Berdini's project makes no pretension to even the most tenuous relations with empirical reality. But let us suppose that, by a bizarre decision, the Warburg Institute has chosen to establish a secondary headquarters in that provocative landscape which extends itself northwest of the Lago di Bolsena. And could *this ever happen? The likeliness is more than extremely remote. However, how much* does *this matter? For, in the format of a town in which Nicolas Poussin (in Italian Nicola Pussino) might have found himself at home, Berdini's thesis presents what Thomas Jefferson would probably have called an "academical village," a romantic* stazione di villeggiatura *to which, as an escape from London, Warburgian scholars might retreat for study and discourse during the hotter months of the year.*

The architect describes the project as follows:

> *Borgo Pussino is an architectural fantasy. A hamlet-like settlement that in its picturesque presentation would like to be interpreted as a rather familiar blend of village charm and academic distinction.*

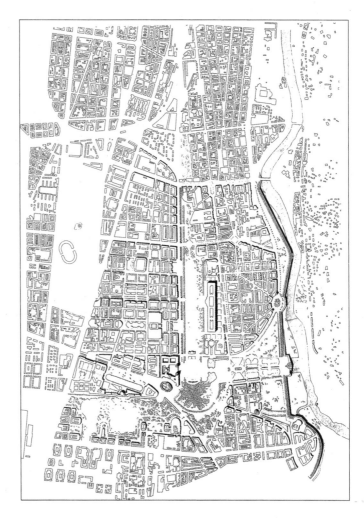

33. Turin, the Lingotto site, proposed shadow plan and figure/ground by Jeffery Klug.

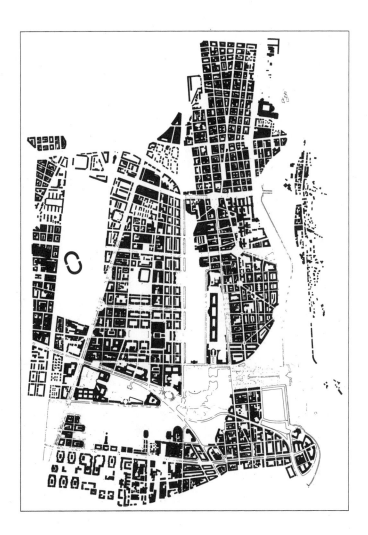

Cornell Studio Projects and Theses

34. Warburg Institute, Pitigliano, by Paolo Berdini, proposed plan.

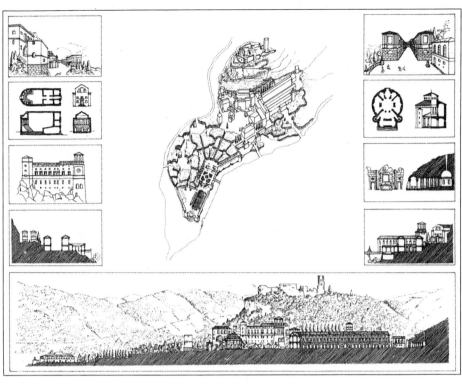

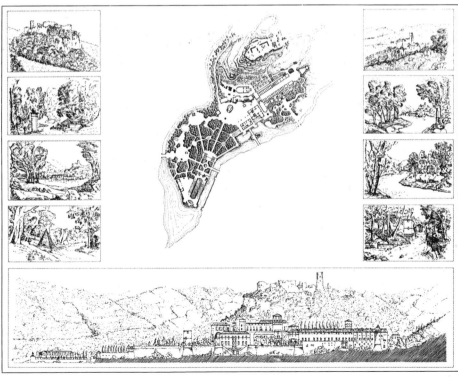

35. Warburg Institute, Pitigliano: axonometric and details (top); garden development and views (bottom).

Like the books in the library of that peculiar institution, the buildings of Borgo Pussino assemble themselves according to the theory (or the practice?) of the "good neighbor," that is, each piece aspires to a significant relation with its neighbors and that the pieces would not easily surrender to an a priori, predicated arrangement. But the analogy should not be carried too far because the range of sentiments which inspire an architectural fantasy demand a correspondence of visual relations, the accuracy of which is pictorial. The imaginary cities of Poussin's landscapes impose themselves as a supreme reference while the wild, primitive, and uncontaminated territory which extends itself north of Pitigliano appears as its actual counterpart. In the end Borgo Pussino is expected to recall that special blend of unimaginative and rustic classicism which contributed much to the austere local magnificence.

I share most of these reactions to this particular landscape; and, after a lot of driving around, I have begun to notice that, while Claude mostly painted situations to the south of Rome—the Colli Albani—Poussin seems to have preferred sites to the north around Monte Soratte and the rugged edges of that great Etruscan plain which is focused upon Viterbo.

C.R.

Boston Redevelopment
Paul Mortensen (1986)

With remarkable consistency and panache this thesis for a highly problematic area of Boston proposes a comprehensive series of several urban sites all at once: first, it provides for the completion by infill development and restructuring of the present ill-defined area to the north of Beacon Hill and of the West End between the Charles River and the Central Artery; second, it presents a new, coherent structure of streets and buildings for the area lying just across the river to the southwest of Bunker Hill and at the head of Boston Harbor; and, third, most importantly, it develops a union, hitherto scarcely considered, between the two sides of the river. As of now the Charles River flows as a more or less continuous, undifferentiated linear sequence; but, with this scheme, it may now be seen as a series of water pieces firmly embedded within the urban fabric. This project is both highly exemplary and extremely suggestive.

C.R.

Firenze: Fortezza da Basso, Stazione Santa Maria Novella, Cascine

Of course, most of the Italianizing projects of the 1980s were rather more down to earth than Paolo Berdini's; and, in this ongoing sequence, I now illustrate an exercise of some months later.

     During the fall of 1987 various members of the studio undertook a project for Florence. Originally they were concerned with Fortezza da Basso and its connections with the city center; but this led to further speculation about the future of the railroad tracks which so brutally impinge upon the fortezza *and so horribly vitiate what should be its orbit of influence. And then a further problem assumed prominence: what to do about the territory extending from the* fortezza *to the river, a territory which includes the beginnings of the city's principal park, the Cascine. The solution for this area which is here published is a composite of individual discoveries, and their extremely smooth assembly must have been the result of a sustained and harmonious group excitement. Students responsible for different parts were: Carter Hord, Thomas Hofman, Andrew Klamon, and Kim Tan, with Matthew Bell assisting in general coordination. The following text is retrospectively written by myself.*

C.R.

The five-sided Fortezza da Basso is a standard piece of sixteenth-century military architecture. There were comparable pentagonal fortresses at Livorno, Parma, Peschiera, Turin, Antwerp, and no doubt many places else. The Palazzo Farnese at Caprarola is a partially domesticated version of the type, and perhaps the Pentagon in Washington, D.C. is a further, and retarded, celebration of the same themes. Also it is just possible that Fortezza da Basso is the only considerable surviving specimen of this species.

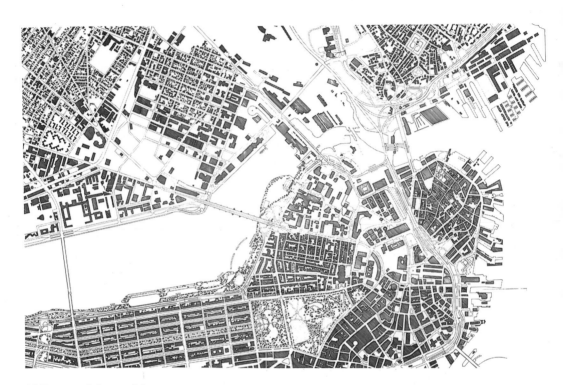

36. Boston, existing condition.

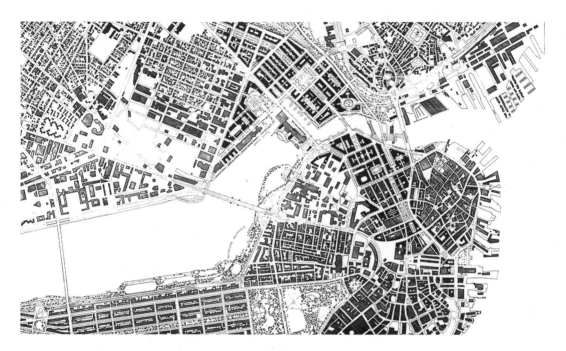

37. Boston, proposed figure/ground by Paul Mortensen.

Cornell Studio Projects and Theses

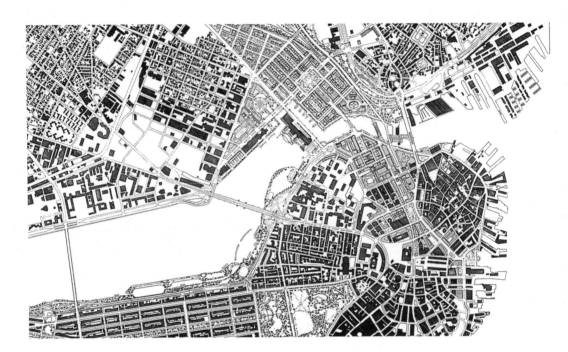

38. Boston, proposed new structures.

39. Boston, axonometric.

Cornell Studio Projects and Theses

A Medici production of the 1530s, for all its external aggressiveness its primary purpose was never so much the defense of the city as the control of its citizens. The Medici were about to become Grand Dukes of Tuscany—an ambiguous destiny for a mercantile family—and this piece of military architecture is by way of being an indication of the shape of things to come.

Never a tourist attraction and, probably, never too much loved, still Fortezza da Basso just *happens* to be there, the city unimaginable without it, an intrinsic part of the idea of Florence; and, hence, it was our assumption that it might be put to prominent, profitable, and agreeable use.

Then, with the Stazione di Santa Maria Novella, we found ourselves absorbed within a different theater of problems. The original station on this site, the old Maria Antonia station, dated from 1848–1857 and was originally built, I believe, as the terminal of a simple local track to Lucca. Surprisingly, this may be almost the same date as the building of an equivalent terminal station in Rome again intended to accommodate the service of such local *villeggiatura* towns as Frascati, Castelgandolfo, and Albano. But this, of course, is pure coincidence, since, even in the 1850s, at least two of the independent governments of peninsular Italy, the Papal States and the Kingdom of the Two Sicilies, had no anxiety to promote any intercommunication by railroad, since railroads could only bring the equivalent of social upheaval. Pio Nono did not speak of *chemins de fer* but of *chemins d'enfer*!

But the Grand Duchy of Tuscany had long enjoyed a more genial reputation. After all there were all those censorious English who had chosen to live in Florence; and both the track to Lucca and the Santa Maria Novella station were almost certainly subsidized by London capital. Then, further, there was that wedge of confiscated monastic land (?) extending from the rear of the church of Santa Maria Novella all the way out to the city walls; and what better place than this could there be for driving tracks into town quite as far as possible? A decision related to London capital and English railroad practice? I suspect so; and, certainly, a decision which established the station in what has become a place of maximum inconvenience—generally inconvenient for traffic, Rome-Bologna-Milan, and locally inconvenient for the volume of traffic which its presence imposes upon a street system inadequate to accept it.

Almost certainly by 1866, in the days of *Firenze capitale* and after the demolition of the city's walls, a more elegant logic would surely have prevailed; and one may imagine the solution which Giuseppe Poggi, architect of the new boulevards which had come to surround the city, might have entertained, a new through station perhaps to be approached by a forecourt from the circuit of his new *viale,* easy access, easy exit, maybe just a bit like the station which was to be built at Bologna, circa 1871? But this was not to be; and even in the 1930s, when ideas of rational *grandezza* were so epidemic and when Giovanni Michelucci came to build his own very superb new station, against all common sense it was still the Santa Maria Novella site which continued to be used.

Question: If Florence is to receive a new through station (as rumor sometimes infers) then what is to be the destiny of the present building, generally conceded to be a work of conspicuous importance; and, if Michelucci's station continues to serve a local usage, just how many tracks is it necessary that it should receive? Apparently, back in the 1850s, the original station was served by only four tracks, and I would now guess the presence of about sixteen. And the question of the number of tracks is of vital importance; and this for the reason that it is the breadth of the railroad viaduct leading to the station which completely compromises the sequence of the *viale* and reduces to irretrievable gloom that whole tract of territory between Fortezza da Basso and the Cascine.

Except for the somewhat exotic nocturnal activities which it supports, the Cascine—I cannot help thinking—is, at present, no great rendezvous of pleasure. Possibly it began its existence as a hunting park lying outside the city; no doubt it achieved its greatest success as a nineteenth-century carriage park—that mobile display of languishing ladies, glamorous uniforms, and opulent horseflesh; but, since we no longer inhabit the world of Marcel

40. Florence, existing condition.

41. Florence, proposed plan (composite).

Proust, and since his alluring combinations of equine and human furniture are no longer available for our entertainment, it must now be stipulated that, as a twentieth-century pedestrian promenade, as a place *per fare la passeggiata,* it is scarcely an overwhelming focus of attention.

No doubt its shape is against it. It is a very long park without any very apparent destination. Its frontage to the *viale* is all too short. Penetrated from its east end, flanked to the south by the river, to the north there seems to have been almost a concerted attempt to exclude any spreading of its influence; and, to the north, the elements of its enclosure are particularly disgusting—a stretch of dilapidated industrial building serviced by a virtually abandoned railroad, now quite embarrassingly useless—all this backed up by a gridding of indifferent housing which is to be imagined as almost panting to receive at least some breath of the more benign and salubrious air of the park.

This, then, is the Cascine as it happens to be. It is a very long park painfully not provided with the variety of animation which a series of lateral entrances might help to supply. It tends to look as though, ever since the horse was displaced by the automobile, it has been the subject of benign neglect; and its best feature must be the long straight *allée* which extends from its entrance for some third of its length.

After which exposition of problems now briefly to review the story of our interventions; and to begin with the Cascine where they should be the most obvious.

So, basically, we eradicated that mini-industrial quasi-wasteland with all its accessories; and, by doing so, we acquired an extended southern-facing frontage envisaged as a site for development for apartments and hotels. A site with almost sublime dimensions—distant views of Bellosguardo and near views of the park—one can imagine no other site in Europe, no other site in either of the Americas, as equipped with such potential, and a potential which might be realized without conservationist protest and without undue social divisiveness. For would not the presence of money on the park lubricate and benefit what would now become the park's most intimate hinterland?

But not to sound like a real estate man enjoying an epiphany! Because this simple operation of making visible the northern enclosure of the park not only enlarges the Cascine but also amplifies its presence along the line of the *viale.* Allowing a somewhat rudimentary boulevard to appear as an extended frontier, by allowing the Borgo Ognisanti to continue as the north face of the park, we also hope that this move will promote a reciprocity between the solids of the city and the voids of the park, and, to assist this interchange, we have introduced a type of *rondell,* ostensibly as a setting for Vittorio Emanuele and his horse.

But, apart from this, our operations have been few. We have prolonged the line of the Lungarno by a series of *boschetti;* we have surrounded the *rondell* with another *boschetto,* itself integrated with the urban fabric to the north; and then we have attempted to convey some semblance of order to that random collection of buildings which have intruded themselves in the middle of the park.

But, around Fortezza da Basso, our interventions are of a different order. We have located Stazione Centrale, a through station with forecourt, immediately to the north; and, then, we have allowed the prevailing grid, the oblique face of the *fortezza,* and the presence of existing railroad land to describe the outline of a new piazza, which (because we don't know enough about the underground course of the River Mugnone at this point) we have decorated with a reminiscence of the always useful Prato della Valle from Padua.

Fortezza da Basso itself we envisage to be internally reconstructed as a center for performance, exhibition, and meeting; and this can only lead to the problem of how to get into it from the city's center. And, at the present, it resists approach. A large hunk of building or, if you prefer it, a monument, it is equipped with no spatial preface, not even the most perfunctory gesture of welcome; and one imagines how deeply distressing this must have been to Giuseppe Poggi, prone to such gestures, and here, most likely, inhibited by the contiguity of the railroad viaduct.

However, if, for purposes of research, we suppose that the railroad tracks are no longer with us, and if, in their imaginary absence, we begin to scrutinize the site in front of the *fortezza,* this may discover highly suggestive information; and it derives from the alignment of the city's postmedieval grid which impinges upon the direct frontal approach to the *fortezza* not so very far before this building is reached. So, if two streets, major and minor, may be said to converge at this point, then and for the sake of some equality of input, how about a third? And, of course, as a further reward for scrutiny this is waiting to be discovered among the further coordinates of the postmedieval grid as it extends itself along the river. And, thus, to look along the Lungarno from the Ponte Santo Spirito westwards, there, waiting for discrimination, can only be this third component, about halfway between Piazza Ognisanti and Villa Favard.

At this point there is a little bridge followed by a little street which points, quite implacably, to the place of convergence we have already identified! And it was in this way, and obedient to the promptings of circumstance, that, in front of Fortezza da Basso, we educed—we did not impose—the existence of a trident which, to us, presented itself almost as an embryo awaiting a very natural delivery. Like all tridents just a bit of magic; but, at this place, we also thought a useful trident for assisting a more complete reading of the city.

For us this made our case complete; and, at a smaller scale, we added a little more to the postmedieval grid. And so *what* of Michelucci's station which we have completely obliterated? And are we just a gang of cultural innocents who have, inadvertently, committed a very horrible crime?

And what to do about Michelucci's station, so very respectable and so very unfortunately located? To get a taxi there and to be driven up that squalid street to the *fortezza,* or to suffer the miseries of that railroad viaduct, these are not agreeable experiences; but can they be enough simply to condemn Michelucci? The Futurists might have thought so; but ourselves do not. And, therefore, we speculate: could Michelucci's station be reassembled as a further stopping place out at Riffredi? Or, much better and following the example of the Gare d'Orsay in Paris, could its more significant parts be put to use as a Museum of Transportation?

Three Projects for Rome: Largo Argentina, Quartiere dei Banchi, Piazza del Cinquecento
Cheryl O'Neil (1987), Matthew Bell (1987), Robert Goodill (1987)

These three theses are to be related to further work done by their authors at the same date. This was for a contribution to the exhibition "Nove Progetti per Nove Città" which opened in Milan in early 1987 and for which we had been asked to make interventions in the vicinity of the Mausoleum of Augustus. Our project for Piazza Augusto Imperatore (see below in this volume) was an attempt to redefine and reconstitute an area of the city which had suffered serious damage from ill-considered demolition and rebuilding; and such was also the objective of the proposals which follow.

For the most part these were independent of my criticism, though I did see these projects briefly for the hanging of our exhibition piece at the Triennale.

The Largo Argentina project by Cheryl O'Neil is an attempt to render accessible and visible the four republican temples in the sunken enclosure isolated by the streets. At the same time it proposes a perimeter addressed to the general scale of the centro storico.

The project by Matthew Bell is a response to the confusion which has existed for approximately a century in this area of Corso Vittorio Emanuele II, Ponte Sant'Angelo, Via dei Coronari, Via Giulia, and San Giovanni dei Fiorentini. In addition, like the Piazza Augusto Imperatore project at the Lungotevere it attempts to establish a clear relationship between river and city.

Finally Robert Goodill's project offers a reduction in size of the enormous territory which intervenes between the Stazione Termini and the Baths of Diocletian. The ensuing space is structured so as to respond to the great thrust of the station's canopy.

42. Largo Argentina, Rome, views of the project by Cheryl O'Neil.

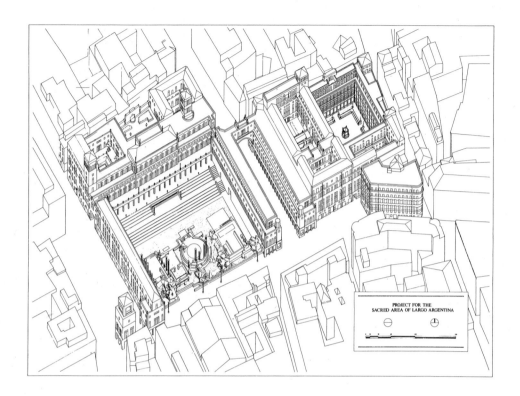

PROJECT FOR THE
SACRED AREA OF LARGO ARGENTINA

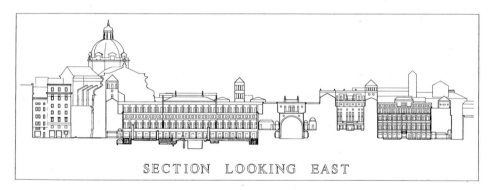

SECTION LOOKING EAST

43. Largo Argentina, proposed axonometric and section.

Cornell Studio Projects and Theses

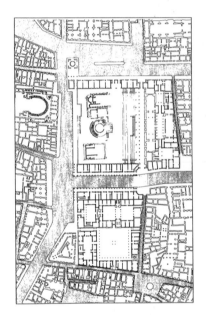  

44. Largo Argentina, proposed ground-floor plan; existing and proposed figure/

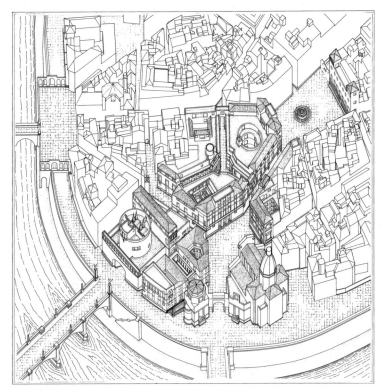

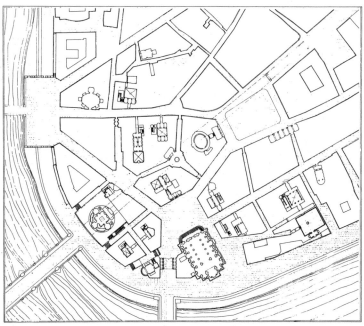

45. Quartiere dei Banchi, Rome, proposed axonometric and plan by Matthew Bell.

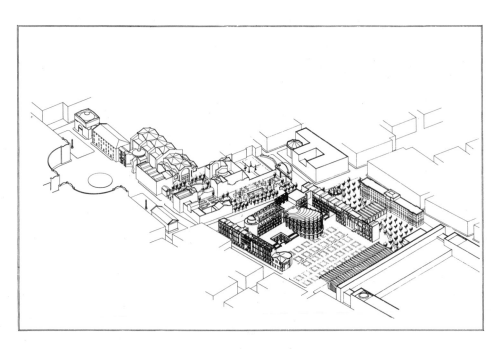

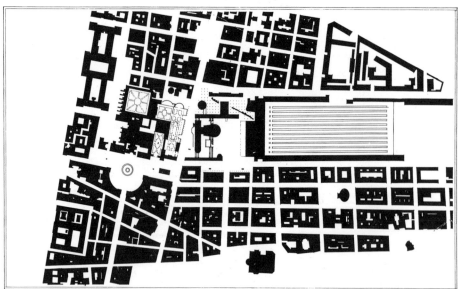

46. Piazza del Cinquecento, Rome, proposed axonometric and plan by Robert Goodill.

After these Roman performances, the following year there were two thesis projects for New York and Chicago; and it was with these that, effectively, the Urban Design Studio came to an end.

C.R.

Manhattan: Object/Fabric
Carter Hord (Thesis, 1988)

This surprisingly discreet project relates to a site west of Lincoln Center and extending along the Hudson which has lately attracted much attention. On the whole—and like its author—it is so extremely modest that it tends to escape notice; but other projects for this same site have been much less suave and far more noisy.

C.R.

Chicago: A Plan for the Central Area
Mark Weintraub (1988)

The thesis proposes a synthesis of the influences of the Chicago grid, the river, and the lake. Together with past historical models and new inventions the scheme responds to the nature of individual districts while creating an identity for the central area as a whole, and, in so doing, focuses on the following objectives:

1. the linking of the Pilsen, Chinatown, South King Drive, and University of Illinois communities with the north side of the central area,
2. the establishment of a network of pedestrian and vehicular paths to allow for and to enhance their respective activities,
3. the creation of a sense of arrival through points of entry from the south, and
4. the unification of the entire lakefront as a continuous park system linked to the supporting urban fabric.

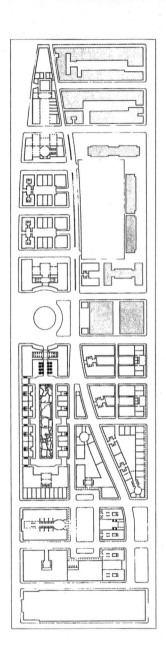

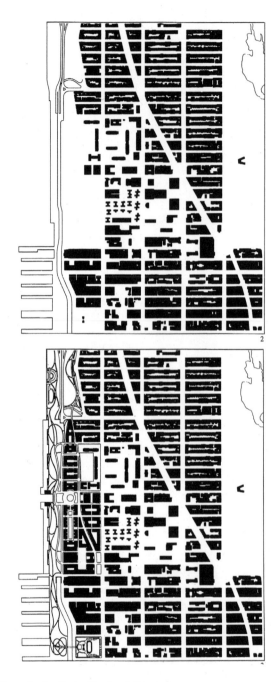

47. Manhattan object/fabric, proposed ground-floor plan by Carter Hord; existing and proposed figure/ground.

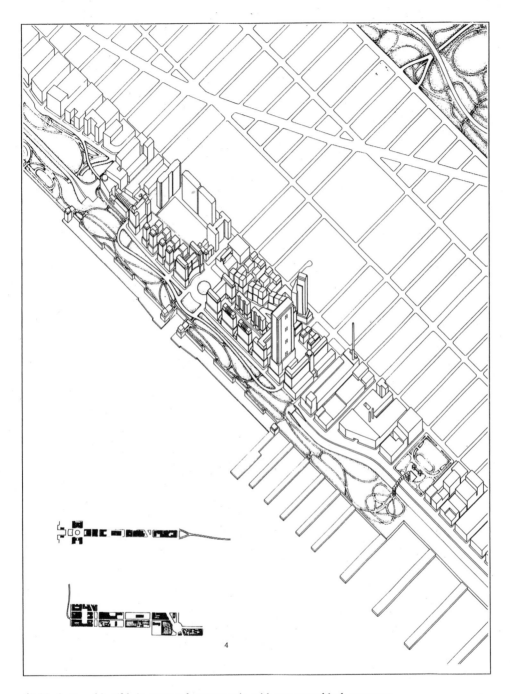

48. Manhattan object/fabric, proposed axonometric, with two street block sequences.

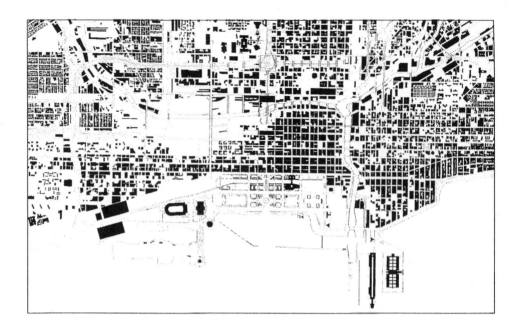

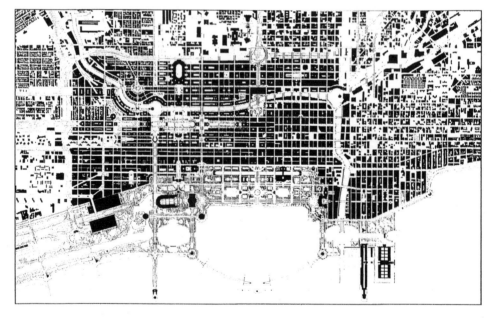

49. Chicago central area, existing and proposed figure/ground (Mark Weintraub).

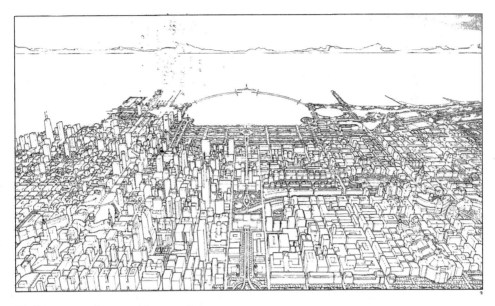

50. Chicago central area, aerial perspective.

It is proposed, then, to accomplish a restoration of as much of a regular grid as possible; imposed upon it is a series of urban figures creating spaces and generating activities. A cross-axial system of parks and boulevards is introduced in conjunction with an east-west canal to organize the southern central area. The completion of Burnham Park and its related harbor is then a move intended to unify the north and south sides of the principal urban figure.

{edited from Weintraub's thesis introduction}

The New City: Architecture and Urban Renewal

During the years 1967–1987 five exhibition projects were executed by myself and groups associated with me. Respectively these were: for the Museum of Modern Art, New York; the Albright-Knox Gallery, Buffalo; the Walker Art Center, Minneapolis; rather improbably for the Mercato di Traiano in Rome; and, finally, for the Milan Triennale.

In 1967 the Museum of Modern Art sponsored an exhibition titled "The New City: Architecture and Urban Renewal." Ostensibly, it was Arthur Drexler's show; but, more privately, it was Peter Eisenman's. Peter's incandescence and, I suppose, his innate competitiveness had prevailed over Arthur's more cautious intelligence; and this has resulted—typical of Peter—in the idea of an urbanistic/academic confrontation, almost the equivalent of an Ivy League football game. Representatives of three universities, Princeton, Columbia, and Cornell—in other words of where Peter had been teaching since his return from Cam-

bridge, England, of where he had done his graduate work, and of where he had been as an undergraduate—were to make presentations to display the possibilities of a less ad hoc *approach to urban renewal in New York City than that which currently prevailed. Which, for practical purposes, meant: from Princeton, Eisenman and Graves; from Columbia, Jacquelin Robertson (shades of Yale and Cambridge and close to the politics of Mayor Lindsay); and, from Cornell, myself.*

And so we met at MoMA in the late summer of 1966 in order to discuss possible sites; but, as it turned out, in the reality of the meeting there could scarcely be too much discussion. Drexler insisted that the sites be contiguous; Robertson wanted to make a linear structure over the New York Central tracks from 97th to 134th streets; Eisenman and Graves wanted a Riverside Drive site from 125th Street to, approximately, 155th; and these different insistencies and wishes, both spatially and topographically, seemed to place the focus of the exhibit on Harlem—perhaps unfortunately since Harlem does have its own sociological cross to bear.

Then, while accepting the central Harlem site, I also made the suggestion that an invitation to contribute should be extended to MIT and this was agreed upon. MIT received the very detached job of Riker's Island.

The Cornell team comprised Colin Rowe and Thomas Schumacher; Jerry Wells and Fred Koetter; with assistants Steven Potters, Michael Schwarting, and Carl Stearns. The text that follows is modified from that published for the exhibition.

How can we modify the existing grid plan to improve circulation, encourage the development of parks and new neighborhoods, and clarify the order implied by the terrain itself?

There are at present two major urbanistic conceptions: the traditional city—a solid mass of building with spaces carved out of it—and the city in a park—an open meadow within which isolated buildings are placed. The traditional city fails to meet our needs for open space. The city in the park, an early twentieth century invention, lacks the density and vitality we associate with the urban expe-

51. Harlem redevelopment site plan. The plan preserves the central spine of existing grid-plan buildings, while flanking this with "corridor" extensions of a park system.

The New City: Architecture and Urban Renewal

rience. Both of these alternative and contrary concepts are already present within the area north of Central Park, and this project is designed to mediate between them.

Implicit in the site is a division into three zones. And, of these, the central zone most completely retains its original nineteenth century characteristics while the two outer zones have been extensively, though not consistently, redeveloped as project housing, or as cut price versions of 'the city in the park'. With this statement in mind, it is here proposed that these facts should be recognized and their consequences clarified. And this is to argue as follows: that the central zone be interpreted as, more or less, an area of conservation or preservation, its existing format to be enhanced; and that, in the two outer zones, a wholly different strategy should apply.

Or such is the general idea: the central zone would become a protected environment and the two outer zones would be encouraged to accomplish the entirely different destiny which, since the 1940s, urban renewal, without any conscious intention (?), has attempted to impose upon them.

But this does not involve any infatuation on our part with Le Corbusier's *ville radieuse*. In terms of empathy, Louis Kahn used to speak of *what a building wants to be;* and his attribution of likely-to-be-frustrated ambition to a building is among the happier of his perceptions. Then, by extension, it may be possible to speak of *what a part of a city wants to become.* In any case it was a 'logic' of this sort that we followed; and it is this process of thought which the illustrations represent. Fundamentally we attempted to produce two corridors of greenery and continuous space: the east corridor bounded by Lenox and Madison avenues and the west corridor extending from Eighth Avenue to the boundary made irregular by the presence of Morningside Park, St. Nicholas Park, and Colonial Park.

A fatuous and excessive daydream? But the skeptical should notice that it involves no extensive *tabula rasa,* that constructions and demolitions required to bring it about are, as a matter of fact, surprisingly few—in the end, apart from a little patching here

52. Harlem redevelopment, model. Central Park in the foreground.

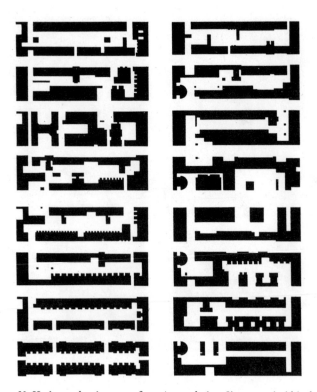

53. Harlem redevelopment, figure/ground plan. Sixteen typical blocks lying between Lenox and Eighth avenues in the area that the general scheme proposes to preserve and improve without destroying the clarity of the street grid. A possible strategy for local development converts backyards into playgrounds; potentially adequate existing housing is rehabilitated; public buildings acquire the appropriate settings that their social importance might suggest.

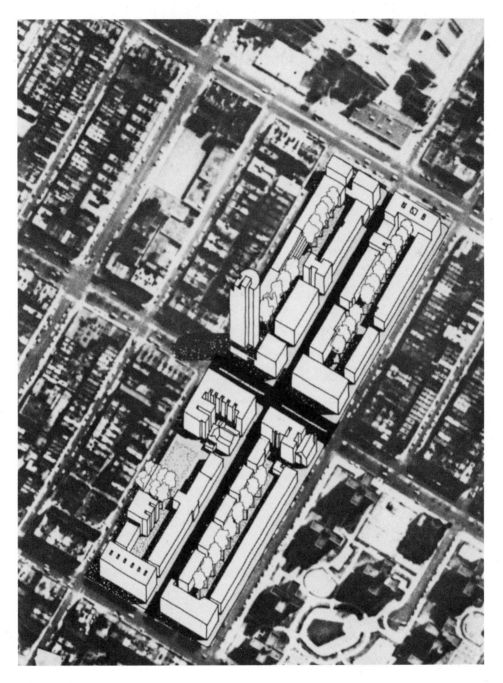

54. Harlem redevelopment, perspective. Four such block renovations in the context of the existing city.

The New City: Architecture and Urban Renewal

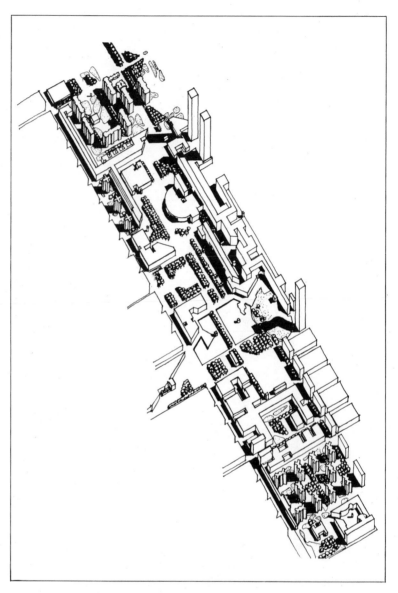

55. Harlem redevelopment, isometric, showing new construction in the "corridor" park zone incorporating Mt. Morris Park. The long building complex combines residential, commercial, and possible light-industry facilities serving this and adjacent areas.

56. Harlem redevelopment, view of Manhattan Island looking south.

The New City: Architecture and Urban Renewal

and there, the removal of vestiges of row housing which have become painfully deprived of their context, and just a number of residential towers hopefully envisaged as being slightly better than current New York specification 1967.

Such, then, was the basic diagram; but it became complicated in the east corridor by the approach of 125th Street to the elevated Park Avenue railroad tracks and, compounding the problem, by the relentless mega-machine which the Columbia team proposed to build there. Now, perhaps this building offered a protracted solid rather than a protracted void; it had something of a tendency to steal the show. It was entirely itself. I do not remember that it made any local concessions. It was without useful ambiguity. And, with hindsight, I believe that the Cornell team was too deferential towards it, that it was inhibitions about what Columbia proclaimed which sponsored the most doubtful of our proposals—that excessive spatial elaboration focused upon 121st Street between Lenox and Madison avenues. Our procedures may be studied in detail by taking a look at our rehabilitation of blocks of traditional housing where interior yards are converted to become quiet courtyards opening off the street. This project was an attempt to demonstrate the incipience of an order which awaits extraction from the city's confusion.

Buffalo Waterfront

This project dates from 1965–1966 and is a collaborative work of the Cornell Urban Design Studio of that time.

It was prepared by Richard Baiter, Richard Cardwell, David Chan, Wayne Copper, Harris Forusz, Alfred Koetter, Makoto Miki, El-pidio Olympio, and Franz Oswald; and the critics were Colin Rowe, Werner Seligmann, and Jerry Wells.

It was taken to Buffalo for a brief showing in 1966; and, then, three years later it became the subject of an exhibition at the Albright-Knox Art Gallery, June 23–September 1, 1969.

This exhibition was prepared under the supervision of Alfred Koetter and Steven Peterson; and those who assisted were Paul Curtis, Harris Feinn, Richard Gelber, Jerry Kreider, Henry Richardson, Terence Williams, and Priscilla Wilson. Advice on the graphics was given by Klaus Herdeg and photographs of the model were the work of Hadley Smith of Ithaca.

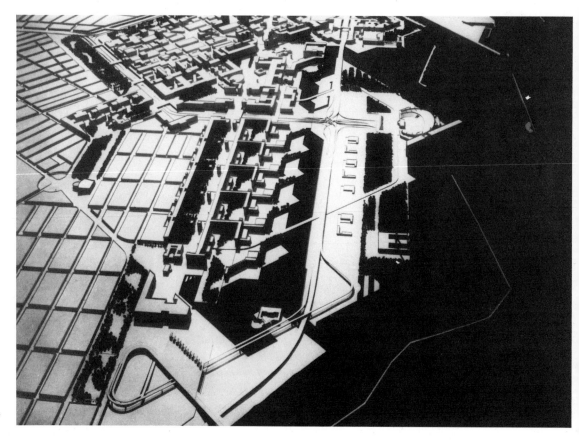

57. Buffalo waterfront, views of model looking southeast and northeast.

Buffalo Waterfront

In many ways Buffalo, New York, was an absolute gift. In its plan it was almost an ideal city, but, an ideal city vitiated by a failure to confront either lake or river, it seemed to clamor for both 'restoration' and 'correction'; and this is what we attempted to supply. Over-ambitious as our proposals may seem, and even megalomaniac as they must have appeared to many who saw the show at the Albright-Knox, as a matter of fact we made very few demolitions and mostly restricted ourselves to a development of land which had become abandoned and, more or less, derelict.

But, of course, no such guidelines possibly could have been followed by the planning establishment; and the result has been a further degradation of the original plan, the obliteration of one of the diagonals converging on Niagara Square and the ruthless destruction of a number of very high quality nineteenth-century buildings—a process which defeats understanding.

The text which follows was written for the Albright-Knox exhibition of 1969.

This project, prepared by members of the urban design class at Cornell, is offered as a commentary upon the potential of Buffalo's waterfront. It assumes that a basic strategy for the area must, first of all, recognize the real and symbolic significance of Niagara Square and must attempt to place this space in some explicit relationship with Lake Erie and the mouth of the Buffalo River; it further assumes that the entry from Canada and the diagonal of Niagara Street are among the valuable determinants of any significant solution; while, in addition, it implies that Symphony Circle with the layout to which it relates ought to be recognized as an important urbanistic achievement which, of necessity, must modify any immediately adjacent new developments.

These issues are here considered as being vital ones if the waterfront area is to be in any way integrated with the Buffalo city center as it at present exists; but, obviously, no less vital must be the nature and constitution of the area itself and, in this connection, a variety of recreational, residential, commercial, and civic facilities

101

58. Buffalo waterfront, master plan.

Buffalo Waterfront

are proposed. These, which are intensively interrelated, include: a stadium with adjacent installations for athletic activities; public and private docking for pleasure craft; a diversity of high- and low-rise housing; a provision for a full range of shopping and hotel possibilities; and office space for the use of both private and public establishments. Further to these are supplied a community college, a convention and exhibition center, a library, an opera house, and an international museum. In the absence of a specific program of requirements projects such as these are proposed as possible but by no means the only developments which might occur within the waterfront area; and obviously, they are not presented as the rigidly definitive components of a static and unchangeable plan. Instead they are introduced as the variable details of a model which now requires to be submitted to empirical criticism. It is a physical model: but, while it is primarily envisaged as a logical development of factors inherent in the site, it is believed that the generalizations which it suggests need not be in contradiction with conclusions derived from sociological, economic, and other criteria.

1810

In 1804 Joseph Ellicott established the plan for the town of New Amsterdam, which took the name of Buffalo in 1813. The centralized plan with its radial streets was extended by the linear common and was intercepted by the boundary of the New York State Reservation, later incorporated into the city as Black Rock. The immediate area of the central square early became highly developed while the outlying lands to the east were planned as farm lots. (See Diagram A in fig. 59.)

1910

The general grid of the city, after various twists, has aligned itself along a north-south axis. Intensive development remains at the original core and continues along the radials in a linear fashion; but, as early as the 1850s, a park and boulevard system had been proposed to the north of the core and it was this system which became the setting for further residential development. The Pan-American Exposition of 1900 was an extension of this park system. It was planned according to the principles of the City Beautiful movement with an emphasis upon such civic amenities as fountains, symmetry, and monumentality of structure.

Meanwhile an extension of the Erie Canal has penetrated the city and, as the transportation of goods switches from barge to train, it has shortly been followed by the arrival of rail yards. Buffalo c. 1910 shows an area of apparently self-conscious urbanistic activity—the city core and the park system—in the grip of a seemingly uncontrollable transportation happening.

1969

The self-conscious urbanistic initiative of 1910 has scarcely been maintained though the stranglehold of the railroad has significantly diminished. Transportation by rail is now supplemented by auto and truck, while arterial highways now penetrate the city along the old canal and rail lines. The need to replace decayed housing and to provide more open space has resulted in the construction of large tower complexes set in open lots. The linear definition of the street is thus destroyed, while the steady sprawl of the suburbs has consumed the open land once existing between subsidiary rural centers and the city proper. As the city has expanded the memorable Buffalo of the early twentieth century has been reduced in importance and, correspondingly, has entered into a process of decay.

Analysis of Buffalo discloses a composite of complementary and conflicting elements, of deliberate acts of will and of incongruous accidents—all of which factors are evident from the very beginning in Joseph Ellicott's original plan, Diagram A.

Evident in Ellicott's plan are not only a highly ambitious orchestration of streets and spaces, but also the clear indication of a conflict between an ideal city model and specific circumstances

Buffalo Waterfront

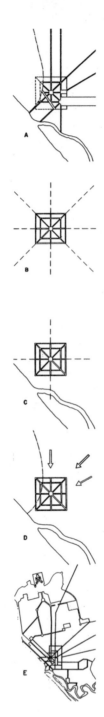

59. Diagrams A, B, C, D, E.

which this model *cannot* accommodate. The ideal model which
seems to be implied is presented in Diagram B. A distinct and self-
contained community is equipped with a central square and is penetrated by major orthogonal and minor diagonal axes. It is generally
reminiscent of Washington, D.C. and is ultimately derivative from
the Utopian speculation of Renaissance theorists.

Diagram C illustrates certain topographical conditions of
the site which necessarily acted to modify what we might call Ellicott's Platonic idea. The grid of Ellicott's layout is aligned neither
with the Lake Erie waterfront nor with the course of the Buffalo
River. Also the closeness of his central square to both lake and river
suggests that any major expansion of his community will result in
lopsidedness and a consequent erosion of its basic centralized
theme.

Diagram D indicates some other factors which promoted
further distortions of an ideal state. To the northwest the presence
of the New York State Reservation prohibits a logical development:
to the northeast, the lines of the present Genesee and Broadway introduce still more elements of disturbance.

As a diagonal axis in Ellicott's layout, Genesee is conceptually of less significance than the 'major' axes of Court and Delaware,
but, as an important entry into town and as a street leading directly
to the lake, Genesee competes in importance with the 'ideally' more
prominent Delaware. Thus its functional values are wholly at vari-
ance with the status assigned to it, and this is a condition which
seems destined to render still further ambiguous the southeast quar-
ter of the scheme where Busti Terrace (see Diagram A) has already
introduced an entirely erratic condition.

Some of these conflicts between ideal concept and empirical
conditions Ellicott was able to resolve; but some issues he could
not. Diagram E, showing Buffalo c. 1900, reveals the continuing
importance of his dispositions—and their insufficiency.

Primarily through the agency of Delaware, Main, and Genesee, his city has been able to extend itself throughout the northern

Buffalo Waterfront

sector; but, along the waterfront, the confusion which might have been anticipated has now come to prevail. Thus this area preserves itself as both major problem and major opportunity.

The nature of the opportunity is suggested by the examples of waterfronts elsewhere, but the solution to the problem can only be derived from the fabric of Buffalo itself; and the drawings which follow are presented as a minimum examination of this fabric.

Points and Lines of Prominence

The plan of Buffalo discloses a number of locations of conspicuous importance. Such are: Niagara Square, Lafayette Square, Soldiers Place, Symphony Circle, which may be regarded as the intersections in a lattice of important streets. It is thus possible to speak of a basic structure of prominent points and lines. Some of these have been consciously organized as such: but there are other points of either functional or topographical relevance which have remained unexploited. The approaches to the Peace Bridge and the mouth of the Buffalo River are obvious instances of two of these unorganized conditions; but it must also be noticed that, from the existing lattice, it is possible to infer a more complete development. Thus, a projection of the lines of Court and Virginia suggests that the place of their intersection is one of great latent significance; a projection of Genesee towards the lakefront suggests another such situation; while a rerouting of Porter Avenue to bring the Peace Bridge area into direct relationship with Symphony Circle presents itself as another move which seems to be implicit in the Buffalo plan. The diagram in figure 60 shows the existing lattice and its potential extension. It indicates a network of places requiring particular attention. The example of Paris below suggests that prominent parts within such a structure are likely to become the generating cores of equally prominent development.

60. Buffalo, points and lines of prominence (top); the example of Paris (bottom).

Buffalo Waterfront

Areas of Collision

Within the plan of Buffalo it is possible to discriminate the presence of a variety of grids. These distinct grids or fields tend to sponsor conditions of development which are generally coherent but which at their extremities or frontiers are likely to produce areas of confusion and disorientation. These are areas where the activities of distinct grids become impacted and thereby produce situations of collision. Such situations in Buffalo lie to the lake side of City Hall, in the zone extending northwards from City Hall to Symphony Circle, and along Michigan Avenue southwards of its intersection with Genesee (fig. 61). Such situations, which are areas of extreme difficulty because of their manifold inputs, are also places of great potential. Also illustrated is a nineteenth century solution of such a collision condition in the city of Munich.

Parks

The points and lines of prominence already noticed comprise one aspect of Buffalo's park system. The areas of collision suggest the possibility of its further extensions. From the combination of these there emerges the idea of a more comprehensive development which, via Squaw Island, Front Park, La Salle Park, and a Niagara Street Boulevard, could link an architectonic area to the lakeside of City Hall with the complementary and scenic values of Delaware Park. Parks are of two sorts—naturalistic and rectilinear—and common to both may be the presence of water. The diagram in figure 62 presents Buffalo's existing and latent park system. Implied is the contrast between the naturalistic lake of Delaware Park and a more formalized marina in the area of the waterfront. Below are illustrated extreme versions of the two basic park types.

61. Buffalo, areas of collision; the collision condition in Munich.

Buffalo Waterfront

62. Buffalo, parks (top); the two basic park types (bottom).

URBANISTICS

Waterfront Area

This area, encompassing the waterfront from the Buffalo River to
the Peace Bridge, is envisaged as an extension of the existing park
system to the north and is proposed as the primary recreational and
public use area of central Buffalo. Facilities projected include a stadium for 80,000 people with related athletic club and sports fields,
a community college at the point adjacent to the mouth of the river,
and a pleasure craft watercourse with adjacent yacht club and ma-
rinas.

The watercourse is located on the site of part of the Erie Canal. It connects the vicinity of the Peace Bridge with the proposed
City Hall plaza and, being inland, is protected from prevailing
winds and also capable of controlled purification.

Auxiliary to this elaborated La Salle Park are connections
along the line of the present Carolina Street back to Symphony
Circle and a development to accommodate the Peace Bridge and to
place this gateway from Canada in explicit relationship with Niagara Street, and, hence, with Buffalo's central square. The greater
part of this area is either open land, land containing dilapidated
structures, or land reclaimed from the lake. Its proposed functions
are public, and its early development seems to be highly plausible.

City Hall Area

The area of 'collision' to the lakeside of City Hall is potentially Buffalo's point of greatest prominence. Inputs in this area are from the
adjacent downtown, from the residential districts to the north, from
the waterfront, and from the river, while the presence of the Thruway adds a further element of intrusion.

Architecturally, the problem of this area becomes one of reconciling these various confrontations, of mitigating the conflict between the 'ideal' Ellicott plan and the direction of the lakeshore and
of resolving the diagonal attack of the highly 'accidental' grid
which Niagara Street supports. Symbolically, the area requires to be

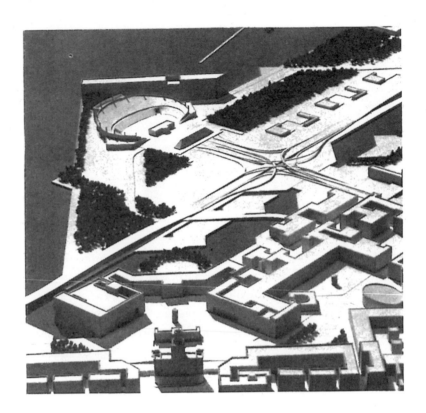

63. Waterfront area, model and perspective view.

considered as of maximum civic importance. And, functionally, a variety of further uses—commercial, residential, and recreational—suggest themselves. A recognition of these conditions could produce a major group of linked plazas, accommodating the line of the Thruway and leading from Niagara Square through to the waterfront and the mouth of the river.

Residential Areas

Areas which are adjacent to downtown Buffalo and proposed as primarily residential include the waterfront site north of Virginia Street and the Ellicott project site east of Michigan Avenue.

The waterfront housing comprises block-long segments or neighborhoods which are arranged so as to let local streets enter the site as service streets. These segments define Niagara Street as a major civic connection between the Peace Bridge and City Hall and to the west relate to the pleasure craft canal and the central recreational waterfront area.

In addition to housing of various types, each segment contains covered parking, small commercial establishments, professional office space, kindergarten facilities, recreational areas, and boat docking arrangements.

A pedestrian network related to the commercial and recreational facilities connects the residential areas with the City Hall plaza. Generally, the architectural intention is to retain the advantages, in terms of light, air, and view, of present-day, tall, freestanding residential building types and at the same time to reestablish the street-defining characteristics and multi-use vitality of traditional urban building configurations.

Illustrated in figure 64 are a few of the combinations of buildings possible within the housing areas. Important to such variations is the maintenance of Niagara Street and the canal as recognizable parts of the large-scale structure of the city. Thus, these buildings must perform in two ways. They must make reference to the city structure as a whole and at the same time they must relate

Buffalo Waterfront

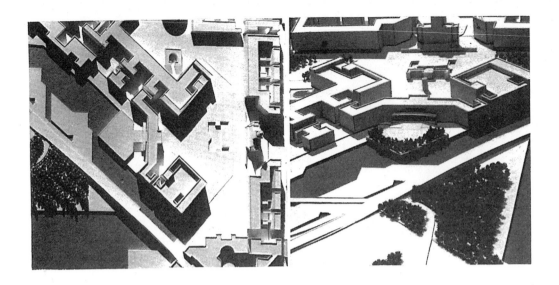

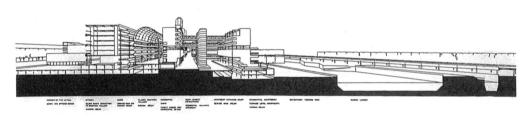

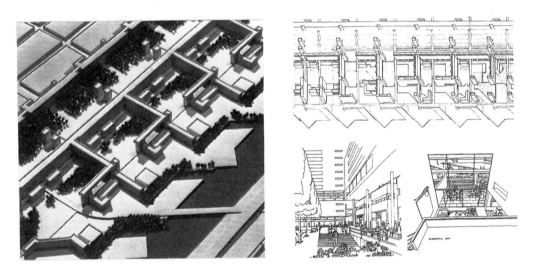

64. City Hall area (two views, top); section through area north of City Hall showing residential and commercial spaces (center); residential areas, with illustrations of possible residential combinations (bottom).

to the more particular characteristics of the immediate area. It can be seen that while the line of buildings defining Niagara Street remains fairly constant, those towards the waterfront are free to vary as circumstances dictate.

Circulation

Circulation is divided into three basic categories: vehicular, pedestrian, mechanical. The vehicular circulation system is a function of the existing road layout and includes a high-speed through system, an intermediate-speed ring road system, local streets, and a pleasure drive circuit relating to existing and proposed parks. Local streets relating to primary public activity areas and landmarks are developed as tree-lined boulevards.

The pedestrian system is independent of vehicular traffic and connects residential areas with civic, commercial, and recreational functions.

Mechanical transport includes a subway system serving the suburban areas with shuttle lines in the city center and a pedestrian travelator system relating to the general pedestrian layout.

At points of convergence between the various systems and close to commercial areas transport centers are located. These centers contain large municipal parking facilities, bus docks, major subway stops, commercial establishments, and office space.

Texture

Together the preceding illustrations imply a skeleton of points, lines, and fields which could provide a basic strategy for attack upon the waterfront problem; but they leave as an open question the issue of any further detail or texture.

As regards texture, when we think of older cities, the major image we have in mind is that of a continuous solid from out of which a structure of spaces has been carved (fig. 67, top). But we may also think of the suburb as a context of grass and trees within

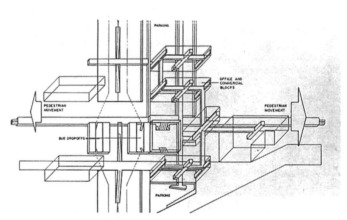

65. Circulation; circulation diagram.

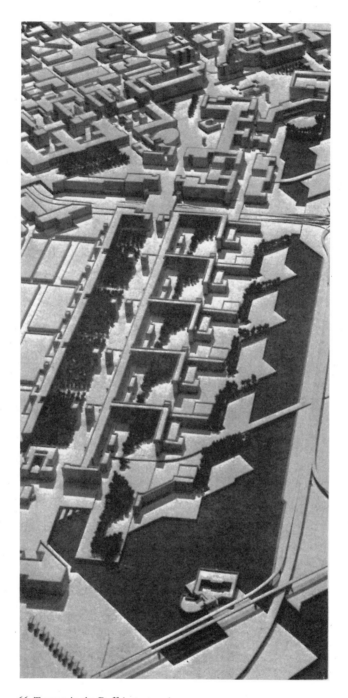

66. Texture in the Buffalo proposal.

Buffalo Waterfront

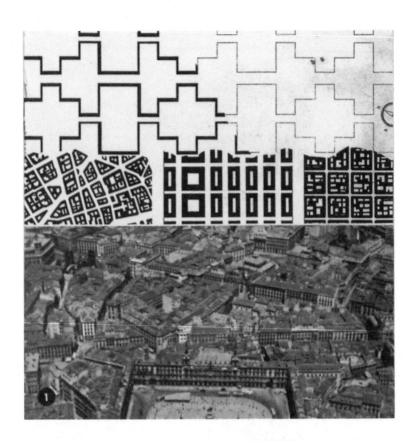

67. Urban texture (top): continuous solid/structured space. Suburban texture (bottom left): continuous void/freestanding buildings. Modern texture (bottom right): towers in the park.

which freestanding buildings are located (fig. 67, bottom left). These are the two traditional extremes, the one represented, in Buffalo, in the area of Main Street and Niagara Square, the other to the south of Delaware Park. But Buffalo also shows a third and specifically twentieth century urban texture. This is that produced by the typical renewal project involving the idea of the city as an accumulation of isolated towers (fig. 67, bottom right).

None of these textures seems appropriate in the waterfront area. The solid city fails in terms of space, light, and air; the suburban variation fails in terms of density; and the city of isolated towers in its inability to supply the varieties of interest which are needed.

For these reasons a basic pattern of long wall-like buildings enclosing spaces and defining streets has been adopted, and it is this procedure which has determined the project in detail.

Buffalo Waterfront

Nicollet Island, Minneapolis

A contribution to an exhibition, "The River: Images of the Mississippi," sponsored by the Walker Art Center, Minneapolis, 1976. Catalogue published as Design Quarterly, *no. 101/102.*

Judith DiMaio and Colin Rowe for the Institute for Architecture and Urban Studies assisted by John Hartley, Stephen Potters, Martin Kleinman, Livio Dimitriu, Bill Strawbridge, Andrew Anker, and David Buege.

Other projects for Nicollet Island were submitted by Studio Works and the Hodne Stageberg Partners, Inc.

The authors of this project believe it should be regarded primarily as a study rather than a prescription for Nicollet Island and its adjacent shorelines. It is some sort of attempt to discriminate configurations which seem to be latent, almost to be visible; and, by awarding them the priority which they appear to require, to sponsor

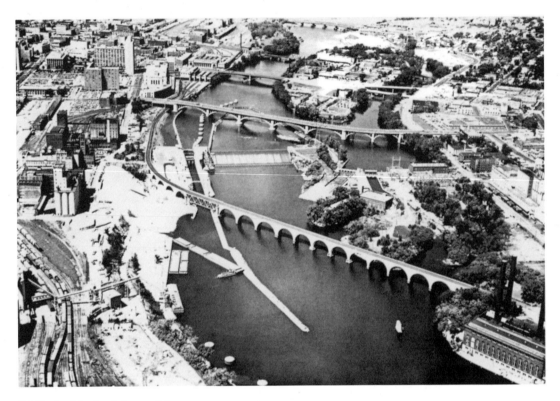

68. Nicollet Island, existing condition.

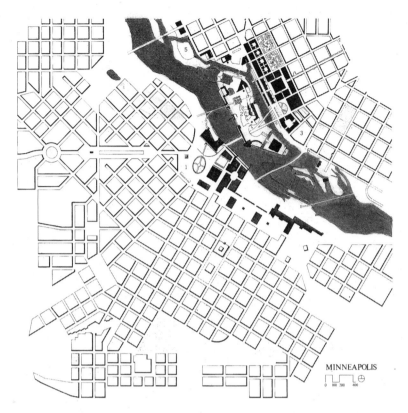

69. Nicollet Island in the Minneapolis context: plan. The Institute's project anchors itself to central Minneapolis, St. Anthony, and East Hennepin by an extension of the
skyway system. In Minneapolis a reconstructed depot, providing a multipurpose internal environment, serves as a point of departure for the island skyway, which travels alongside the railroad bridge, crosses the island at a low level, and arrives at the
St. Anthony side of the river at what is thought of as a community focus—a shopping district and housing.

intimations of identity, direction, and place. In the language of
Louis Kahn, it is an attempt to discover what things wish to be;
and the authors of this project believe that this wider mode of
investigation (which is also a discovery of clues) is neither entirely
Utopian nor wholly gratuitous. Instead their mood is that of
conservative-radical. They neither despise Utopia nor exalt the status quo; but, though they are very much concerned with the dialectic of novelty and tradition, they have no anxiety to present their

Nicollet Island, Minneapolis

larger proposals as, in any way, definitive. Nor do they wish their proposals for Nicollet Island itself to be regarded as any more than a strategy of approach. Nicollet Island could, for instance, become just another state park. It could, just possibly, thrive as no more than a rustic theater for family barbecues and frisbee; it could even become a bird sanctuary; but, if such might be among its only too predictable fates, it may still be imagined that the interest of Minneapolis could better be served by the entertainment of more arresting fantasies. Islands in cities! Very few cities are privileged to possess them. Paris but not London, Rome but not Florence, St. Petersburg and Berlin but not St. Louis—Memphis—New Orleans; and the city so lucky as to possess an island has always been prone to regard it as something emblematic and representational—never as a casual throwaway but as something intimately related to its idea of itself.

But if traditionally one may think of the urban island as a focus of the public realm, as equipped with a cathedral or a stock exchange or several museums, the situation in Minneapolis does not allow us so to envisage Nicollet. For all this kind of thing is provided elsewhere; and, short of another university, what to do? Should the whole outfit be leased to Walt Disney Enterprises?

The Institute's team does not disparage this possibility. Indeed it is more than apt to imagine its own contribution as providing a framework for something very like this—for a pedestrian resort, a spectacular urban garden, celebrating the theme of water but also capable of presenting a variety of further stimuli—cultural, recreational, commercial, residential. The Institute's team assumes that an idiosyncratic mix of all these uses is desirable; but, obviously, its argument is based not so much in terms of functional consideration as of archetypal image. Its members suppose that a successful interpretation of Nicollet Island will be one which stresses not so much matter of fact but rather a magical (and extravagant) profusion of reminiscence.

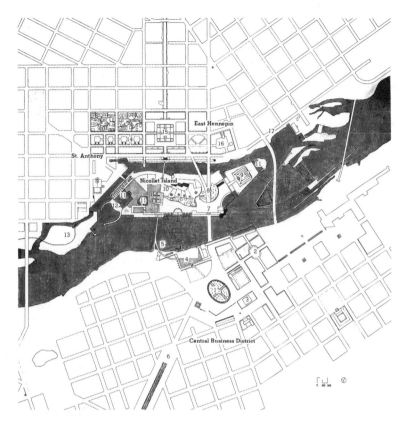

70. Nicollet Island and its adjacent shorelines, plan.

Nicollet Island, Minneapolis

Axonometric View

71. Axonometric.

URBANISTICS

Roma Interrotta

Contribution to an exhibition organized by Incontri Internazionali d'Arte in 1977 and displayed in Rome at the Mercato di Traiano, May–June 1978.

Other participants in the exhibition were Piero Sartogo, Costantino Dardi, Antoine Grumbach, James Stirling, Paolo Portoghesi, Romaldo Giurgola, Robert Venturi, Michael Graves, Robert Krier, Aldo Rossi, and Leon Krier, and contributions to the catalogue were made by Giulio Carlo Argan, at that time mayor of Rome, and Christian Norberg-Schulz.

The program for the exhibition was based upon the plan of Rome published by Giambattista Nolli in 1748 (fig. 72) and upon the argument that, after Nolli, the urban tissue of Rome had been 'interrupted', that is, that something assumed to be implicit in the urban texture of Rome had become lost. In other words, since nothing very important in Rome had happened between 1748 and 1870—except for

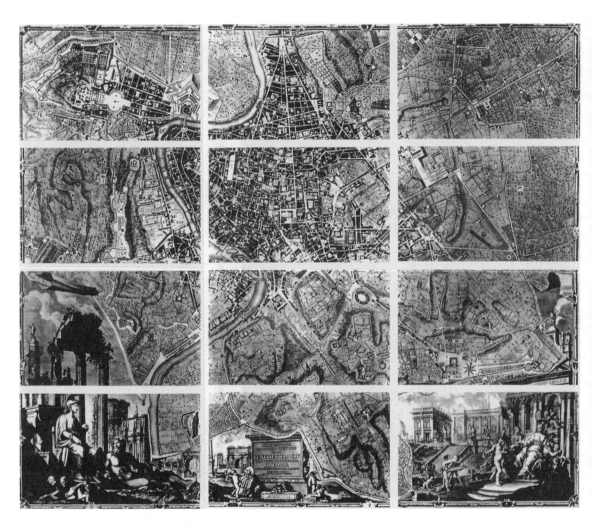

72. Plan of Rome, 1748. Giambattista Nolli.

Valadier's intervention in the Piazza del Popolo—the exhibition was an ostensible critique of urbanistic goings-on since the overthrow of the temporal power of the Papacy.

Participants—many of whom, I think, failed to understand the message—were each assigned one of twelve plates which make up Nolli's plan, and from it they were asked to extrapolate their own developments.

An interesting idea but one which could scarcely lead to any successful issue; and this because Nolli's twelve plates, when they are presented as sites for development, are not equipped with any equivalency of complication. And thus, up north—when confronted with the Vatican, the Borgo, and the Piazza del Popolo—just what do you do? And thus, down southwest and south—the plates given to Robert Venturi, Robert Krier, Aldo Rossi, and Leon Krier—since these are occupied by the decorations of Nolli's plan, then, yet again, except for producing new decorations, just what do you do?

Anyway, as things worked out, we were given a center site, the Palatino, the Aventino, and the Celio, that most difficult theater of ancient Roman debris; and it is now that I should say who we were.

From the beginning we were Judith DiMaio and myself, with the assistance of Peter Carl (Lexington, Kentucky, July 1977); and Judy's mark is registered in the circular garden (the Orto Botanico from Padua) on the Aventino. But, when Judy left to go to the American Academy in Rome, it was with Steven Peterson and Barbara Littenberg that I resumed work on this project; and, by it, we were all highly stimulated.

Presuming that the idea of Rome Interrupted required a fake history of Rome to explain our developments, I wrote such a fake history; and I am amused to say that I still receive letters from such persons who assume that at least my footnotes must be genuine. "Just where do I find that article by Françoise Choay which you called out?"

So it is an imaginary history of development which follows.

The following is excerpted from the catalogue of the exhibition "Rome: The Lost and the Unknown City (Roma Ignota e Perduta)"

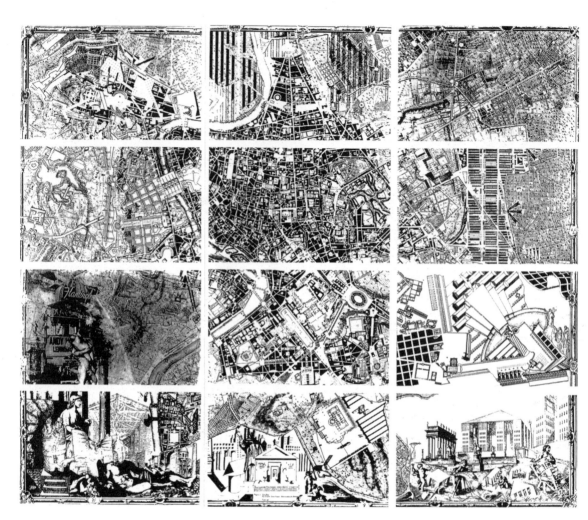

73. "Roma Interrotta," the twelve sectors (left to right, top to bottom): Sector 1, Sartogo; Sector 2, Dardi; Sector 3, Grumbach; Sector 4, Stirling; Sector 5, Portoghesi; Sector 6, Giurgola; Sector 7, Venturi; Sector 8, Rowe; Sector 9, Graves; Sector 10, R. Krier; Sector 11, Rossi; Sector 12, L. Krier.

organized by the Museum of Art, University of St. Francis Xavier, Great Falls, Montana in the summer of 1974. This exhibition continues to be little known and was, at the time, regrettably unadvertised; but we believe that we can state with certainty that the catalogue is the product of the late Father Vincent Mulcahy, S.J. In instructed circles Vincent Mulcahy's knowledge of Roman topography is, needless to say, recognized to have been as extensive as it was minute. Indeed, Mulcahy, who was always a fount of generalizations, was simultaneously so devoted to the arcane and the abstruse as to have rendered much of his very solid information highly suspect to those many scholars whose only ideal is the never to be interpreted accumulation of what, without undue epistemological concern, they presume to be no more than irreducible fact.

Incipient criticisms of Father Mulcahy's more extreme speculations are already to be found in the catalogue of the exhibition "Papal Urbanism and Numismatology," Museum of Fine Arts, Waxahachie, Texas, 1972, in which, with something approaching an excess of critical apparatus, certain of his conclusions are found to be less than accurate; but in this disagreement of authorities we would prefer to remain neutral. Indeed, because we feel more than highly indebted to Vincent Mulcahy—and because we prefer to consult the visible evidence of available drawings and monuments—though sometimes skeptical of his more elaborate findings, we would prefer to stipulate our own dependence upon his incomparable exegetic capacity.

> We are so familiar with the area of the Palatine, the Aventine, and Celio in its present appearance that it becomes difficult for our minds to reconstruct its earlier aspect—an arid and deserted region of ancient remains, unkempt vineyards, malarial *villini,* and battered monastic foundations. But such was the landscape known to Poussin and to Claude, known also to Gaspar Van Wittel; and while we may mourn its loss, we may also salute the present appearance of these hills, which in their gentle and brilliant green-

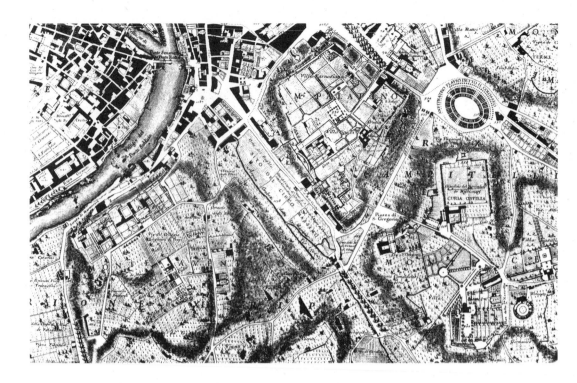

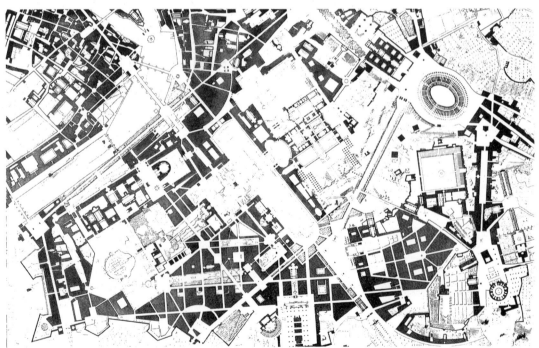

74. Sector 8: fragment of the Nolli plan; proposal by the Cornell team.

ness, are apt to suggest a fragment of the Veneto posturing as an ideal and a better Rome, as a Rome of the Northern imagination.

The present Venetic, and almost English, character of this territory, which has so long displeased archaeologists, was, needless to say, the result of a deliberate policy. The Acqua Buonaparte, later to be known as the Acqua Pia and, still later, as the Acqua Sabaudia, was a primary result of the French administration of the city during the years 1809–1814, but, though mostly an affair of the Ecole Polytechnique, this great hydraulic undertaking demonstrably betrayed a symbolic purpose. For if ostensibly there was here proposed no more than a rational program of irrigation, in the profusion of water which was supplied the bounds of reason were extravagantly exceeded. And therefore (and almost like the cataract of eighteenth century rationalism itself) this particular aqueduct might lend itself to interpretation as a 'scientific' critique of an assumed Papal retardation.

However, if the Acqua Paola and Acqua Felice were, here, both put to shame, this is to anticipate our account, since modern developments in this area may be said to have begun at a slightly earlier date, with Cardinal Albani's purchase of the Orti Farnesiani from Charles III of Naples.

The building of Capodimonte and Portici, not to mention the impending construction of Caserta, had, one supposes, begun to place too great a strain upon the narrowed Bourbon resources; and, since there was the additional expense of the excavations at Pompeii (however many vases might later be bought by Sir William Hamilton and others), the disposal of superfluous Farnese estates in Rome was perhaps the inevitable result. The exact date of the sale of the Orti Farnesiani and the exact price paid are still not known;[1] but Cardinal Albani's purchase might be considered as having been doubly happy. For, while it re-lieved the house of Naples of an embarrassment both genea-logical and financial,[2] it equipped the Cardinal with an archaeological foyer of unexampled richness. The villa al-ready built by Marchionni at Porta Salaria (Villa Albani as it is *still* sometimes called) became now a merely minor the-ater of display; and, in the new Villa Albani del Palatino, we should be called upon to imagine the enthusiastic builder dispensing hospitality and patronage to Robert Adam, Jacques Louis Clérisseau, Hubert Robert, Raphael Mengs, Antonio Canova, Benjamin West, and others.

Though never elaborate,[3] it is now recognized that this new Villa Albani provided one of the principal 'forcing houses' in the early history of neo-Classicism,[4] and, as such, we are indebted to Goethe for some record of its appearance and contents on the occasion of his Roman visit of 1786. But, fresh from Weimar and highly susceptible to all appro-priate impressions, Goethe's encomium of the Villa Albani is too famous to require record; and, as we recall it, we can only experience regret for what, substantially, is lost—a most brilliant and precocious demonstration (the youthful John Soane must have known it well) which could only have prepared the way for the more exacting archaeological tastes of circa 1800.[5]

However, in spite of Cardinal Albani's remarkable incentive and in spite of its art historical celebrity, as already intimated, for further developments we are com-pelled to wait for the French Revolution and the subse-quent impact of the Napoleonic Empire; and here we are faced with a major problem. The Emperor's projects for Paris are well known, but largely uninvestigated is the his-tory of his projects for Rome; and, no doubt, a prime rea-son is the received idea that Buonaparte himself never visited peninsular Italy which, in his days, slumbered so happily outside the major theaters of European dispute.

The subject of Napoleon and Rome, so crisscrossed with the internment of Pius VII at Fontainebleau, has of course been lately illuminated by Françoise Choay in her exemplary *Interventions Napoléoniennes à Rome;*[6] and this study has made us, yet again, aware of the fantastic plan of Scipione Perosini (involving an ensemble of palaces extending from Piazza Colonna to the Colosseum) and the less ambitious proposals of Raphael Stern (involving no more than a reconstruction of the Quirinale).[7] Mme Choay also makes abundantly clear the roles played in these projects by the Comte de Tournon and the Maréchal Daru, respectively Prefect of Rome and Intendant of the Imperial Palaces; and it is, therefore, highly unfortunate that her researches were unable to take cognizance of that great body of Valadier drawings which, until 1972, remained unknown. For these drawings, so recently revealed by the Cabinet des Estampes et des Desseins of the Bibliothèque Nationale, still largely unpublished and still waiting detailed exploration, introduce an entirely new evidence; and involving as they do a 'reconstruction' of the Palatine and the Circus Maximus, a monumental cemetery (the present Uomini Illustrissimi), a *sistemazione* of the Aventine, an Egyptian Temple,[8] and, as a pendent to the Arch of Constantine, an Arco Napoleonico, their ultimate interpretation may well inspire a major revision of our ideas as to Imperial policy—as, quite certainly, they may reinforce the stubborn legend, hitherto dismissed, of the Emperor himself having visited the Eternal City on at least two occasions.

Legend and rumor, though insubstantial, are never to be wholly wished away; but, meanwhile, the record of Buonaparte's movements during the years 1809–11 would seem to be established quite beyond dispute. Do we, therefore, assume a *Doppelgänger* in Paris (or wherever) while the alleged Roman visits took place? Mariana di San Silvestro and Luigi Primoli would encourage us in this fantasy[9] but,

these apart, if we know that the Valadier drawings are anno-
tated by the Emperor himself and if the same evidence
leaves us in no doubt as to his firsthand, though not intimate, knowledge of the relevant topography, then what are
we to postulate?

We will leave aside the possibility of a clandestine
visit which Napoleon may have paid to Rome in the years
1809–11 (could the visit have been paid on his return from
Egypt in 1799?); but we will assume the probability of his
reviewing and condemning the projects of Perosini and
Stern at about this date; and we will then assume a new
incentive on the part of Tournon and Daru resulting in the
Valadier propositions, which, apparently, secured Imperial
approval in May 1810.

However, to interpret what was here presented
and, conditionally, accepted will require on our part a willing suspension of disbelief. For, if the Imperial iconography
is eloquent, ourselves are apt to view this Greco-Roman apparatus rather as a period piece, its outlines softened by ret-
rospect, than as what it was designed to be: a hard-edged
politico-theatrical propaganda intended to elicit enthusiasm for a universal rule.

But to place ourselves in the position of Napoleon
circa 1810: his new wife is an Austrian archduchess; Pius
VII, to all intents and purposes, is a prisoner, the news
from Spain, though scarcely happy, is dismissable; and
meanwhile, since Russia remains unattacked, the future
sequence of catastrophe—Moscow, the Beresina, Leipzig,
Waterloo—is not to be conceived. Indeed, triumph is absolute; the new Caesar's fantasies are at their most elaborate;
and it is into this arena of possibility that we would wish
to place the evidence of the Valadier drawings of which, as
yet, we have very imperfect knowledge.

To repeat: the time is 1810; and, while we are confronted with the meaning of Valadier's project, to be taken

into account there are also those six colossal statues intended to represent Alexander, Julius, Augustus, Constantine, Charlemagne, and Napoleon himself, known to have been ordered from Canova's studio in 1809;[10] and then there is the more surprising image of Cola di Rienzo, apparently intended to be part of a fountain, provided by Thorvaldsen in the following year.[11] But if, by themselves, the Rienzi piece, recently put on exhibition by the Accademia Carrara at Bergamo, and the Canova commission may constitute a difficulty, then, related to Valadier, all these problems diminish. For, simply, the Valadier drawings seem to suggest themselves as the preparation of a stage, a stage for the ultimate Napoleonic settlement of Europe which was to be dictated from Rome possibly in 1819 and, probably, on the occasion of the Emperor's fiftieth birthday, August 15.

One may imagine the anticipated scene of the Congress of Vienna in reverse operation. The Russians and the English are exhausted; the gently heroic Pius VII has yielded; there is to be much coming and going between the Vatican and the Palazzo Imperiale del Palatino; there is to be a major concordat; the King of Rome is to be crowned; possibly Beethoven is to contribute a symphony; there are to be acclamations, parades, pyrotechnics, fountains running with wine, *feux de joie,* all the rest—and the whole is to be conducted in a setting of heroically romantic neo-Classical architecture.

The Valadier drawings are, therefore, an ironical commentary upon possibility and prediction (man proposes, God disposes); but, if the Dictate of Rome did not come about, the idea of this 'triumph' was to be not without its future influence. The Foro Buonaparte, otherwise known as the Piazza d'Armi del Circo Massimo, was of course constructed, complete with Palladian reminiscences, in 1811; by the same date work was under way on the Pala-

tine;[12] and by the following year the great terrace of the
Aventine with its accompanying bridges was also building;
but since the rest of this plan remained unaccomplished at
the time of Pius VII's return in 1814, one may still be surprised by the longevity of its skeleton—a longevity which
clearly excludes politics. Otherwise, how could Valadier's
great Piazzale dell'Aventino, put forward as Napoleonic gesture, be later converted into the setting for Santo Spirito
della Restaurazione, that *chiesa votiva* so embarrassingly presented by the Czar Alexander to the Pope?

And, of course, this masterpiece of Quarenghi,[13] a
highly accomplished Pantheon and not completely a crude
monument to reaction, must now be recognized as a major
secondary impulse in the development of the area. For, in
the 1820s, to that opulent English and Russian society
which increasingly flooded Rome it provided an irresistible
magnet. Fashionable (dare we say corrupt?), at Santo
Spirito spectacle, religiosity, and the Almanach de Gotha
were all simultaneously entertained; and if, to the Russians,
the church suggested St. Petersburg and, to the English,
Regent's Park, it should not be at all surprising that this society (with its miscellaneous German clients) increasingly
gravitated to the vicinity.

The various villas—Monmouth-Bariatinski,
Demidoff, Beresford-Hope, Storey, Casamassima,[14] Curtis-
Winterhalter—built in this area attest to this Anglo-
Russian, later American, and always foreign influence.
Partly because of Santo Spirito the Aventine became a
quartier-de-luxe. But, if so much is part of knowledge, there
might have still been almost nothing had it not been for
the genius of Aldo Rossini, the Czar's chef, like his more
famous namesake a native of Pesaro, who in 1817 retired
from the snows of Russia to establish what may well have
been the first of grand hotels.[15] The great and almost Geno-
ese bulk of the Albergo della Russia, then so eccentrically

located, might today be considered as having established the ultimate cachet of the neighbourhood. . . .

Footnotes to the Text of Father Vincent Mulcahy, S.J.

1. Perhaps, with the destruction of the Neapolitan archives, never to be known. But see Heinrich Schreiber, Winckelmann, and Kardinal Albani, *Preussische Jahrbuch für Künstegeschichte,* vol. XXV, 1913.

2. The illegitimate descent from Paul III Farnese had begun to constitute a problem.

3. Cardinal Albani was able to acquire little more than the Farnese property.

4. See Jacquelin Tannenbaum, *Cardinal Albani as a Patron,* Princeton, N.J., 1958; and, for a different opinion, see Martino Scolari, "Un Cardinal Dilettante," *Connaissance des Arts,* 1964.

5. Friedrich Gilly also visited the Villa del Palatino, unfortunately during its decadence; and, of course, to Karl Friedrich Schinkel we are indebted for yet another survey. Indeed we are indebted for a survey so accurate that we may be eager to acknowledge some of its traces in that brilliant sequence of apartments executed by Schinkel for the Berlin Schloss. In which context see Mario Praz and Giuliano Briganti, *Illuminismo e Romantismo,* Bari, 1953.

6. Françoise Choay, *Interventions Napoléoniennes à Rome,* Paris, 1969; and particularly pp. 97–115.

7. See also A. La Padula, *Roma e la regione nell'epoca napoleonica,* Rome (?), 1970; and Vittorio de Feo, *La Piazza del Quirinale,* Rome, 1973.

8. Napoleon's regret at not having built an Egyptian temple in Paris is recorded in Las Cases, *Mémorial de Sainte Hélène,* vol. II, p. 154, ed. Paris 1956. "Il regrettait fort, du reste, de n'avoir pas fait construire un temple égyptien à Paris: c'était un monument, disait-il, dont il voudrait avoir enrichi la capitale, etc." And, from the same source, see also vol. I, p. 431: "L'Empereur disait que, si Rome fut restée sous sa domination, elle fut sortie de ses ruines; il se proposait de nettoyer de tous ses décombres de restaurer tout ce qui eut été possible, etc. Il ne douter pas que le même esprit s'étandant

dans le voisinage, il eut put en être en quelque sorte de même d'Herculaneum et de Pompei."

The Egyptian temple located at the head of the Circus Maximus and destined for the purpose of a cult as yet unknown is, of course, the present church of Saint Catherine of Alexandria.

9. See Mariana di San Silvestro di Castelbarco della Verdura, *Mémoire Inédite,* Turin, 1872. Born in 1790, during the French interregnum, her grandfather self-exiled to Sardinia (Luigi di San Silvestro, 1738–1817, remained one of the most intractable ornaments of the court of Turin), the Contessa di San Silvestro, in her youth acquainted with Mme de Staël and, later, allegedly, more than a friend of Cavour, can only be a reliable witness. Though somewhat divorced from her proper niche in time, she was a person who saw and knew; and, if her own record may still be insufficient, there still remain the *Saggi Napoleoniani* of Luigi Primoli, Livorno, 1905; and Primoli, again from the point of view of an eminent insider, amply corroborates the San Silvestro rumors.

10. See Janos Szechenyi, "A Hitherto Neglected Project of Antonio Canova," *Art Bulletin,* vol. XVI, 1972.

11. See Bertil Gyllenstierna, *A Republican Monument to Empire,* Uppsala, 1970.

12. The Hellenistic bust of Apollo presented by Pius VII in 1817 to the Prince Regent is a record of this building campaign. One of the few significant discoveries made in construction work on the Palatine, before being transferred to Windsor, it was for many years incongruously housed among the *chinoiseries* of Brighton.

13. A posthumous masterpiece sometimes, alternatively, attributed to Japelli. Quarenghi, of course, died in Bergamo in 1806.

14. For the background of the still surviving Villa Casamassima see Henry James, *Roderick Hudson,* London and New York, 1875; and Michael Manfredi, "A Nineteenth-Century 'Replica' of Pirro Ligorio's Villa Pia," *Facciata,* vol. V, Geneva, N.Y., 1973.

15. For a full appraisal of Rossini's culinary genius see Joseph De Maistre, *Les Soirées de Saint Petersbourg,* 5th ed., Lyon, 1845. But Aldo Rossini deserves also to be celebrated as the probable inventor

of that notorious Manhattan dessert, named for a Russian foreign minister of Portuguese birth and Anglican background, the Nesselrode Pie.

At this stage we will leave Father Mulcahy to both his footnotes and his fantasies. To us he has provided an indispensable guide; but he has also left us in the position of old-fashioned classical archaeologists attempting to reconstruct a shattered monument or statue from the most fragmentary debris and, while it has been useful, his information is sometimes a little too selective for our purposes. Thus, while he makes brief reference to the monumental cemetery of the Illustrissimi, Father Mulcahy is strangely reticent about further developments on the Celio which Valadier's proposals seem to have sponsored. We refer to the elegant Quartiere Mattei, achieved without any great mutilation of the Villa Mattei itself; to the sequence of spaces (the present Piazza Giuseppe Terragni and Largo Cattaneo) leading in from the Colosseum; to Von Klenze's manipulations of Santo Stefano, which have often been considered doubtful; and then, and unlike our Jesuit guide, we suggest that the same architect's Accademia Bavarese, located immediately to the rear of the church in the former *vigna* of the Collegio Germanico, is a building which—with all its later Nazarene associations (frescoes by Schnorr von Carolsfeld, etc.)—increasingly clamors for record and recognition.

But, if these proofs of nineteenth century Bavarian piety have not been noticed by Father Vincent, then how much stranger is his account of developments upon the Aventine! For there he concentrates exclusively on the great terrace and its later Russian appendages and fails entirely to make any commentary upon much else which surely deserves attention. We refer to the Orto Botanico with its decidedly Paduan overtones (was this executed by Japelli?); to the interesting but apparently decorative sequence of fortifications extending from the bridge of Porta Portese; to the public park, the Pineta del Monte Testaccio, which protrudes into the area; and to the sequence of villas and other buildings, vaguely recalling

Giulio Romano, Pirro Ligorio, and Claude-Nicolas Ledoux, which, rising out of their context of trees, comprise the southwestern enclosure of the Circus Maximus. But, even with regard to Santo Spirito, Father Mulcahy, who clearly detested the whole program of this church, is also mysteriously quiet with reference to its iconography, the great Piranesian Terrace of the Aventine! Its references to Diocletian and to Robert Adam! Its superstructures so suggestive of Durand! The essence of this great terrace, so well conceived by Alexander I, seems completely to have evaded Mulcahy's scrutiny. Had too many years in the American Midwest dulled his native Irish percipience? At one end of the terrace the Cavalieri di Malta; and at the other (as a replica of the Castello Savelli) the new *priorato* of the Cavalieri della Restaurazione—that order which, deriving mostly from the Baltic provinces, was for so long unduly favored by Pius IX and Leo XIII!!

Correspondingly, Father Mulcahy, whose instincts were always compassionate and expansive, chooses also to ignore the proposed conversion of Santa Francesca Romana and the temples of Venus and Rome into a barracks for the Gardes Impériales. Indeed, while frequently concerned with minutiae, such rather large minutiae as these he often affects to disdain; and possibly, we too should be glad that this particular project was never even attempted. However, Father Mulcahy's silences with regard to much else, we must confess, do place us in a situation of great difficulty.

As to be expected, his interests altogether cease as of September 20, 1870; and even after 1848 he is scarcely disposed to be highly attentive. For with all his midwestern democracy, Father Mulcahy was no friend to the Risorgimento, the Garibaldini, or the House of Savoy. In 1870 he would have been the implacable enemy of all those who assembled themselves around the strangely assorted court of the Quirinale. But if almost constitutionally he was anti-Piedmontese, his unwillingness to make commentary upon what he regarded as usurpation does result in some grave injustices; and we allude to his apparent refusal to discuss the present condition of the Circus Maximus and the Palatine.

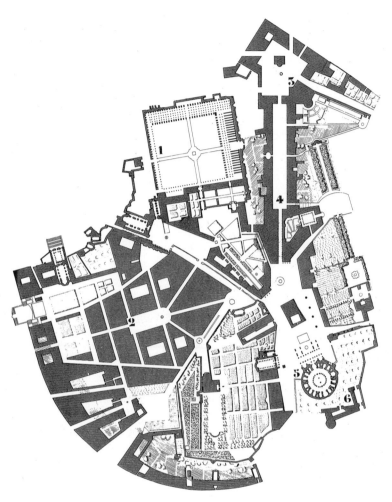

75. Celio.
1.   Cemetery of the Uomini Illustrissimi
2.   Quartiere Mattei
3.   Piazza Cattaneo
4.   Largo Giuseppe Terragni
5.   S. Stefano Rotondo
6.   Accademia Bavarese

Roma Interrotta

The Circus Maximus, though it was never simply an unembellished *piazza d'armi,* down until the later 1870s retained a somewhat astringent neo-Classical character. Surrounded by Valadier with a shallow canal registering its original outline and equipped with an apparatus of balustrades, bridges, obelisks, and statues, it is tempting to attribute to its format during these years a further Paduan source; and Stendhal, when he compared it with the Prato della Valle, of course made this connection. But though the role of this source is still visible, as the area was revised around 1880, it is impossible not further to interpret it as both a tribute to Hadrian at Tivoli and a large-scale commentary upon the water garden at Bagnaia.

An arcadian valley, crudely suggestive of the magic garden of the *Hypneroto-machia,* densely enclosed by a framework of pines, palms, oleanders, and rhododendra, perhaps the most seductive of all Roman celebrations of water, the Circus Maximus, in its present role of nymphaeum and *boschetto,* though it has always displeased the erudite, became immediately one of the most popular of resorts; and as such, it could only instigate further important local activity—in the first case the Viadotto Margherita of 1893.

This bridge, which is usually considered less than happy and which connected the garden of the former Villa Albani with the Piazzale del Aventino, seems suddenly to have been found indispensable; and its engaging stucco and cast-iron construction is directly relatable to further building campaigns upon the Palatine.

Father Mulcahy publishes Valadier's proposals for the Palazzo Imperiale, notices that work began upon them, but disdains to comment upon their subsequent evolution; and, needless to say, during the period 1814–70, this unfinished building could only constitute a grave Papal embarrassment. "Part sacrilege and part nostalgia," to quote from Sigfried Giedion's characterization of Schinkel's palace on the Acropolis for King Otto of Greece, the buildings of this Napoleonic *mise-en-scène* were already too advanced and too solid to permit even the idea of demolition. There are some indications that here the Czar envisaged the seat of the Holy Alli-

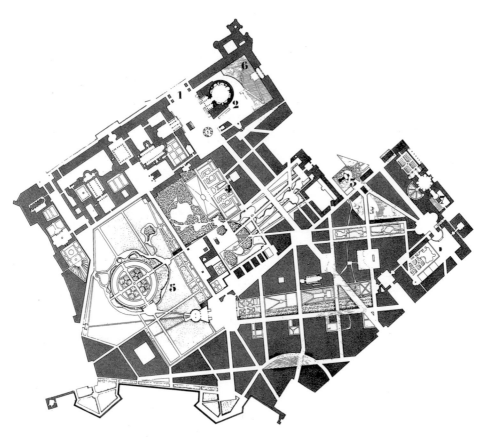

76. Aventino.

1.   Terrace of the Aventine
2.   Santo Spirito della Restaurazione
3.   Villa Casamassima
4.   Albergo di Russia
5.   Orto Botanico
6.   Palazzo dei Cavalieri della Restaurazione
7.   Palazzo Laetitia

ance; and, as all the world knows, Lord Byron spent one extremely uncomfortable winter attempting, in the company of Teresa Guiccioli, to inhabit these unheatable halls; but we will leave aside the comparable circumstances of Richard Wagner's occupancy in 1865 (the buildings were then rented to him by Monsignor de Merode) because what might well be called the *crisis of the site* begins now to approach.

The mode of the Piedmontese entry into Rome (via the Porta Pia) undoubtedly contributed to the 'convenience' of the Quirinale (it was the first adequate house to be reached); but to the old Papal residence there always adhered something of an inappropriate atmosphere—the flavor, no doubt, of illegitimate acquisition— and, consequently, the idea of the Palatine could only remain enticing. Indeed, if the ruins of Rome have always implied a program of *renovatio,* the circumstances were now almost more than perfect. The shell of the buildings was approximately available; they awaited only an incrustation of ornament; and we owe it to the good sense of *il rè galantuomo* that this extravagant policy was not pursued. Vittorio Emanuele was content with quiet, if slightly wild, domesticities; and thus it was not until his daughter-in-law began to exert her influence that projects for the Palatine came to be revived.

We are not historians and as to an accurate sequence of events we entertain no clear idea; but we are told—and can believe—that quite shortly after 1878 there were projects on the boards for a monument to Vittorio Emanuele upon the Palatine— even, in some cases, taking the form of a completion of Valadier's proposals. It seems to us appropriate that the first king of a united Italy should have been so commemorated; and we would like to think of the contemporary remodeling of the Circus Maximus as related to these ideas. However, after 1882, it became apparent that the Vittoriano was not here to be built; and, apart from a disastrous refurbishing of the Villa Albani (to which the Viadotto Margherita is directly related), for further works on the Palatine we are compelled to await the twentieth century and the sequel to the terrible events of that evening of July 1900 at Monza. For, with the tragic

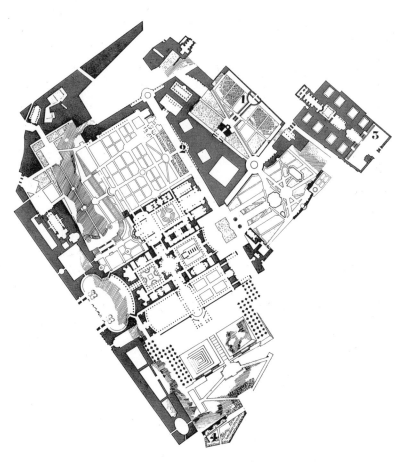

77. **Palatino.**

1.   Orti Farnesiani
2.   Villa Albani al Palatino
3.   Gardes Impériales
4.   Septizonium

Roma Interrotta

assassination of the second king of Italy, the question of a monument again arose; and, if there could be no question of the Umbertino competing with the Vittoriano, it was still under these circumstances that the international conspiracy of archaeologists was defeated and a site on the Palatine made available.

One need not be altogether exhilarated by the results—though doubtless taste will change. Whether Sommaruga and Sacconi were the most harmonious of collaborators is scarcely an open question; but the decision to rebuild the exedra of the Domus Augustana and to establish behind it the Galleria Nazionale d'Arte Moderna was surely prompted by a reasonable ambition and a conspicuous wisdom. For, if its classicism is, in parts, a little bit too Puvis de Chavannes, and if its details are, occasionally, uncomfortably reminiscent of the Italian Pavilion at the St. Louis Exposition of 1904, from a distance, certainly, the Umbertino is surely more than adequate; and, excessive purism apart, it can be claimed that this white marble apparition helps pleasingly to complete the architectural furniture of the Circus Maximus.

There is little more that now remains to be said. In spite of the strenuous manipulations of Queen Margherita, the Palazzo del Palatino still awaits completion. However, as a ruin imposed upon ruins, it is not without a certain poignancy; and, in our accompanying plan, we have chosen to present it had it been built according to intentions. In other areas, too, we have taken comparable liberties—by adding to the plan of Valadier contributions by later architects (Santo Spirito, the Accademia Bavarese, etc.) which seem to suggest or to augment its themes and by not showing the Viadotto, which was, after all, demolished in 1937. We are inclined to suspect that, although approved by Napoleon, by Valadier's own standards the urbanistic scenery of the Piazzale di San Gregorio remained unsolved and subject to emendation; and particularly we are conscious of the problems which he must have experienced at the termination of the Via Appia.

Along with the church of Saint Catherine of Alexandria (the Egyptian temple which Father Mulcahy conveniently foot-

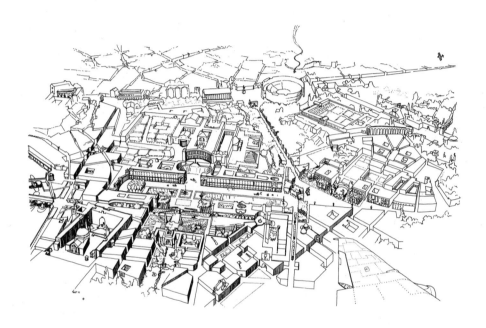

78. Aerial perspective: Circo Massimo, the Palatino, the Celio, and the Colosseum.

Roma Interrotta

notes) did he here propose a university, or following the model of the Invalides, was it a hospital that was here intended? A private source of information (which we cannot divulge) has made us aware that, in this area, the drawings at the Bibliothèque Nationale are invariably redundant, imprecise, and overlaid with contrary suggestions; and so much we would have expected. In any case, we present the area as the academic precinct which it now is—in many respects curiously precursive of the plan of Rockefeller Center (did the architects of Rockefeller Center have an early access to the Valadier archive?); and we notice that adjacent to all this, aligned with the Septizonium and opposite to it, Valadier did project a building, the Palazzo Laetizia, somewhat reminiscent of the Villa Madama and destined at that time to be the Roman establishment of Madame Mère. Or at least such are the fragmentary indications which we have derived from Mulcahy's indispensable catalogue; and, accordingly, we have reproduced this building (formerly the Villa Monmouth and now the Canadian Embassy) as something of a hybrid—with both concessions to Valadier and concessions to its present condition.

The foregoing rather too protracted diversion is prompted by the solemnity of the occasion and the site. To both it would be possible to adopt a casual attitude and to make either a simply ironical or laconic gesture. But we have chosen otherwise.

We suppose that a purpose of this exhibition is an oblique criticism of late nineteenth century and, particularly, present day urbanistic strategies; and we can only agree with this intention. We could have proposed that on the Palatine be erected a fragment of the *ville radieuse,* on the Aventine a figment of Ludwig Hilberseimer's imagination, over the Colosseum and the Circus Maximus a space frame; but, in the name of mere amusement or dubiously avant-garde proclamation, to protract the errors and the later irresponsibilities of Modern architecture does not appear to us to be a very useful procedure. We assume that, on the whole, Modern architecture was a major catastrophe—except as a terrible lesson best to

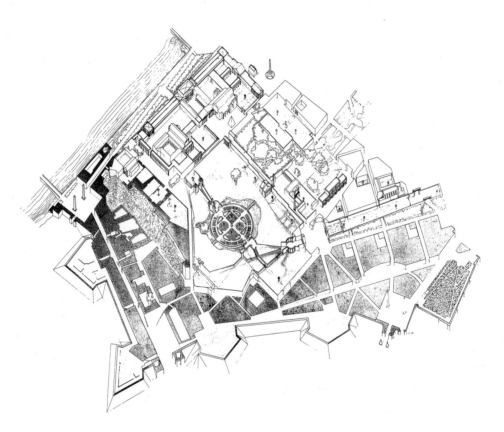

79. Axonometric: the Aventino and the Orto Botanico.

be forgotten; and, though we sometimes wonder how an idea—apparently so good—could so easily have been betrayed, we see no reason to indulge in pseudo-regrets or quasi-satirical demonstrations.

Instead, since a purpose is to extrapolate from Nolli a Rome that could have been but never was, we have invented a history that might have been but never was. We apologize to the real Vincent Mulcahy for the hypothetical, and somewhat erratic, Jesuit scholar whom we have dared to invent in his name. Likewise we apologize to the shades of Cardinal Albani, Giuseppe Valadier, Napoleon, and Queen Margherita for the different uses to which we have put their separate reputations. Along with Father Vincent, they have been our lifesavers; but had we been dealing with another area of town—less sacrosanct and less central—no doubt we should not have needed them and, almost certainly, we should have deployed an entirely different category of argument.

However, as it is within the limitations of the Nolli format, we have attempted to make a plausible Rome, a city belonging to the category of the impossibly probable; and our fictive history has, for the most part, been an alibi for a topographical and contextual concern. For, assuming, that "Roma Interrotta" infers a condemnation of most of the horrors which have been perpetrated since 1870, we have attempted to constitute a fragment of the city which could appear as no more than a 'natural' extension of the 'old' Rome of the Campus Martius, a city of discrete set pieces and interactive local incidents, a city which represents a coalition of intentions rather than the singular presence of any immediately apparent all-coordinating ideas.

We can say no more except that we offer extended thanks to Bryant Baker, Susan Power, Cecile Chenault, Steven Leet, Robert Szymanski, and others who wish to remain anonymous, who have participated in the production of our drawings.

I was never wildly excited about our solutions for the Palatino (difficult to do anything) and the Aventino (which, I think, requires something far less uptight). But, on the other hand, the Celio, where I began by celebrating the lines of the old garden of Villa Mattei, and to the south of the Circo Massimo (which Steven has always insisted is a version of Rockefeller Center— though I don't understand why), I believe that we were elegantly lucid.

Rome: Piazza Augusto Imperatore

A contribution to the Milan Triennale of 1987, "Nove Progetti per Nove Città." Colin Rowe, Matthew Bell, Robert Goodill, Kevin Hinders, Brian Kelly, and Cheryl O'Neil, with Paolo Berdini as occasional critic. The text that follows was written retrospectively in 1995.

In 1986 I was invited by Franco Purini to make a project for exhibition in the Milan Triennale in the following year. It was to be a project for an area in Rome; and, if I were interested, how about the general vicinity of the Mausoleum of Augustus, the Augusteo?

At a small scale the project seemed to follow quite logically from "Roma Interrotta." Also it seemed to be quite vital for the entertainment of those students whom I had met in 1980–1981 while teaching for the University of Notre Dame in Rome and who, after graduation, had followed me to Cornell. These knew the city very well and this was the sort of exercise which would completely involve their absorbed attention. Then the fee was sufficiently large to allow everyone concerned—when work was done—a free trip to Milano for the opening of the show. But what Italian largesse*! And, therefore, should it be surprising that I responded to Purini's proposition with an emphatic affirmative?*

So Nine Projects for Nine Cities! And, apart from Rome, the cities involved were: Ancona, Bologna, Firenze, Milano, Napoli, Palermo, Torino, Venezia.

Rome shall become such as to amaze the peoples of the world: vast, well ordered, powerful as in the days of Augustus. You shall relieve the old oak of growths that cling to it. You shall clear the area around the Theater of Marcellus, the Augusteum, the Capitol, the Pantheon. All that sprang up in the ages of decadence shall vanish. The millenary monuments of our history shall stand out as giants in solitary splendor.

Benito Mussolini, 1926

And he was almost as good—or as bad—as his words.

> Divert the canals to flood the cellars of the museums. Let the glorious canvases swim ashore. The picks and the hammers! Undermine the foundations of venerable towns.

This is not Mussolini although it almost might have been. Instead it is the voice of Milanese Futurism; and it may permit the intrusion of yet a further quotation:

> Prophets and forerunners of the great Italy of today, we Futurists are happy to salute in our not yet forty year old Prime Minister a marvelous Futurist temperament.

From Marinetti to early Mussolini is, of course, but a step, and there is surely a strand of early Fascist rhetoric—that exaltation of dynamism and violence—which may be seen to disclose its only too likely origins in Futurist Milan. But those Milanese Futurists, who imagined themselves to be on "the promontory of the centuries," to

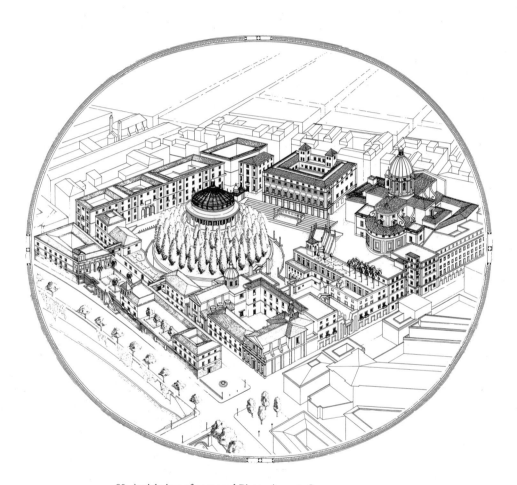

80. Aerial view of proposed Piazza Augusto Imperatore.

Rome: Piazza Augusto Imperatore

81. Piazza Augusto Imperatore, existing figure/ground (left) and proposed figure/ground (right).

Rome: Piazza Augusto Imperatore

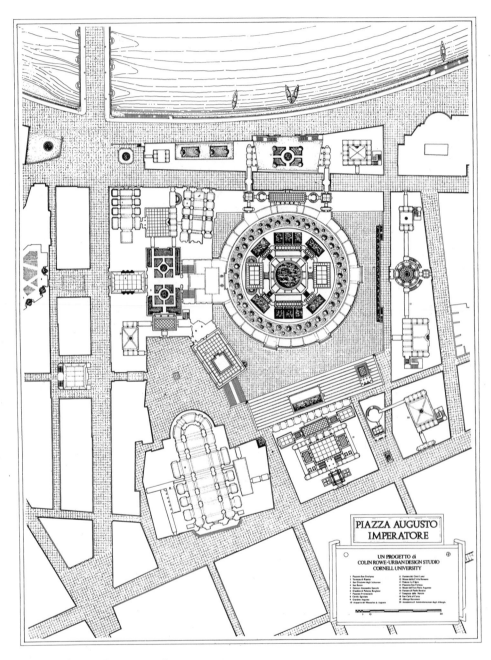

82. Piazza Augusto Imperatore, plan.

VEDUTA DEL PIAZZA AUGUSTO IMPERATORE

83. View of the piazza.

Rome: Piazza Augusto Imperatore

be the cutting edge of continuous becoming, of never to be impeded change, who could conceive of both life and the city as an unceasing frenzy of demolition and construction, whose delirium contributed so much to the psychological set of Modern architecture; did they also contribute something of their frenzy to the psychological set of Benito Mussolini? And, with a significant modification, the answer must surely be that they did. However, as regards building, in Rome the message from Milan could only become somewhat changed. For, if in Milan it was history *in toto* which was to be seen as a contaminant, in Rome Mussolini could only be more selective. For, after all, in Rome there were those "millenary monuments" only waiting decisive action so that they could "stand out as giants in solitary splendor." A bad history and a glorious history, respectively the Rome of the Papacy and the Rome of the Empire, such was the problem of Rome as Mussolini seems to have perceived it; and, while the relics of Imperial Rome were waiting to be exalted, then—inevitably—the huge residues of the so many years in between were, very largely, to be considered as dismissable.

Futurist fervor curiously compounded with whatever might be the characteristic zeal of the classical archaeologist, the determination to reveal every trace of antiquity whatever the cost might be. Such seems to have been the state of mind which inspired Mussolini's literally devastating demolitions, his *sventramenti*, of which that made to facilitate the route of the Via dei Fori Imperiali was emphatically the most extreme. Almost it fulfilled the Futurist ambition to "undermine the foundations of venerable towns." Inaugurated in 1932, extending from the Piazza Venezia to the Colosseum, for the purpose of this indifferent avenue a whole community was wiped out—eleven existing streets with all the accessory apparatus of houses, palaces, and churches. Almost it was Rome's rather belated response to what had been Milan's most extravagant demands; and, by comparison, the site to which we were asked to address ourselves, the Piazza Augusto Imperatore, is a very modest little *sventramento* indeed.

In his book *La Piazza del Popolo* (Rome: Officina, 1974) Giorgio Ciucci emphasizes that, by the early eighteenth century, the northern section of papal Rome had come to involve a triangulation of three highly spectacular events: the Piazza del Popolo itself; the Scala di Spagna; and, on the river, the Porto di Ripetta. These were the points of orientation, the places of destination which an air view would have disclosed; and so they survived until the late nineteenth century when the Porto di Ripetta was demolished for the building of a no doubt necessary bridge; and a result of this was to diminish the cogency of the entire area. Simply one of the corners of the triangle had been eliminated.

A conceptual problem no doubt; but also not without perceptual implications. For, if one stands at the obelisk in Piazza del Popolo and looks down the three streets which present themselves, one is compelled to recognize that the Via del Babuino and the Via di Ripetta were never equal. Almost certainly Via del Babuino has always been preferred and, almost certainly, Via di Ripetta has always been avoided. Via del Babuino leads to the allure of Piazza di Spagna; and, after the destruction of its romantically baroque little port, Via di Ripetta can only lead to not very much.

And now to approach the Mausoleum in itself. A circular building, too big to be interpreted as a mere *tempietto*, too small ever to be thought of as a rival to Castel Sant'Angelo, during the course of its long history it has been at different times a fortress, a platform supporting an elevated garden, a bull ring, and—earlier in this century—a concert hall, all this before it was stripped of its accretions to become the difficult object, the restored ruin which it is today.

This then is the Augusteo; and, as of now, it is not exactly a highly gratifying sight. Located in what appears to be a left-over space, it has required excavation down to the original level in order properly to disclose it; and, further to this, it stands in compromising proximity (though at a different level) to that large glass box built in the late 1930s, at the expense of further degradation of the Via di Ripetta, to permit a display of the Ara Pacis.

Rome: Piazza Augusto Imperatore

And so much is a brief summary of the problems with which we were confronted: problems of level; problems of access and animation; and problems of alleviating the disruption of the urban fabric.

So, to the west, we were concerned with a restoration of Via di Ripetta; and, for this purpose, we removed the Ara Pacis to a position adjacent to the splendid apse of San Carlo al Corso. And, then, we proceeded to reline this much-abused street with an apparatus of buildings and terraces—buildings connected at the upper level by bridges and terraces commanding views of the river with limited return views from across the river of the Augusteo.

Then, to the south we propose two entrances: one from the existing piazza on Via Tomacelli which would lead to what we call the Piazzetta San Carlone; and the other to a new piazza which would lead to the entrance of the Augusteo.

Then, to the north, we propose a long building (in that area, where San Giacomo degli Incurabili is so close, a building can only be long) which might house apartments or offices; and, to the west and next door to San Carlo al Corso, we suggest a grand hotel, which we call the Albergo Borromeo, the lobbies of which would lead to a *caffè* overlooking the Augusteo and its surrounding space.

The Augusteo itself we have surrounded with circles of cypresses and, perhaps with insufficient reverence, we think of it as becoming, up top, an aviary and, down below, an aquarium.

These were the major moves; but in the process of drawing all this up there was one unexpected little mishap. I failed to stop the group before they drew their own, highly imaginary plan of the mausoleum!

The Present Urban Predicament

A lecture delivered June 18, 1979, at The Royal Institution, Albemarle Street, London, this was the second Thomas Cubitt Lecture and was the first published by The Architectural Association Quarterly *during the course of the following year. It was then republished in* The Cornell Journal of Architecture, *no. 1 (Fall 1981).*

Alberti's statement that the house is a small city and the city is a large house perhaps *should* be true; but, certainly, there scarcely seems to have been any such correspondence between the architecture and the urbanism sponsored by the Modern movement. A quasi-private world of mostly domestic architecture which often disclosed an elaborate concern for contingency and spatial involution, with a more public world which usually displayed an almost complete impatience with the empirical fabric of the city, with any existence of idiosyncrasy: such is the seeming paradox, complex house—simple city, which seems to have been promoted; but which, for the most part, remained unobserved. For the simple city was, of course, not so much a city as it was a psychological construction.

> I have a vision of the future, chum.
> The workers flats in fields of soya beans,
> Towering up like silver pencils, score on score,
> While surging millions hear the challenge come
> From microphones in communal canteens
> No right, no wrong, all's perfect, evermore.

To quote John Betjeman is to make more or less appropriate commentary upon the city propounded by Modern architecture; and to add another question is to make still more appropriate commentary upon the present day. The second quotation is from Baudelaire: "There may be a subtle joy in deserting an old cause in order to find out what one will feel like in serving a new one."

So it might be supposed that, as of now, many persons involved with architecture and urbanism are experiencing this "subtle joy." For we are, presently, the witnesses of a great *dégringolade*. Modern architecture, which was once to be seen as among the conspicuous hopes of humanity, has suddenly come to seem, at best, incredible, and at worst, a lamentable aberration. And although this cannot mean that all notions of Modernism have been flushed away—(notions of Modernism are too complex to be readily dismissable)—it must mean that all kinds of old certainties are vanishing and that neither action nor observation can any longer rely upon the simple faith of what it is sometimes tempting to call the heroic days. The vision of the future, the fantasy of the infallibly programmed society in which unhappiness and tragedy are forbidden, has dimmed. Modern architecture and the city which it proposed no longer elicit "a willing suspension of disbelief."[1] And so we have the Art Deco revival, the exponents of Postmodernism, of super-Mannerism, of Architettura Razionale, and of all the other practitioners of Baudelaire's "subtle joy." We have the threats of

Modern architecture's impending demise, alternatively the information of its extinction; and, though much of all this may be journalistic and graphic manoeuver and much, because of its gratuitous
triviality, may inspire yet another wave of revulsion, we have still acquired a little crop of possibly premature obituaries; and, though I
have scarcely read them (I find Postmodernism a somewhat opaque
concept), I must now attempt, as an opening strategy, to imagine
one of my own. Its conclusion might read something like this:

> We may ascribe her death (Modern architecture is surely a
> she) to the ingenuousness of her temperament. Displaying
> an extraordinary addiction to towers and completely un-
> constructed spaces, when young she possessed a high and
> romantically honorable idea of life and her excess of sensi-
> bility could only lead to later chagrin. Like one of Jane
> Austen's more extreme heroines—though she was simulta-
> neously morally reserved, passionate, and artless—it was
> her juvenile notion that, once she was perfectly wedded to
> society, this so much desired husband would, by the influ-
> ence of her example, become redeemed of errors, tractable,
> pliant, and ready to act with her in any philanthropy which
> she might have in mind. But the marriage did not prove to
> be a success. Modern architecture was admired by society
> but not for what she conceived to be her inherent virtues.
> Her spouse was attracted by her many external charms but
> was utterly unwilling to award recognition of what she con-
> ceived to be the ethical principle of her being. And, in
> spite of the elevated model which she offered, he remained
> stubbornly confirmed in his old ways. Moral regeneration
> he did not seek. For him the ethical posture of modern ar-
> chitecture was too much like that of a Victorian heroine
> and, correspondingly, he looked for his delinquent plea-
> sures elsewhere. He, society, was in no way ready to envis-
> age those limpid possibilities of the New Jerusalem which
> she so enthusiastically advertised and, as she continued, he

increasingly became fatigued. Indeed, he (society) came to discover that, though admired, he too was not accepted; and, gradually, the rift became irretrievable. Not surprising, therefore, should be modern architecture's agitated and long decline; but, though this death was to be expected, it is greatly to be regretted and the extinction of this once pristine creature (with her elaborately Victorian standards) has been desperately sad to witness. But, a late nineteenth-century character and never fully knowing it, she addressed herself to a moral condition of permanent rapture, to an ecstatic condition which could only endanger her frail physique; and, to repeat, excessive sensibility abused by inadequate experience, motivated by a quasi-religious sentiment not well understood and complicated by the presence of physics envy, *Zeitgeist* worship, object fixation, and stradaphobia must be considered the greatest factors contributing to the demise.

Physics envy, *Zeitgeist* worship, object fixation, and stradaphobia, I believe, are none of them yet known to the clinical diagnosticians of what used to be called "the faculty." I owe the first term to Denise Scott Brown and the second to David Watkin.[2] A number of years ago, speaking at a symposium in the Museum of Modern Art, Denise Scott Brown proceeded to attack quite violently a state of mind which, with obvious derivations from Freud, she designated "physics envy," the idea that architecture could ever be elevated, or reduced, to the level of that most certain of sciences. David Watkin, in criticizing the Hegelian component of Modern architecture's apologetic, the conception of the architect as sensitive antenna, humble pencil, obedient *planchette,* just simply transcribing the utterings and mutterings of the spirit of the age, has spoken of *Zeitgeist* worship.

We will consult only the facts (physics envy) and we will experience no serious epistemological concern as to what the substance of these facts may be. Simultaneously, and without any sense

of incongruity or inhibition, we will happily submit ourselves to
the will of the epoch (*Zeitgeist* worship) without too many questions
as to whether this will is substantial, singular or manifold, or indeed anything other than a highly unempirical, historical abstraction.

So physics envy and *Zeitgeist* worship, which together (let
us wait for direction from outside ourselves) constitute an implicit
denial of free will, are almost certainly to be related to our present
incapacity to innovate (but I am merely the agent of science and destiny)—to our present conception of ourselves as victims.

However this is to digress, since it is not so much with the
morale of Modern architecture as with the physique of its related
city that this present discussion is concerned. And if Scott Brown
and Watkin have, as I believe, correctly diagnosed the most debili-
tating of Modern architecture's psychoses, I must now attempt to
give substance to my own terminology. Two images—the corner of
the unbuilt Library and Administration Building at IIT, which excited so much enthusiasm circa 1950, and the corner of the courtyard of the Ducal Palace at Urbino—might serve to initiate a
preliminary discussion about the style of attack and the physical
limitations of Modern architecture (fig. 84).

We are here presented with both an outer angle and an
inner angle, and both conditions are argued with almost obsessive
clarity. However, though one may admire them both, for present
purposes this parallel is equipped with a prejudice which might be
quite simply stated: Modern architecture and, following its lead,
related urban practice, has been enormously preoccupied with
the outer angle, presumably aggressive and protuberant, and has
scarcely been able to involve itself with the inner angle, possibly passive and recessive.

Now, no doubt, this statement could be made to bear a
completely monstrous overload; but, instead of that, all that I here
wish to extricate from it is that the tradition of Modern architecture
has tended to produce objects rather than spaces, has been highly involved with problems of the built solid and very little with prob-

The Present Urban Predicament

84. Palazzo Ducale, Urbino, courtyard corner; Library and Administration Building, IIT, Mies van der Rohe, corner.

lems of the unbuilt void, that the inner angle which cradles space has scarcely been among its concerns. Which further statement may introduce the pressing question: just how to make a city if all buildings proclaim themselves as objects, and how many object-buildings can be aggregated before comprehension fails?

Ingenuity versus Contingency

Although the principle victim of Modern architecture has been the city, its first victim was surely the garden.

At the beginning of this century there existed a very great concern for the garden as support and extension of the house. The house was to be surrounded by a variety of enclosures and parterres and preferably the whole condition was not to be symmetrical, the idea being rather a symmetry of local episode associated with a general randomness supposed to be justifiable as accommodation of functional or topographical contingency.

It is in such terms that one might interpret many of the architectural/horticultural compositions of Frank Lloyd Wright, Edwin Lutyens, M. H. Baillie Scott, Charles Platt, Jacques Gréber, Werner Hegemann, and others who were all of them highly concerned with what, at the Ecole des Beaux-Arts, would have been designated *entourage*. This meant that, in the early years of this century, there was a widely distributed conviction that house and garden should exist in the most animated, interactive relationship. Garden was to be structure for the exhibition of house as event. Or, alternatively, house was to be event for the presentation of garden as structure. But, if about such fluctuations of reading as these we can never be sure, then, as we contemplate such an organism as Lutyens's Grey Walls at Gullane (fig. 85), we can scarcely be uncertain that we are in the presence of a highly constructed field from which figure emerges into prominence precisely because of the existence of the ground so thoughtfully provided. Which is figurative—garden or house—is, I think, immaterial. But, as we withdraw attention from Grey Walls and proceed to contemplate Gerrit Rietveld's

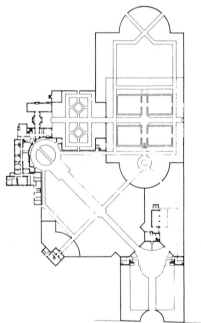

85. Grey Walls, Gullane, view and plan. Edwin Lutyens.

URBANISTICS

Moisten glue strip, fold over, and seal.

PREFERRED DISCOUNT VOUCHER

COVER PRICE	YOU SAVE	YOU PAY ONLY	FREE
$139.00	$64.05	$74.95	Online Access

Your Preferred Subscriber Benefits:

- Exclusive subscriber-only access to the current issue — Included
  plus five years of archives at nybooks.com

- Special issues, including:
  - Spring Books — Included
  - University Press — Included
  - Summer Reading — Included
  - Fall Books — Included
  - Holiday Books — Included

- Money-back guarantee: if you ever choose to cancel

Schroeder House at Utrecht (fig. 86), any ambivalence as to what is figure and what is ground evaporates. Both Grey Walls and the Schroeder House are pieces of the greatest virtuosity. At Grey Walls both garden and house are, possibly, a little too tricky. Ingenuity is, maybe, a little too evident. But, at the Schroeder House, for all of its elaborate quotations from Constructivism and De Stijl, there is a complete absence of any supportive apparatus or enframing field. One might have hoped for a few cedars of Lebanon in the style of John Claudius Loudon (faint and hyper-English hope!) but even these are not provided. Instead, one discovers the paradigmatic architecture piece; belligerent, isolated, responsive only to the most abstract of contexts, not at all responsive to local contingency, but quite excessively so to what are presumed to be the more active contingencies of time and culture. At Grey Walls it is the spirit of the place that is the primary idea, at the Schroeder House it is the spirit of the age; and, in this shifting of criteria from *genius loci* to *Zeitgeist*,[3] it is notable that while as object, the house becomes aggressively intensified, as space, the garden becomes correspondingly reduced to no more than a very vague and tributary accessory.

Now, if the Schroeder House and Grey Walls may be considered as indicative of two states of mind, one directed to the built solid, the other toward the unbuilt void, then the argument may proceed, from the garden to the city.

In spite of the present revival of interest in his production, I am only a very reserved admirer of the architecture of Sir Edwin Lutyens; but, though most frequently I find him a little too charming, for me, his version of Hyde Park Corner (fig. 87, top) will always rank among what should be considered his most celebrated performances. For I am never driven through the present absurdities of Hyde Park Corner, never observe its present degradation, without thinking both about Lutyens and about what this part of London used to be, with Park Lane emerging through Hamilton Place, the engagement of Apsley House to the general facade of Piccadilly, and then the gradual decrescendo into Knightsbridge. It was all without calculation; it all possessed great understatement and reserve; it

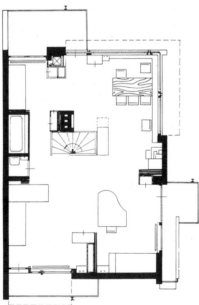

86. Schroeder House, Utrecht, view and plan. Gerritt Rietveld.

all belonged to the happiest category of London accidents; it was
something of almost insuperable delicacy. And now, parts of the debris of that situation, with the fatuousness inherent to bureaucrats,
are ineptly entitled Duke of Wellington Place.

But, if one imagines the first Duke of Wellington revolving
round and around in his tomb at what has here been executed in his
name, it might now be reasonable to desert the pragmatics of the
incompletely educated highway engineers for the idealist decorum
and the spatial concern of Lutyens. For, simply in terms of pragmatics, the Lutyens proposal would surely have worked quite as well
as the present dispensation. Indeed, could it possibly have worked
worse? Inherently no doubt, it involved the celebration of an empire
about to be lost; but, if in this area Lutyens was scarcely clairvoyant
and if there were to be no more imperial celebrations, *could* his proposal have involved a more timid confusion than what we find, a solution which owes very much to a cynical reception of *some* of the
precepts of Modern architecture?

Perhaps comparable remarks cannot be made about the Lutyens proposal for Piccadilly Circus (fig. 87, bottom), for the simple
reason that nothing has been done there from that date to this; and
here Lutyens is perhaps a little too excited, a little too suggestive of
some impossible Edwardian epiphany. However, as initial reactions
cool, as one contemplates this project, one might still be disposed
to wonder whether, for all its inflation, it still does not focus and exhibit *some* of the aspects of the 'truth' of the place. No doubt it is as
though Lutyens were rather tired. At Hyde Park Corner we are presented with a species of Hippodrome or Circus Maximus. But, if
something very like this is to be served up at the other end of the
street, then one should also recognize that proposals such as these
are highly provisional. To make the Hyde Park Corner that Lutyens intimated did not really need two versions of Apsley House
and two versions of Decimus Burton's screen; and, comparably, the
Lutyens *idea* of Piccadilly Circus may be stripped of its profusion of
palaces and still be perceived as an exceptionally suggestive explora-

87. Hyde Park Corner, London, Edwin Lutyens; Piccadilly Circus, London, Edwin Lutyens.

tion, intrinsically a far more pregnant proposition than any made since.

All the same, it is perhaps too literal, too less than ingenious; but, if one may imagine it being rendered susceptible to local circumstance and gaining thereby, then, to find a major piece of unbuilt London, which both grandly stipulates the ideal and elaborately engages the empirical, we must be prepared to retreat way back into the late seventeenth century, to the setting which a disappointed Wren conceived for St. Paul's (fig. 88).

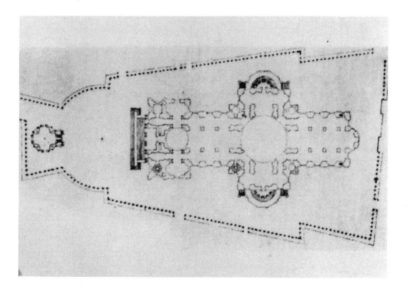

88. Wren's proposal for St. Paul's Churchyard, London.

The Present Urban Predicament

It may be a source of astonishment that this Wren project, simultaneously modest and assertive, is not more acclaimed. Had it been built, it would surely long ago have been advertised as among the great Baroque pieces of accommodation, a large London equivalent of such Roman miniatures as Piazza Sant'Ignazio, Piazza della Pace, and Porto di Ripetta.

No local contingency has been violated. Ludgate Hill approaches without any reorientation. Likewise the lines of Watling Street (preceding the present Cannon Street) and Aldersgate follow their familiar traces. Comparably, the eastern trapezoid was always approximately present and the western trapezoid, a product of Ludgate Hill intended to accommodate a Hawksmoor/Vanbrugh chapter house/baptistery, is the only significant novelty. It is all enormously economical and persuasive. We accept what exists. We build from it. We also try to transcend it. The place is both the customary point of convergence which it always was and is something quite different. It is not what Wren initially wished. It is far better. The original idea of 1666, a-spatial, abstract, doctrinaire—like Washington, D.C. at its worst—has experienced all sorts of empirical vicissitudes and has gained in ideal density by this experience.

Was there any possibility, after 1945, that Wren's St. Paul's Churchyard might have been realized? Theoretically, yes; practically, no. Had it been presented as a possibility one might imagine a conservative and retarded consensus wishing it; but one can also imagine the defeat of any such consensus by the massed ranks of the architectural and planning intelligentsia to whom a sin against the *Zeitgeist* was, at that time, far more outrageous than any sin against the Holy Ghost. And so it is that we acquired the present bizarre setting of St. Paul's: to the east cheap commercialism and, to the north, a labyrinthine and silly *coup de théâtre* of the most bland and dubious state-sponsored townscape.

The prospect of what is and what might have been is embarrassing; but the accumulation of prejudices which destroyed Hyde Park Corner and vitiated the possibility of any setting for St. Paul's was, evidently, something endemic throughout the world;

and if, in London, there has been no significant urban space produced during the course of the twentieth century, this should be no
occasion for surprise. For, out of the whole scenario of twentieth-
century urbanism we are probably left with only one highly convinc-
ing space; and that is, strangely enough, in New York, where the
tradition of space has never been elaborate and where the prevalence
of object has always been extreme.

But Rockefeller Center (fig. 89), for all of its attenuated
Art Deco externals (and probably because of these), is the only
twentieth-century urban space one might dare to put into competition with spaces of the textbooks. Like Wren's setting for St. Paul's,
Rockefeller Center involves both an ideal of normative procedure
and an ideal of empirical concession. One supposes that the architects of Rockefeller Center were French-trained and distrusted their
French training, that they had received certain restricted information as to what Modern architecture was supposed to be about, but
were in no sense illuminated by the findings of Cubism, Constructivism, and De Stijl. In other words, one imagines that, in
their minds, there were no fantasies about diaphanous building, no
exaltations of a crystal city, no obsessions about space-time composition. And, as one looks at their details, one is obliged to observe
that their stylistic ideal was not very far removed from that of the
nearly contemporary Palais de Chaillot. Down below, it is all tre-
mendously Paris 1925. Up top, it is all New York mildly subdued.
But, more than this, inherently, it is a confrontation between two
sorts of reason; the reason of the mind and the reason of the purse;
and it is the ever-valid arguments of money which detach Rockefeller Center from its French origins, introduce the absolutely necessary empirical pressures, and render it an indisputably American
piece.

Rockefeller Center is scarcely photogenic. It is apt to be
dour and, architecturally, a little banal. But, as a presentation to
Fifth Avenue, as a succession of highly ordinary spaces (the word is
used in Robert Venturi's sense), as an inevitable emanation of the
Manhattan grid (one should observe the very ingenious relationship

The Present Urban Predicament

89. Rockefeller Center, New York City, plan and view. Associated Architects.

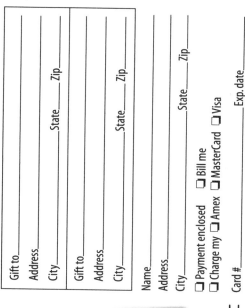

...st two of the pavilions on ...rch and recapitulating the ...ilions flanking its apse, the ...Center itself, and the gener-...space below and something ...ter is superb and unrivalled. ...nks about London and also ...how it could be that, in the ...e remained so completely un-...del so comprehensive and so ...g without imitations.

...e found as responses to this ...ill quite obvious. During the ...ory has placed enormously ...ulated object (fig. 90, left), ...e disappearance of the gar-...n prone to follow suit (fig. 90, ...ble. This bubble is perfect and ...enly distributed from the in-...interior." [4] "In contrast with frontality sanctified by a rigid static concept of life, the new architecture offers a plastic wealth of multi-faceted temporal and spatial effects." [5] "Modern functional planning distinguishes itself by dealing honestly and competently with every side, abolishing the gross distinctions between front and rear, seen and obscene, and creating structures that are harmonious in every dimension." [6]

Such are specimen illustrations of an attitude which is only too well known: Le Corbusier rather ingenuously reiterates an old and primary French argument; Theo van Doesburg, with his "temporal" and "spatial," provides the same argument with a fashionable, post-Einsteinian and post-Cubist trim; and Lewis Mumford reiterates all this in the concerned voice of a sympathetic liberalism for

The Present Urban Predicament

90. Santa Maria della Consolazione, Todi; *Counter-Construction,* Maison particulière, Theo van Doesburg.

The Present Urban Predicament

which any idea of facade, any idea of necessary interface between the *res publica* and the *res privata* is a final and terrible dissimulation.

And, of course, to these illustrations of an attitude once related to intelligence there are many others which might quite well be annexed. And here one might think of Leonardo Benevolo writing in the 1960s and addressing himself to the regularities of Chester Terrace and the Rue de Rivoli (fig. 91): "But architectural regularity was only an expedient to give uniformity to a branch of building activity which, even here, escaped administrative control. Behind the uniform facades, individual contractors continued to work when and how they pleased, unconcerned with any comprehensive plan."[7] So much is part of a caption in Benevolo's *The Origins of Modern Town Planning,* and, as an instance of vivacious, old-time prejudice become contemporary, dull folklore (that famous "comprehensive" with which everything is to be "integrated"!), it may stand as a significant exhibit.

However, attack upon facade and promotion of building as object can only become attack upon street: "We must kill the street! We shall truly enter into modern town planning only after we have accepted this preliminary determination," said Le Corbusier. "Against all sense the present practices [are]: alignment on the streets and enclosed courts and light wells, two forms entirely contrary to human well-being, and to which the Athens Charter has opposed the principle of architectural development from within to without." And, "We must destroy the impenetrable web of streets, passages, house rows, courts . . . avenues or boulevards, enjoyed by pedestrians, walks, traffic lanes, full of noise and smell of cars, buses, and motorcycles."[8] Further: "We have, of course, killed the corridor street, the street of any and every town in the world. Our dwelling houses have nothing to do with the street."[9]

It is in the context of such hysterically overstated values as these that it becomes possible to recognize and to speak of Modern architecture's "object fixation" (obsessive overestimation of the built solid) and "stradaphobia" (obsessive underestimation of any linear, constructed void).

91. Chester Terrace, London, John Nash; Rue de Rivoli, Paris, Percier and Fontaine.

The Present Urban Predicament

Visually oriented architects and planners abetted by callously pragmatic capitalists, all of them preoccupied with the spurious representation of an implausible public realm, had hopelessly compromised the possibilities of both decency and life; and, as the outward and visible sign of their moral hideousness, the street could only stand condemned as a disgrace to civilization, as (more or less) the psychopathic symbol of its discontents.

Naturally, in terms of so heated a critique, that there might be good streets and bad streets could scarcely be a concern; but, if the Lutyens monumental avenue from Victoria Station to Buckingham Palace might, in the framework of such a polemic, stand as a very obvious target, then it could also follow (and quite automatically) that van Eesteren's brilliantly sober and diversified project of 1925 for the Unter den Linden (fig. 92, left) would, almost like Rockefeller Center, remain scarcely a visible model. In fact, the street—often so confusing, so popular, and so necessary—was coming rapidly to be regarded as an instrument of repression; and therefore, in Berlin, where in late Weimar days the pace was so hectic, it should not be surprising that when, circa 1930, Ludwig Hilberseimer came to make a project also related to the Unter den Linden, his propensity was altogether to deny its existence (fig. 92, right).

So one contemplates the Hilberseimer proposal. It is interjected into what, at that time, was one of the most delicate areas of the city. In front of it there is Schinkel's Schauspielhaus with its two adjacent churches and, to its north, there is the great processional avenue (the city's primary virtue?) which van Eesteren was at such pains to reinforce. But, for Hilberseimer, the monumental continuity of Unter den Linden is clearly a theater of only bad meanings and, evidently, in a better world, it is destined to be superseded, presumably in the name of rational, and abstract, equality; and it should be of interest that, even as late as 1961, the strategies of Hilberseimer still prevailed. For an inspection of the contributions to the Berlin competition of that year will clearly illustrate that most of the competitors were still inflamed by the same *parti pris,* that for nearly all of them Unter den Linden was something to be diminished, one might almost say to be violated, by a series of flank attacks, by (again and again) an extreme preference given to the line of the Friedrichstrasse.

Now, in what way Hilberseimer's project is to be considered superior to English by-law housing of the late nineteenth century may not be clear. Nor can it be clear how much more adequately its linear buildings might have been expected to service the requirement of human well-being. That it was thought to be socially benevolent there need be no doubt; but then, so also was English by-law housing which, with never very successful results, was at least conciliatory to the community of the street. However, these doubts only introduce a not very useful parenthesis. For, if what Hilberseimer presented has operated as one of the most pervasive of twentieth-century models, the time is now come to desert the *Zeilenbau* and to approach the point block.

With the point block, just as Hilberseimer selected one of the most fragile and elaborate parts of Berlin in order to make his demonstration, so Le Corbusier proposed to obliterate one of the most complex and closely detailed quarters of Paris in the interest of what he clearly conceived to be a Cartesian version of New York (fig. 93). In both cases there is a certain gruesome excess of conviction. But now, even more than with Hilberseimer (in whom one senses a certain Prussian doggedness and desperation), with Le Corbusier one is confronted with the vision of a completely reconstructed, happy society, happy but also efficient beyond any possibility of belief. For the dogma of permanent, universal happiness, combined with universal managerial expertise, reigns predominant; and, if one knows to what horrors this dream leads, if the fantasies of Lutyens, by comparison, are beginning child's play, it must still be insisted that, between the two of them, Hilberseimer and Le Corbusier, both publishing dubious poetry which then became accepted as even more monstrous prose, provided the basic paradigms against which we still wretchedly struggle.

The city as an accumulation of isolated solids in largely unmanipulated void and the new city within the city as primarily a

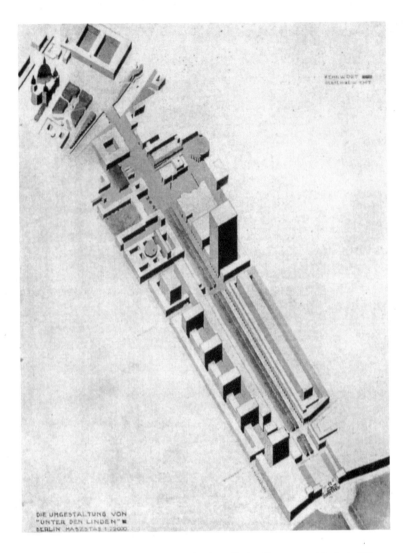

92. Unter den Linden, Berlin: projects by Cornelis van Eesteren and Ludwig Hilberseimer.

The Present Urban Predicament

93. Plan Voisin, Paris, Le Corbusier; Peter Cooper Village, New York City.

URBANISTICS

Phoenix symbol—as an emblem of a new world superior to any previous life and, therefore, physically quite discontinuous from its immediate environment—this favorite theme of Modern architecture has persisted with remarkably few energetic indications of protest. Indeed, with all of its iconographic special pleading, until lately the idea of the new as largely discontinuous from any physical setting has survived among the unexamined norms of what has been widely regarded as progressive practice. In terms of such remarks it is interesting to notice that the detachment of Le Corbusier's Plan Voisin, its independence of any local clues or promptings, is curiously reproduced on almost the same site by the Candilis, Josic and Woods Bonne-Nouvelle project of some forty-five years later (fig. 94, top). And this same highly perfunctory approach to any pressures of context continues to be visible even in quarters where one might least expect it—as for instance, in this project of not so very long ago from Milan (fig. 94, bottom).

However—not to make further commentary upon questions of physical context which, if they are scarcely yet among the everyday assumptions of practice, are still apt to have become among the platitudes of criticism—it remains to notice the very positive virtues of such proposals as the Plan Voisin and, doing so, to iterate some of the very defensible presuppositions of Modern architecture which, otherwise, may soon be forgotten. Rational equality, light, air, movement, aspect, prospect, hygiene, recreation, a general limpidity, no confusion; all of these are among the spiritually refreshing virtues of that city of Modern architecture which has been so crudely exploited and which, unhappily, can never be built. And it remains to confront this enlightened and somewhat eighteenth-century condition with the opposite and rather messy virtues of the traditional city, of which confluence and convergence are among the greatest benefits.

To select, not quite at random, a traditional city, Vigevano to the west-southwest of Milan (fig. 95) illustrates how the continuous fabric of the buildings acts as a species of urban *poché* giving

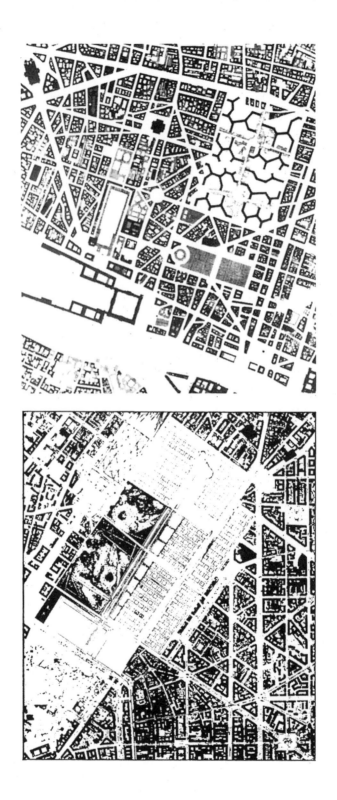

95. Piazza Ducale, Vigevano. Bramante.

94. Facing page: Bonne-Nouvelle, Paris, Candilis, Josic and Woods; Porta Venezia, Milan, Faccoltà dell'Architettura di Milano.

energy and legibility to its reciprocal condition, the structure of specific spaces; and how the inherent versatility of this fabric, as a condition of more or less continuous and unprogrammed building, is relatively free from most of the dictates of function and is, correspondingly, available for the accommodation of all kinds of transient local uses.

But if so much is very obvious, and if such virtues are every day more loudly acclaimed, and if the object building, when interpreted as a universal proposition, represents nothing more than a demolition of public life, it must still be suggested that neither the city of Modern architecture nor the city which Modern architecture hoped to supersede is likely suddenly to vanish away. They both represent important emotional, vested interests, and, recognizing their separate merits, it should not seriously be beyond human ability to facilitate their profitable intercourse. Or such could be the implication of the plan of Wiesbaden as it was around 1900 (fig. 96) in which the city presents the spectacle of an elegant hybrid, of two complementary fields, one largely a solid equipped with local spaces, the other largely a void in which objects have been encouraged to proliferate, each of them giving value to its opposite condition.

Cause versus Cure

However, with these remarks which envisage a situation of intelligent urbanistic detente, we have begun to move away from our somewhat premature obituary of Modern architecture, from our psycho-biographical diagnosis, to the consideration of palliatives and prescriptions. If it is possible to agree with Le Corbusier that "between belief and doubt it is better to believe,"[10] then it might also be possible to assume that matters are not quite so desperate as they are often said to be, that neither physics envy nor *Zeitgeist* worship, object fixation nor stradaphobia is irremediable, and that an exacting analysis with a distinctly more varied diet may yet effect the cure. For, however psychically disturbed and intellectually sclerotic,

96. Wiesbaden, figure/ground.

The Present Urban Predicament

the patient *may* yet recover. A few basic prescriptions might now be proposed for Modern architecture (and, by implication, contemporary urbanism).

One

In order to reduce the mental inflammation which has always demonstrated itself as moral excess and undue preoccupation with over-articulated solids, the patient should be encouraged to consult the visual evidence and the empirical constitution of the traditional city. For the purpose, what better or more obvious exhibit is there available than an overview of Rome (fig. 97)?

For here we are presented with the greater part of the story; a more or less uniform ceiling height; a dense matrix, tissue, or texture, from out of which relatively neutral field certain spaces are subtracted and certain objects are allowed to erupt; and so, in this aerial view of Rome, among spaces, we are primarily likely to be impressed by Piazza Venezia and its Mussolinian dependencies, by the decisive cut of the Corso and Via Flaminia, by Piazza Navona (if we look for it), by Piazza del Montecitorio, and, in the distance, by the great spaces to be associated with the Villa Borghese. And, in this view, objects are the reverse of anything primary. There are, of course in the foreground the Vittoriano and a variety of quasi-vertical pieces (Torre Milizia, Column of Trajan) related to it; then, in the middle distance, one is able to discern (though not too well) the domes of the Gesù and of the Pantheon; and, finally, in different parts of the background, the Villa Medici leaps into prominence and the Palazzo di Giustizia emerges from a nineteenth-century grid of streets in order to make a confrontation with the river.

However, if we are now willing to descend from the airplane (which homogenizes) to a more normal elevation (which articulates), we can begin to find ourselves confronted with a profusion of objects: Santa Maria di Loreto (fig. 98), Santa Maria del Nome, the two towers of Piazza Venezia, the dome of the Gesù, the dome of the Chiesa Nuova, the Borrominian outfit (just what do you call

97. Rome, view.

The Present Urban Predicament

98. Santa Maria di Loreto, Rome.

it?) which rises about Sant'Ivo della Sapienza, and, in the background, the Papal superdome. And, of course, one may descend still further; and, once looking into the streets from the rooftops, one may begin to discern how certain phenomena, propounded up top as objects, ultimately relinquish any such ambition and, finally, present themselves as a mediation between object and prevailing tissue/texture. For which purposes, as illustration of the building which emerges from the texture of a vertical surface to assume the characteristics of object, Sant'Agnese in Piazza Navona could well serve as a prime instance (fig. 99).

But the condition to which attention is being directed in Rome may also be discriminated by two views of Canaletto's London, and, necessarily, the condition of London cannot be quite so condensed as that of Rome. So Canaletto's London, as we look from Somerset House toward the City, is a slightly defused, Baroque-Rococo presentation. Emphatically, the dome of St. Paul's is not the dome of St. Peter's and the different spiky pieces (mostly Wren) scarcely possess the memorability of their Roman precursor. Nevertheless, though in the Rome-London comparison certain issues are faded, muted, and lost as one looks toward the City, one may still be astonished by the behavior of St. Paul's; and, as one looks toward Westminster, one may still wish to observe the preponderant roles of Banqueting House and Abbey. For, in both cases, and much more so in the City, there prevails the idea of ceiling (related to texture) and the contrary idea of object, protruding above this particular plateau of building and announcing itself in the style of grand, magisterial cadenza.

And something like this condition of horizontal datum, below which assertions are few and invariably circumspect, and above which plastic excitement, virtuosity, take over, is also to be illustrated in a carefully selected view of the Yale campus (fig. 100). Most of this is a fake London of Wren and Canaletto; but then, acknowledging the fake, apart from topography, it might still be suggested that, nowadays, there are very few English views quite so 'English' as this professes to be. Wren-Gibbs represented with some

99. Sant'Agnese, Piazza Navona, Rome; Giovanni Antonio Canaletto, views of the Thames from Somerset House Terrace, looking toward the City (left) and toward Westminster (right).

strange, atavistic enthusiasm? Possibly; but not to mock. Because to move from Rome to London, to New Haven, and, finally, to Manhattan is still to receive a version of the same message.

For, in Manhattan, the earlier skyscrapers (almost everything built before 1950) are still obedient to the principles observed in Rome. No doubt New York City is a vertical excess, but, until very recently, almost every skyscraper behaved approximately like Sant'Agnese in Piazza Navona. The Woolworth, the Chrysler (fig. 101), the Empire State buildings all behave this way. Below a certain level they are reticent and no more than street furniture; and at this level while they accommodate the street, they make no insistence. At street level they are quiet. They are not big and bold and

100. Yale University campus, New Haven, Connecticut.

The Present Urban Predicament

grand. Instead, they only display what they intend to become above a certain highly calculated elevation. Below this, they are tranquil; and above this, they are disposed to be exuberant. The set piece, the celebration of object, the *fioritura,* belong up top.

All of which was both loved and hated by Le Corbusier: "In New York then I first learned to admire the Italian Renaissance. . . . It is so well done that you could believe it to be genuine."[11] He admired a tightness of profile, a laconic contour, a graphic stringency, never virtues of London and none of them virtues of Paris since circa 1860. But, at the same time, while immensely excited by what he conceived to be inadvertent Cartesian values, he thought that "a skyscraper should not be a coquettish plume rising straight up from the street. It is a wonderful instrument of concentration; to be placed in the midst of vast open spaces."[12] Le Corbusier was equally empathetic to what he supposed to be American turbulence, violence, dynamism: "Here the skyscraper is not an element in city planning but a banner in the sky, a fireworks rocket, an aigrette in the coiffure of a name henceforth listed in the financial Almanach de Gotha."[13]

And, infatuated with roofscapes of New York, with those versions of Mont-St.-Michel, those Gothic extravagances, those Trianons, those belvederes which, more often than not, are no more than the disguises of the water cisterns and the elevator mechanisms, Le Corbusier was led to propose that the ground level of Manhattan should be raised so that the whole island might become simply a large version of Central Park with such poetical versions as these standing around in it.[14]

Two

But perhaps the divorce of object from texture, the results of the abrupt proclamation of object and then the attempt, out of a repertory of idealized objects, to insinuate some version of town center as structured receptacle, could not be better illustrated than by Le Corbusier's plan for St.-Dié and its comparison with an aerial view of

101. Sant'Agnese, Rome, Borromini and Bernini; Chrysler Building, New York, William Van Allen.

The Present Urban Predicament

the Spanish town of Vittoria (fig. 102). For, at Vittoria, with great simplicity, we are presented with a wholly ideal space, whose facades are entirely internal and whose external elevations appear to be little more than happenings, with a wholly enclosed environment which is yet able to accept outside pressures and to deliver further pressures of its own; while at St.-Dié is exhibited, as clearly as possible, the dilemma of the object-building, the space occupier attempting to operate as space definer. And it is a dilemma from which there ensues the production of a curiously unsuccessful labyrinth, in which it seems that ideas of centrality and hierarchy are simultaneously intimated and retracted and in which, while convergence is an explicit aim, divergence is an implicit result. Thus the four or more faces of all the buildings at St.-Dié, a series of more or less futile gestures which effectively isolate each from each, are particularly interesting when viewed alongside the enclosing wall of buildings, one side smooth, the other corrugated, which is all that Vittoria offers.

So the few remaining devotees of orthodox Modern architecture should be required to observe Vittoria, which is a relatively easy and (in design hours) painless solution; and, in terms of Vittoria, these same persons should further be required to consider the almost equivalent constitution of the Place des Vosges. For here again, a type of inverted palace is made up of buildings bumpy on one side and smooth on the other, of buildings which mediate the opposed requirements of privacy and publicity, buildings which, with the most casual of gestures, are apt to engage external contingency but which, internally, after some slight emphasis upon their independence, only collaborate to enforce a reading of regular and platonic void as prime figure.

This strategy, for practical purposes, is the inversion of the strategies to which we are now accustomed; and the degree and intensity of such inversion is most succinctly to be explained by the comparison of a solid and void of almost identical proportions. If, to illustrate prime solid, nothing will serve better than Le Corbusier's Unité (fig. 103), then, as an instance of the opposite and reciprocal

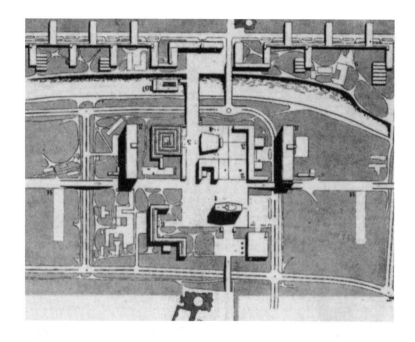

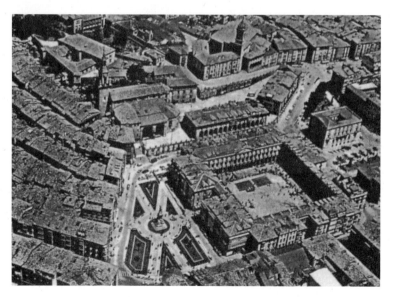

102. St.-Dié, Le Corbusier; Plaza mayor, Vittoria, Justo Antonio Olaguibel.

The Present Urban Predicament

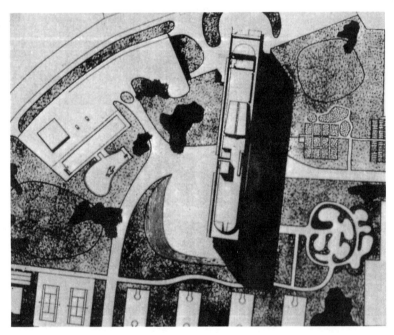

103. Unité d'Habitation, Marseilles, view and plan. Le Corbusier.

URBANISTICS

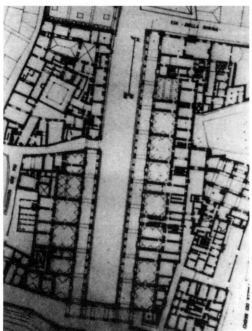

104. Galleria degli Uffizi, Florence, view and plan. Giorgio Vasari.

condition, Vasari's Uffizi is surely its inevitable complement (fig. 104). For, if the Uffizi is Marseilles turned inside out—if it is a jelly mold for the Unité; if it is the dock for the Unité's boat—it is also void become figurative, active, and positively charged; and while the effect of Marseilles (contrary to intentions) is to endorse a private and atomized society, paradoxically, the Uffizi is much more completely a collective structure. While Le Corbusier presents a private and insulated building which, unambiguously, caters to a limited clientele, Vasari's model is sufficiently two-faced to accommodate a good deal more. A central void-figure, stable and obviously planned with, by way of entourage, an irregular backup which may be loose and responsive to close context: a stipulation of an ideal world and an engagement of empirical circumstance; unlike the Unité, the Uffizi may be seen as reconciling themes of self-conscious order and spontaneous randomness and, while it accepts the existing, by also proclaiming the new, the Uffizi may be said to confer a value upon new and old.[15] Urbanistically it is far more active.

Three

But, apart from suggesting to the still-surviving protagonists of Modern architecture the usefulness of the Uffizi–Place des Vosges–Vittoria model, a further prescription which might suggest itself is the scrutiny of long, skinny buildings, the equivalent in thickness to the *Zeilenbau* structures of Hilberseimer or the Maisons à Redents of Le Corbusier (fig. 105) but, unlike these, operating rather more as special cases than as parts of a general system. Operating perhaps like parts of the Munich Residenz (fig. 106, top) to discriminate certain conditions of texture or landscape; or like the Grande Galerie of the Louvre (fig. 106, bottom) as it behaved during the eighteenth century, acting as a means of physical communication, as an instrument of field recognition, and (like the walls of the Hofgarten at Munich), as sometimes filter and sometimes facade.

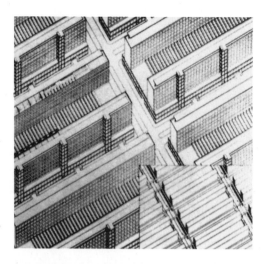

105. *Zeilenbauen,* Berlin, Ludwig Hilberseimer; Maison à Redents, Paris, Le Corbusier.

The Present Urban Predicament

In which sequence there should also be considered, from Rome, the Palazzo del Quirinale and its extension, the improbably attenuated Manica Lunga, which might be several Unités put end to end; but which in its *engagement* of the fabric of the city also acts with great decisiveness (fig. 107). For, while the Unité continues to enforce its object quality, the Manica Lunga is both object and space definer, permitting both street and garden to exert their separate and independent personalities; and the economy of the operation, all done so laconically and with such directness, may very well stand alongside the courtyard of the Palais Royale as a criticism of present-day procedures.

Four

But the courtyard of the Palais Royal (fig. 108), its walls a type of habitable *poché,* itself a species of secluded, urban room, might now be allowed to introduce the topic of the garden (first victim of Modern architecture?), which may comprise yet another prescription for the overcoming of object fixation.

Toward the end of the preceding Thomas Cubitt lecture, Giancarlo de Carlo noted Baron Haussmann's dismissal of a group of architects and, in their place, the substitution of the great Second Empire gardener, Alphand.[16] Alphand was presumably considered more capable than the architects. Had he, by then, already made his book *Les Promenades de Paris,* which disclosed that much covering up may be done with trees?

However, no great matter, since the issue is not dates but trees; and if, as already noticed, in the early 1920s the disappearance of the highly constructed garden is to be regarded as precursive to the dissolution of the city, perhaps a reverse operation might still be applicable. In the time of Louis XIV the park and the gardens of Versailles were almost exactly the same size as the city of Paris. But, some sort of critique of the city as it was, they also became a model of the city as it was to become. The *allées,* the *rond-points,* the *pattes*

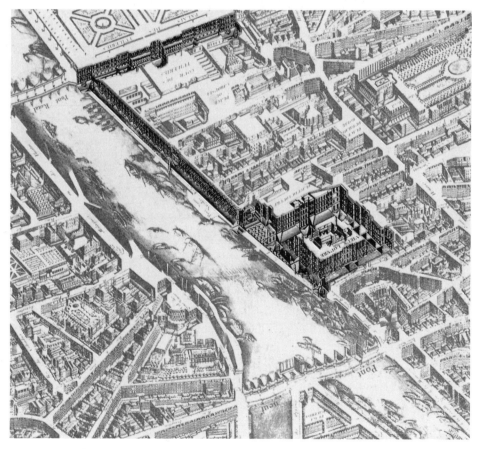

106. Residenz, Munich, figure/ground; Louvre, Paris, Grande Galerie.

108. Palais Royal, Paris.

d'oie of Le Nôtre at Versailles all find some sort of reflection in Haussmann's Paris; and, in this ecologically self-conscious age, *could* it not just be possible that the architecture of trees, articulating spaces, *might* provide both a palliative for the present and a paradigm for the future?

"Architecture is in deep trouble, whereas landscape architecture thrives": this is the opinion of Geoffrey Jellicoe as expressed in Boston in 1988;[17] and, of course, he may almost be right. But I should say with one proviso about the trees. Within the park of Versailles there are the two Trianons (fig. 109). There is the Petit Trianon located in a lyrically English garden, and we should be

107. Palazzo del Quirinale, Rome.

The Present Urban Predicament

prepared to give it only a very brief inspection. This because not too far away there is the Grand Trianon—a series of vertical planes arising from a highly constructed field and enclosing a pair of very carefully specified voids—and we should be prepared to give it a fairly protracted scrutiny. Sociologically, it may be an odious building; but morphologically, it may be useful.

109. Petit Trianon, Versailles, Anges-Jacques Gabriel; Grand Trianon, Versailles, Louis Le Vau.

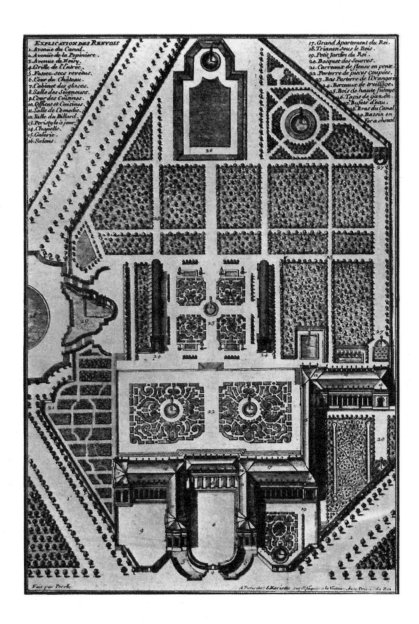

The Present Urban Predicament

This lecture might quite well have been entitled, as I now recognize, "Object Fixation: Cause and Cure"; and the condition of what might be called "space shyness," the basic condition of twentieth-century urbanism, is all the more remarkable when we allow ourselves to consider that in no previous century has there ever been so much talk about space as in the present. And could one, therefore, suggest that the critical use of this term has inhibited the production of the thing itself?[18]

Among the various therapies which I have proposed, those which I find most credible are: the Uffizi strategy, the long skinny building game, and the reconstitution of the garden; but, if none of these was to operate as remedial, then, needless to say, I regard a revival of the city as far more important than any survival of Modern architecture. However, I also assume that, given diminished passion and increased tolerance, both survival and revival are to be considered as just possible, though never to be considered if the architect continues to insist that all buildings should be considered works of architecture; that all buildings grow from the inside out; that all design should be total; and that the architect is the Messiah of the future.

As a final conclusion, might one consider the argument between Mondrian and van Doesburg, which is the long-ago issue that inspired my own interest in matrix? Van Doesburg is the master of the axonometric approach, invariably separating figure from spatial matrix. Mondrian invariably maintains spatial matrix and figure in a reciprocal and constantly fluctuating relationship. And it is because, to my mind, the relationship of figure to matrix in *Victory Boogie-Woogie* (fig. 110) is the relationship of object to texture, solid to void, randomness to order, incident to norm, even individual to state—because *Boogie-Woogie* allows figures to augment and to contract, to congeal and to dissolve, to erupt from matrix and to return to it again—that, in terms of the imaginary city which I have been examining, I feel compelled to cite this Mondrian performance as what I believe to be the instigation of anything useful which might have been said here.

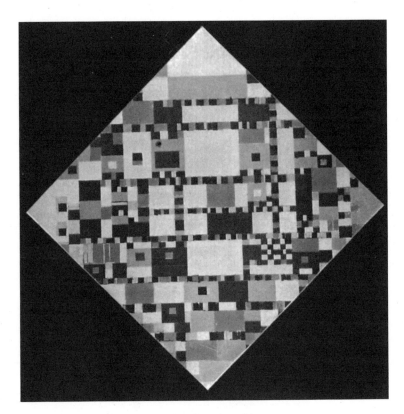

110. Piet Mondrian, *Victory Boogie-Woogie*, 1943–1944.

The Present Urban Predicament

Notes

1. Coleridge's definition of a successful work of art, as that which elicits a willing suspension of disbelief, is probably still the best.

2. David Watkin, *Morality and Architecture* (Oxford: Clarendon Press, 1977).

3. I am indebted to Patrick Pinnell for certain observations with reference to *genius loci* versus *Zeitgeist.*

4. Le Corbusier, *Towards a New Architecture* (London: Payson & Clarke, 1927), 167.

5. These sentiments are persistently apparent in van Doesburg; and when do they first occur? In any case, in 1924, van Doesburg expresses himself as follows: "In contrast to frontalism—arid in origin [with] a rigid, static way of life, the new architecture offers the plastic richness of an all-sided development in space and time."

6. Lewis Mumford, *The Culture of Cities* (New York: Harcourt, Brace, 1938), 136.

7. Leonardo Benevolo, *The Origins of Modern Town Planning* (Cambridge, Mass.: MIT Press, 1971), caption to illustrations 4 and 5.

8. Le Corbusier: these three quotations are taken from Sybil Moholy-Nagy, *Matrix of Man* (New York: Praeger, 1968). Moholy-Nagy did not specify their origins.

9. Le Corbusier, *Concerning Town Planning* (London: Architectural Press, 1947), 22.

10. Stamo Papadaki, *Le Corbusier* (New York, 1948), 137. An excerpt from *The City of Tomorrow,* tr. Frederick Etchells (London: J. Rodker, 1929).

11. Le Corbusier, *When the Cathedrals Were White* (New York: Reynal & Hitchcock, 1947).

12. Ibid., 51.

13. Ibid., 41.

14. The source of this quotation evades retrieval. Is it merely hearsay? Almost certainly not; and, in any case, a letter to the *New York Times* (Francis Brennan, March 31, 1978) which has lately been brought to my attention might serve to corrobo-

rate the persistence of Corbusian fantasy. The time is the early 1950s, the place is the twenty-third floor of the Time-Life Building, and the relevant part of the letter reads as follows: "Peering out across Manhattan through his heavy hornrimmed spectacles, Corbu shook his head in wonder and, to the best of my recollection quietly asked: 'Have you ever imagined what a marvelous sight this island would be if one could bury it up to say, the 20th or 30th story, put in some trees, some nice curving roads and make it all into a kind of park?' Answering himself, he went on: 'Then one could take charming little tours through a fabulous collection of architectural *folies de grandeur*—late Gothic and Romanesque chapels, French chateaux, Greek temples, Zigurat towers, shrines of all sorts, even immense allegorical murals done in colorful mosaics. Ah, what an enchanting museum!' then shaking his head again: '*Mais maintenant c'est vraiment une architecture pour les pigeons.*'" This letter, entitled "The Pigeon's Gain," is primarily an oblique criticism of Philip Johnson's AT&T Building.

15. The foregoing paragraph is, rather more than less, a quotation from Colin Rowe and Fred Koetter, *Collage City* (Cambridge Mass.: MIT Press, 1978).

16. Giancarlo de Carlo, "The Cubitt Lecture 1978," *Architectural Association Quarterly* 10, no. 2 (1978): 28–40.

17. See Michael Spens, *Gardens of the Mind: The Genius of Geoffrey Jellicoe* (Woodbridge, England: Antique Collectors' Club, 1992), p. 12.

18. It seems almost certain that space-talk made its decisive entry into the critical vocabulary of American and English architects with the publication of Sigfried Giedion's *Space, Time and Architecture* in 1941, and Nikolaus Pevsner's *An Outline of European Architecture* in 1943. Certainly, before the early 1940s, English-speaking readers appear to have been relatively underexposed to the analysis of buildings in terms of space and, since then, have come to accept such analysis (Bruno Zevi, *Architecture as Space,* 1957, might be an instance) as a relative commonplace; and, quite possibly, Le Corbusier may be taken as representative of something to the same effect related to French usage. For, while Corbu's earlier publications seem to be distinctly "dumb" as regards space-talk, with him too the new critical vocabulary ("ineffable space") seems to insinuate itself during the course of the 1940s and to become explicitly advertised in *New World of Space* (1948). However this may be, when Anglo-American usage is considered, there remain two, possibly three, exceptions to what has just been stipulated: Bernard Berenson; his disciple Geoffrey Scott; and, maybe, Frank Lloyd Wright.

Berenson's most recent biographer (Ernest Samuels, *Bernard Berenson: The Making of a Connoisseur,* 1979) tells us that in the mid-nineties in Florence he became associated with Adolf von Hildebrand and with the ideas which the latter had published in *Problem der Form in der bildenden Kunst;* and he goes on to suggest that from this source there came Berenson's use of the term "space composition" which emerged among the leading critical motifs of his *Central Italian Painters* (1897). And so much one might have thought; but in *Aesthetics and History* (1948) Berenson appears to have forgotten (or to be anxious to dissimulate) the origin of one of his own critical themes:

> Unfortunately, yet another German professor with a Slav name, August Schmarsow, some sixty years ago initiated an interest in space, not as the negligible void for which it had been taken hitherto but as the one and only existence. Objects, no matter how large or small exist only to make us realize mere extension, and exist for that alone, even though there they are but impertinent interruptions of the mystic void. So the art writing of the German-minded has been more and more dedicated to discussing space determination, space filling, space distortion, space this, space that—but to my recollection never to space composition.

So does one sympathize with the petulance of the aged or does one not? And has there occurred here a genuine lapse of memory? And why the substitution of Hildebrand for Schmarsow, whose Leipzig lecture of 1893, *Raumgestaltung,* is clearly what is here invoked? And in all this is there not a slightly false dealing of the cards? Is not Berenson a little too eager to distance himself from the fashionable, or erudite, criticism of the Viennese *belle époque*? Is he not only too happy to express himself in the amenable terms of English *belles-lettres?* And does not this become so much worse when expressed in the quasi-eighteenth-century accents of his protégé Geoffrey Scott, whose *Architecture of Humanism* still makes no reference to Vienna, no reference (so far as my patience is aware) to Lipps, Hildebrand, Schmarsow?

That Anglo-American spatial discourse became trapped by Berenson and Geoffrey Scott who, both of them relating to Vienna, kept something up their sleeves, should not be a great matter of surprise; but what, in this area, might be the role and the behavior of Frank Lloyd Wright? Was he entirely uninfluenced by Viennese criticism and did he have early and completely individual intimations of what Schmarsow and others had lately been talking about? This is what would be interesting to know. However Cornelis van de Ven in *Space in Architecture* (Assen, Netherlands: Van Gorcum, 1978, 231–238), does seem to suggest that, with Wright, space-talk came late, from 1928 or thereabouts. In any case, and almost certainly, the simultaneous prevalence of both space-talk and space-shyness will surely survive as among the greater curiosities of twentieth-century urbanism.

Comments on the IBA Proposals

After spending the academic year 1980–1981 in Rome with the University of Notre Dame, from the end of 1981 to the end of 1984 I found myself in Berlin on no less than twelve occasions. This was as a guest of Interbauausstellung, *otherwise known as IBA; and I was there as one of eight so-called* Experten *who were summoned to criticize, to advise and, incidentally, to justify. We were the following: Max Bächer, Jaap Engel, Manfred Gehrman, Vittorio Gregotti, Edward Jahn, Egbert Kossack, and myself; and, when we were all present, there was seldom any time for rest and relaxation. It was a business of nine o'clock to five o'clock day in and day out. Indeed, I saw far more of the general texture of Berlin when, in 1967, I was shown around by Matthias Ungers (who took me into bookshops) than anything I saw on these later occasions.*

But how could these sessions not have been stimulating? For, sometimes, we Experten *were obliged to sit through infinitely extended* meetings of social protest—the mothers of Kreuzberg; and then, as an alternative, we could only be solaced by the voices of Julius Posener (always calm) and Otto von Simson, who for years and years had lectured on Gothic architecture at the University of Chicago and who just happened to be the brother-in-law of the English-born Margaret von Hessen und bei Rhein (who with her slightly Virginia intonation—she was brought up in Washington when her father was British ambassador to the U.S.—was likely to say: "But I always call him my brother-in-love").

So this Berlin experience inevitably promoted a little flurry of thoughts and memoranda, no doubt all in the files of Vittorio Magnago Lampugnani. I here restrict myself to only three of these:

1. Proposals which I made with associated diagrams for our second meeting in December 1981. These may have been published in Berlin but I am not sure; and, in any case, they were published in English as "Comments on the I.B.A. Proposals." This was in the number of Architectural Design entitled "The New Classicism" (London: Academy Editions, 1990).

2. A rather less excited piece, possibly addressed to Vittorio Magnago Lampugnani and probably deriving from about a year later. This was published in German by Vittorio as "Modelle für eine Stadt: Ziele und Programme der IBA" (Berlin, 1984); and, in the same year, it made an English appearance in the pages of The Architectural Review as "The Vanished City, or Rowe Reflects."

3. A student project of 1983–1984. This is the thesis of Raul de Carvalho, which may be interpreted as some sort of summation of issues brought up in the two foregoing memoranda. The visuals were published in The Architectural Review (September 1984); the comments included here were written retrospectively for this collection.

I require a quotation in order to set in motion this memorandum; and, since I don't wish to quote from myself, I propose to make use of extracts from an article by my friend and colleague, Werner Goerner, which has come my way today. It is entitled, "Architecture as an Integral Part of the City"; it is mostly about a number of projects for the Ballhausplatz in Vienna; and, published in the *Cornell Journal of Architecture,* no. 1 (1981), my selection of extracts from it reads as follows:

> The scientific and analytic mind, with its tendency to break the world into ever smaller parts, has, during the past 50 years of urban and architectural development, finally succeeded in ending a long and fruitful marriage between architecture and the city. Within the modern movement, both the Neo-Positivistic view of architecture as an a-historical phenomenon, and the view of architecture as exclusively the result of political and economic conditions, dependent on the technological and cultural developments (*Zeitgeist* obsession) finally led to the estrangement of architecture from the city . . . stripped of its civic dimension . . . modern architecture retreated into privacy. . . . [Therefore] in the modern city a meaningful dialogue between the *res publica* and the *res privata* is missing, leading to an impoverishment of the urban spatial morphology. . . . A meaningful orientation within urban public space has become difficult . . . [and] without . . . spatial articulation of the public realm, the city becomes unintelligible.[1]

These remarks specify the present condition of almost any major city in the world; they describe West Berlin, they are indicative of the present day concern to reconcile architecture and the city; and, particularly, they are indicative of the program of IBA. For, I think it no exaggeration to say that IBA's principal concern is to place architecture and the city once more in a condition of fertile intercourse.

The ambition is grand; its realisation is what a large part of the world is waiting for; because it is a trial, it will not be wholly successful; but the historical record will stipulate that it was here, in West Berlin, that a first major attempt was made to reconstitute the city.

Comments on the IBA Proposals

It was several times pointed out by the *Experten* (and, most repeatedly, by Egbert Kossack) that their instruction was incomplete, that, quite simply, they didn't know whether they were supposed to be addressing their attention *to a city plan or to an exhibition.* Nor was the information (as far as I remember) ever forthcoming; and it is to this situation of ambiguity that I now propose to address myself—to these two separate conditions as the separate conditions which they are.

The IBA Proposals as a City Plan

Again, in this context of consideration, the *Experten* were presented with the further traces of a conflict since it was not clear whether they were supposed to be advising on a plan for a part of West Berlin or a plan for a city, at some date, to be reunited. So, here, I shall solve this problem by ignoring it. Ignoring it because I suppose that an adequate plan for a part of West Berlin immediately adjacent to the old city center should in no way be compromised by unification and that a good plan might even act to facilitate such an objective.

However, something must now be said about the prejudices induced by the boundaries of maps. For, surely, the boundaries of a map act, to a large extent, to control what one discerns within these perimeters, i.e.: these boundaries will encourage the reading of certain configurations; but if these perimeters are altered, maybe wholly different configurations will present themselves to the eye and to the mind.

So I make these remarks because of the documentation with which we have been presented. In the first case, as was noticed by several individuals, this documentation has tended to suppress information as to the present condition of East Berlin which, again and again, has been made to look like a large body of water. Then the documentation which was first exhibited could only encourage my eyes, at least, to move laterally (west-east, east-west) more or less along the line of the Landwehrkanal (the result of zoning propositions made way back?). But, if one set of maps will encourage this reading, then another documentation, to which I became alerted by Professor Nagel's remarks in October, could only provoke a consciousness of entirely different movements within the centre part of the same site. For, as something additional—and not contradictory—to the line of the Landwehrkanal, Professor Nagel made a very energetic illustration of the railroad tracks and yards leading to the former Potsdam and Anhalt railway stations.

However, a consideration of the possibilities suggested by north-south movement (whether visual or physical) will be reserved for later attention; and now to approach the specific proposals of IBA:

A. In Kreuzberg North of the Landwehrkanal: Luisenstadt

As I recollect, though the *Experten* heard much vociferous representation from this area (and for very good reasons!), we were not called upon to make particularised commentary; and, accordingly, any remarks here will be of the most general. So far as I can perceive this is, of all others, the section of West Berlin which possesses the most intelligible structure; and, surely, this basic structure should not be infringed or deformed in the name of necessary renewal. From what one has seen and heard, upgrading and renewal of housing *must* occur. But may not such operations be regarded as mostly a matter of urban dentistry—of repair, replacement, and occasional extraction?

Apart from these general remarks, there should probably be noticed the extreme importance of the line of Oranienstrasse, leading from Kochstrasse to the former Görlitzer railway station with its great potential for development as a place of recreation (fig. 111, Diagram 1).

B. Friedrichstadt South of the Wall

This is an area amputated from the urban configuration of which it forms an intrinsic part, and its role is then further diminished by

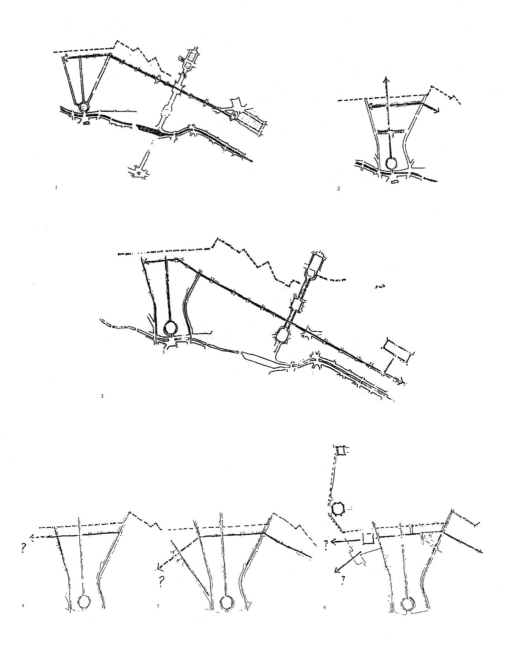

111. The IBA proposals: Diagrams 1 through 6.

the present format of Mehringplatz, which nowadays merely serves as a curious appendage utterly divorced from those functions of convergence which were related to its original Baroque and Roman idea. Then, add to this that the three major north-south arteries of this area—Wilhelmstrasse (Via del Babuino), Friedrichstrasse (Via del Corso), and Lindenstrasse (Via di Ripetta) all terminate to the north as they do; and, then, further consider that Kochstrasse is not exactly the Via dei Condotti . . . and, with these considerations, a sadness about this part of town becomes augmented. It is a fragment. Logically and psychologically, it belongs to the rest of Friedrichstadt; and, taken by itself, its eighteenth-century infrastructure is of nothing like the decisive quality of the mid-nineteenth-century layout in adjacent Kreuzberg. Particularly, Friedrichstrasse can only climax in Unter den Linden. But if, for the moment and the foreseeable future, this is impossible, then what to do?

I think, myself, that the solution is very simple; and, if the IBA plan is not absolutely congealed, I would suggest the following:

1. somewhere approximately midway between Mehringplatz and Kochstrasse, the creation of a direct east-west pedestrian promenade; and

2. at the intersection of this promenade with Friedrichstrasse, the creation of a *very* small *Platz* which, in a better world (with the Wall gone), might serve as a local decoration to the Mehringplatz–Unter den Linden (Diagram 2); and I make these suggestions because of the *necessity* of finding some logical place of convergence within this area.

Apart from these issues, I listened with attention to the arguments about the location of the flower market in this not highly accessible part of the world; and I agreed with those many who think that its present site (the noise and the mess of trucks driving in and out) is more than a little mad.

Comments on the IBA Proposals

However, now to approach the controversial subject of the vanished Prinz-Albrecht-Palais and its related park. In my discussion of Luisenstadt, I have already stressed the high visibility of the connection Kochstrasse–Oranienstrasse–Görlitzer Bahnhof; and, should the flower market be shifted elsewhere, I assume that this could equally be the line Kochstrasse–Junker-/Ritter-/Reichenberger Strasse—though this line would scarcely be equipped with a comparable eastward termination (Diagram 3). But, whichever of these lines is assumed to predominate (and one or the other of them is vital for the integration of Luisenstadt with points west), they are both, of course, approximately blocked at Wilhelmstrasse; and, from then on, everything becomes confused—the prevalent condition in the Friedrichvorstadt.

But should the career of a very important urban ligament (either of the lines which I have itemised) be irretrievably blocked by the horrible associations which accrue to the site of the former Prinz-Albrecht-Palais? And are there not considerations of urban elegance and legibility which would urge a less abrupt solution in this vicinity?

I have seen proposals for the continuation of Kochstrasse to some unspecified point further west (Diagram 4); I have also seen proposals for the routing of the Kochstrasse line through Askanischer Platz and Schöneberger Strasse to some unspecified point further southwest (Diagram 5); but, while I strongly support the examination of both of these moves, I would still like to observe another possibility—and I suggest this with diffidence.

To the north—and in East Berlin—one observes the role of Pariser Platz as entry to Unter den Linden and the comparable role of Leipziger Platz and, therefore, one wonders whether an analogue of these spaces could not be created at this point further south—as an entry to Kochstrasse. The idea would, I think, have certain merits. It would imply the continuity and the intrinsic integration of the urban fabric on both sides of the Wall. It could, in itself, act as a monument. Nor need it be destructive of the present function of this site as a park. For, at this point, one does not propose a building so much as an enclosure of trees through which a continuation of Kochstrasse would travel. And it is to this enclosure of trees (presumably supported by a modest architectural and sculptural apparatus) that a memorial function might then be attributed (Diagram 6).

Such, I believe, might have been the solution adopted by Gilly, Schinkel, and Lenné; and I suggest that it may be a solution which deserves consideration. For I do not think that a proper monument to the victims of the Gestapo is here to be made by simply preserving the site, by nothing more, by pious negation; and, correspondingly, I *do* assume that a monument, *both as a commemoration and as release,* should be a conscious, a grand, and a positive gesture (perhaps in some very minimal and quiet way a present day recall of those neo-Classical monuments which addressed themselves to the recollection of Frederick the Great?).

I would suggest that such a development might be in the best traditions of Berlin; and I would further suggest that such a development must be considered vital for any future animation of Kochstrasse. For, without any other entry places west, what is Kochstrasse beyond a sad and isolated street, excluded from communication, and forever rendered sad by its relationship to Checkpoint Charlie?

Which, otherwise, leaves only to be said that, in southern Friedrichstadt, the IBA proposals represent a triumph of determination. For, although there may be some doubts about the excessive use of perimeter blocks, to have secured the four projects at the intersection of Friedrichstrasse and Kochstrasse, which all combine respect for the existing with introduction of the new, to have combined these with the further project to the east of Lindenstrasse is nothing less than a triumph and so, I am sure, this achievement will be judged.

C. Around the Lützowplatz, South of the Tiergarten, and along the Landwehrkanal

There is, I believe, little which should be said. The sites are separated; beyond a point the area does not presume tight coordination;
and the solutions are invariably more than adequate. So, particularly
within this area one admires Stirling, who has been possibly liber-
ated from his English inhibitions by exposure to the Germanic
lands. Possibly his solution is too Wilhelminian, too Wagnerian,
too Neuschwanstein, too Hechingen, and all the rest. But should
this be a problem? And, in the present situation of Berlin, I think it
should not.

So apart from this, what else? One regrets the absence of
Ungers' Hotel Berlin; and, apart from this, what other objections?
Does one object to the plans of Rob Krier's *urban villas?* I think one
does and, perhaps, Rob Krier should reconsider these.

D. Between the Kulturforum, the Wall, and Stresemannstrasse

This is obviously an area of maximum ambiguity, of maximum con-
troversy, and, not unexpectedly, one in which the IBA proposals
seem to be less happy and accommodating. A comprehensive solution for this area presumably implies a variety of decisions, not all
of them concerned with the area itself; and, as I see them, these are
related to:

- the completion of the Kulturforum;
- the role of the Potsdamer Strasse;
- the role of the Landwehrkanal;
- the future of the Potsdam and Anhalt railway stations;
- a future symbolic access to Leipziger Strasse;
- some improved approach to Kochstrasse(?);
- a location for the Tempodrom;
- and, above all, the ease of north-south vehicular movement through what, for all practical purposes, is, and will surely remain, a major traffic sluice.

Now, with these decisions apparently not made, it should not be surprising that the IBA plan seems here to be a little ad hoc and perfunctory. A little bit stuck together with Scotch tape. For how could matters be otherwise? And do not such decisions lie beyond IBA's mission and sphere of competence?

All the same, to surrender this territory (so central to the city both West and East) to a more or less naturalistic forest would surely be a gesture of defeat; and accordingly, I add a number of notes which are not necessarily addressed to IBA but which are offered as very tentative guides for development.

1. *The completion of the Kulturforum and the role of the Potsdamer Strasse.* I believe it was Alberti's advice that one should not set out to contradict what has already been begun; and this is an opinion which I share. I am only a very reserved admirer of the work of Hans Scharoun; but I can see no good deriving from an interference with his intentions at this point. And, therefore, I am of the opinion that the Kulturforum, so far as possible, should be completed according to Scharoun's idea, with the central residential building which he intended and the axis from the Matthäikirche to a rondel on the Bellevuestrasse which is an extremely important part of his proposals (fig. 112, Diagram 7).

Also, though I can just *begin* to understand why Scharoun chose to use the Staatsbibliothek so as to block the route of the Potsdamer Strasse, I can scarcely believe that he had in mind any six-lane highway which would fatally separate this Staatsbibliothek from the Philharmonie and from Mies van der Rohe's Nationalgalerie on the other side. Scharoun's concept was evidently a version of the Museuminsel, of that cultural complex which, across the Lustgarten, not so long ago faced the Stadtschloss. Which is to intimate that, in the default of a better, the least controversial policy in this territory is to accept Scharoun and to press for the Kulturforum as he presumably intended it to be—traffic-free except for local access.

2. *The Landwehrkanal* is a major asset in the area of the city which the *Experten* were assembled to hear about and to discuss;

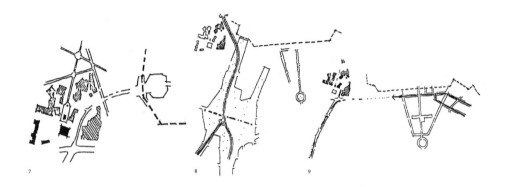

112. Diagrams 7, 8, and 9.

and, quite rapidly, one became convinced that it is the *principal* asset. For what *else* is there to compare it with?

So one believes that the Landwehrkanal is an important and idiosyncratic component of the *idea* of the city; and one also believes that it is 'very special' and much loved. Further, one has noticed that, of its nature, it is equipped with a pronounced *genius loci*. Potentially, it is a linear collection of picturesque episodes; and, if the buildings along its bank are by no means the quality of Amsterdam (or anything like it), still they often comprise highly respectable *ensembles* and, in general, must be considered very much worthy of conservation.

For reasons such as these, the Landwehrkanal surely deserves—and will surely reward—the most sensitive attention. Potentially, it is rich in surprises; and, as one of the few remaining episodes which approach the intimate-spectacular, this potential should certainly be augmented. For the Landwehrkanal presumes a close relationship; and if, along with the late Louis Kahn, one thinks it possible to speak about 'what something wants to become', then one might be tempted to suggest that the most appropriate destiny of this waterway is that of a somewhat reserved enclave, highly accessible but a little private, by no means—in any accepted sense—a park, but still a place of recreation and, sometimes, meditation.

To me, it seems that many persons spoke to this effect; and it even seems that, maybe, there is something of a consensus of opinion that the Landwehrkanal, during most of its length, should become a place a little difficult of vehicular access and should never be degraded to the status of a high-speed east-west artery.

To repeat: a linear sequence which requires the most intelligent and sensitive response.

To observe: if the Landwehrkanal is not to be a major artery, a better access to Kochstrasse becomes of even greater importance.

3. *The Potsdam and Anhalt railway stations* are two sites protruding into the area which was initially exposed to the attention of the *Experten* from a context which the preferred maps do not reveal; and, personally, I am enormously indebted to the presentation of Professor Nagel for his revelation of this enormous, former railroad complex. Indeed, while Professor Nagel spoke, I myself was vividly reminded of the statement of the Abbé Laugier that he who can design a park can design a city. For, from all this huge territory (involving the Gneisenaustrasse and Bülowstrasse, with also points further south), does there not exist the very great potential both for a park and an entry such as no other European city possesses (Diagram 8)?

So, I am thinking neither of an *Autobahn* nor a *boulevard* but of a *parkway,* or a medium-speed drive within a landscape from which close and distant views of buildings may be available. Now the concept of *parkway,* I suspect, is not fully understood in Berlin; and, therefore I feel obliged to enlarge upon it. The concept *parkway* was, probably, an invention of Frederick Law Olmsted; and, as an idea, has probably existed within the United States for approximately a hundred years. In Boston it is represented by the Fenway; in New York, by Riverside Drive and by the approaches to the city via the Merritt and Palisades parkways; and, in Houston, the same strategy is illustrated by Memorial Drive.

To repeat: the *parkway* is not high speed. It is, rather, a *corso* or a *passeggiata* for the automobile; and, as an idea, it is related to late nineteenth-century fantasies about the movement of carriages. But, for these reasons, should it be any less accessible to us? And I think not. For the parkway—apart from its intrinsic amenity—is also a mediation between two important interests—the ecology lobby and *the move vehicles quicker enthusiasm*.

But to qualify these remarks: though one thinks of the *parkway* as an American invention, this cannot be wholly true—since, already, in the 1860s, it does occur in Florence. For, in the days of *Firenze capitale*, what else are Poggi's elegant drives up to Piazzale Michelangelo—the extended drive from Porta Romana and the more compacted ascent from the river—if they are not to be regarded as *parkways*? And, therefore, with the great possibilities of a parkway in mind, I am more than a little surprised that IBA proposes to leave the site of the Anhalt railway station vacant and then indicates a building over the Potsdam railway station site.

Simply, I would have imagined that this was contrary to common sense. The *Experten* were told (I do not know on what authority) that 60,000 vehicles travel through this area every day; and therefore to compound this problem, with what amounts to a restoration of an earlier distribution of streets (in the case of Potsdamer Strasse already interrupted by Scharoun), can only appear to be an ill-advised strategy.

4. *A future access to Leipziger Strasse* is surely a polemical and a conciliatory gesture which West Berlin must make. It would be a representational gesture; and, in this area, its building would be equivalent to a symbolic version of the Brandenburg Gate. It would be a gesture which revealed the potential of communication. Nor need it be elaborate. It could be no more than a hotel, an apartment house, or an office building; but it *could* be arranged—with a *little* rhetoric—to appear as a city gate. So why not?

5. *Some improved access to Kochstrasse*, which I also associate with a destination for Potsdamer Strasse, remains a topic about which I continue to think. That is: if the associations of the Prinz-Albrecht-Palais are not allowed to become obsessive, then could not Potsdamer Strasse and Kochstrasse be seen as connected (Diagram 9)?

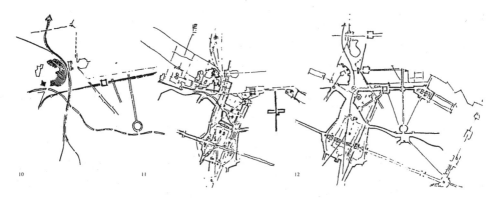

113. Diagrams 10, 11, and 12.

6. *A location for the Tempodrom*[2] should not be a problem. For, without dismay, could not Tempodrom be placed to points either to the north or south of its present situation?

7. *The ease of north-south vehicular movement* is surely a major problem in this area, which is a part of what one might call the north-south corridor; and it is as part of this corridor (as I have already said) that I feel it vital to retain the site of the Potsdam railway station as an open space connected to a larger park on the site of the former railroad yards (fig. 113, Diagrams 10, 11, 12).

Such a park would relieve the density of Kreuzberg and Schöneberg (so often a subject of discussion), might be intersected by the line of Gneisenaustrasse and Bülowstrasse, and, somewhere in the middle of it, one might expect to find a version of that Waterlooplatz which was originally projected for this terrain.

So the perimeters of this park are not, immediately, easy to imagine; but one does conceive that, surrounding it, there might be the equivalent of the Nash Terraces, which in London comprise the enclosure of Regent's Park; and then, projecting into this park from the north, attached to the urban fabric, but also accessible from the Waterlooplatz, one might also think about the possibility of that new Rathaus (town hall) for Berlin which is often said to be so necessary.

Comments on the IBA Proposals

But, meanwhile, to return to the *parkway*. It is to be thought about as travelling through this Potsdamer-Anhalter Park (not to its detriment), as moving through the site of the Potsdam railway station, as swirling around the Potsdam Gate, as extensively screened from the Kulturforum, to cross the Tiergarten as a sunken road (the image here is derived from Olmsted's sunken transverse roads in Central Park, New York), to arrive in a reconstructed version of the former Alsenplatz which might act to give the Reichstag something of the built support which it so badly needs.

So, from there on, one imagines the parkway (or the north-south corridor) leading on in the general direction of Tegel. But not to make comments upon unknown terrain. For one now wishes to return to the Tiergarten and to a sequence of north-south 'decorations' which might be considered auxiliary to the idea of a north-south corridor.

So *can* one think about the Russian monument, at the intersection of Charlottenburger Chausee and Siegesallee, as something in any way positive? And I say this for deliberate reasons. Meaning that the Russian monument is a useful component of the scene which I propose. For why could one not imagine the reconstitution of the Siegesallee as a canal? And beyond this point, I will say nothing further except to suggest that, in terms of the north-south corridor, which it *must* address, the city of Berlin is presented with a major problem, available to elegant solution, with which the city has an obligation to be concerned.

So, to repeat, these remarks are *not* addressed to the IBA. They are addressed to the city; and, with these remarks made, I am suggesting that the city should sponsor a competition for the north-south corridor.

The IBA Proposals as an Exhibition

It has been traditional that an important exhibition be something segregated from the fabric of the city. Such were the buildings for London 1851, Paris 1867, and Paris 1889. After Chicago 1893, it became practice that an exhibition might suggest *the model for a city;* but, all the same, this was a model which could in no way be contaminated by any intercourse with the existing city in which it might be located. The model city was to be framed, isolated (preferably by trees) from any local, empirical infringement; and this is a general exhibition strategy which seems to have persisted down to our own day. The ideal city is to be something aloof and critical; it is to be something *au-dessus de la mêlée,* it is to be Weissenhof-Siedlung or Hansaviertel, and, in choosing to discard this almost one-hundred-year-old tradition, IBA certainly deserves the most prolonged applause. For, while the concept of *exhibition as special enclave* (exhibition as campus) was, for a long time, productive of stimulating results, it now begins to seem that it did serve to promote unnecessary abstraction—the abstraction of Paris 1900 no less than the abstraction of the Hansaviertel.

So, IBA has abandoned the high pedestal on which the former promoters of exhibitions habitually placed themselves. It has chosen to embroil itself within the existing city in all its empirical density; and this conscientious and lucid decision must be emphasised because, quite often, it seems not to be observed. But, to repeat: with the idea of an unsegregated exhibition, the parts of which are to be found scattered around the city, IBA has propounded a significant novelty—an innovation which, in some parts of the world, is already acclaimed, and an innovation which promises to provide a model which no future promoters of exhibitions will be able to ignore. For it is such a model that the Berlin Building Exhibition of 1984 *will* present; and, while IBA is, ostensibly, addressing itself to problems which are local, in reality these problems are worldwide and among the more pressing architectural issues of today.

I am thinking here of the double disasters of war and Modern architecture which have been inflicted upon the European city within the last forty years and which (almost looking like the effect of bombs) have also been inflicted upon the American city—in terms of the slightly contrary designations of 'free enterprise' and

Comments on the IBA Proposals

'urban renewal'. For the joint action of *war and Modern architecture* has been so fundamentally destructive that society now reels under their impact; and, if Berlin still remains the most damaged city then, correspondingly, it is—perhaps—to Berlin that the world looks for some solution.

So it is in this context of anticipation that I would like to place Berlin 1984; but, sitting around as I have done, listening for five, long days, mostly to 'protest' disguised as 'participation', I have also wondered why the programme and the strategy of IBA is not more evident and more visible. Indeed, what I have heard has often caused me to think about London 1851; and, while thinking along these lines, for the predicament of IBA I have frequently substituted the position of Albert of Saxe-Coburg-Gotha in 1849–1850. For Prince Albert, promoting the Crystal Palace, was equally under attack. The whole project seemed strange, bizarre, and foreign; and, on this occasion, the objections came from the Conservatives with their endless refrain of: *this* will never, never do.

But then the triumphant inauguration of the Crystal Palace and Queen Victoria's effusive remarks:

> The sight as we came to the centre where the steps and chair (on which I did not sit) was placed facing the beautiful crystal fountain, was magic and impressive. The tremendous cheering, the joy expressed in every face—the vastness of the building—the sound of the organ—and my beloved husband, the creator of this peace festival 'uniting the industry and the art of all the nations of the earth', all this was indeed moving, and a day to live forever. God bless my dearest Albert, and my dear country, which has shown itself so great today.

Victoria's English remarks are irrepressibly Biedermeier; but, if the situation, nowadays, is somewhat different, is it for all that so very different? IBA is not exactly the consort of Queen Victoria, nor are the professional 'participators' of West Berlin exactly the same as the English Conservatives of the mid-nineteenth century. But something of similarity remains; and how is one to describe it? Or should one try?

I myself do not propose to try. I propose, instead, to comment upon the abundance of IBA's problems and, firstly, upon a problem of communication.

The enmeshing of the concepts *city plan* and *exhibition* is not new; but the enmeshing of these concepts *within the context of the existing city* is so innovative that the promise of a *great exhibition in Berlin* has come to be obscured. It seems to me that the 'participators' (and here I think, again, of the critics of Prince Albert) have addressed themselves to almost every other topic except this one which is so pressing and immediate. An exhibition, apart from its didactic purposes and apart from its values as a paradigm, is also an occasion of public festivity—of fireworks, balloon ascents, acrobatics, dramatics, subsidiary exhibitions, convergence of admiring foreigners, symposia, spectacular concerts, and all the traditional apparatus which it is so easy to imagine. But none of this—all so necessary for any major international event—has ever intruded itself as an issue for discussion; and I suggest that this inhibition of any thought about pleasure (whether vulgar or refined) begins to imply serious consequences.

So is this inhibition the effect of a socio-economic climate or is it something endemic to the city? And, again, these are questions to which I cannot attempt to respond. I notice, instead, that the topic *exemplary exhibition of historical and international significance* does threaten to become reduced to a very local and provincial affair—and mostly an affair of passion related to the intimate format of social housing.

Which remarks may now allow me to suggest that, perhaps, IBA has been too defensive and has not sufficiently loudly advertised what one presumes to be its *dual* mission. By which I mean it is high time that the topic *model housing* should cease to occupy the center of attention and that the topic *exhibition* should be allowed to assume the prominence which it deserves. Because, though

Comments on the IBA Proposals

project after project may be separately discussed and analysed, obviously and in the end, it is the *ensemble* which is going to count.

But, here again, IBA runs into problems which are scarcely of its own making. For how to make an exhibition, let alone the model for a city, out of nothing else but social housing? And, if social housing (or, indeed, any kind of housing) is to be inflated to bear such a burden, is this not to defeat the purpose which is, partly at least, to serve as background for more public urban phenomena? And, just what about these?

I understand exceptionally little of IBA's finances, though I am led to believe that there is little available for what should be considered *the essentials of a great city;* and, by *the essentials,* I understand not simply the details of the *res privata* but, also, the celebration of the *res publica* without which the extended affairs of the *res privata* are apt to become very little more than fatiguing. And the *res publica,* or so I assume, is *not* something to be represented by an infinite multiplication of kindergartens and retreats for battered women.

Serious and necessary, of course, these must be; but an appropriate expression of the public realm, I assume, will absorb and accommodate such details as these. However, with such a remark made, in West Berlin, apart from the still incomplete Kulturforum just what attempts have there ever been made to project any images related to the notions of the state, of the city, of society in general? And I think of the equivalent of such pieces of urban furniture as, in London, the screen at Hyde Park Corner, in Paris of the *chevaux de Marly,* in Munich of the Propyläen, and here of the Brandenburg Gate—all of them, judged by the criteria of the scientific and analytical mind, patently superfluous; but, all of them, intimately related to the *idea* and the *myth* of the cities in which they are to be found. And is it not the absence of such reassuring fragments of urban theater which is, at least, one of the causes of that somewhat interminable theater of 'participation' which it has been a part of my recent education to have observed? For, in default of a built and reliable urban theater, of a theater equipped with traditions and style,

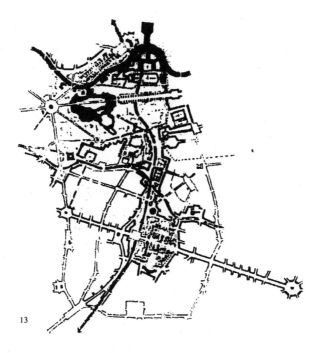

13

114. Diagram 13.

Comments on the IBA Proposals

are we not endlessly obliged to improvise the public realm, to invent it, and to reinvent it, via a series of personal and dramatic interventions? *I am speaking in public and, therefore, the public realm exists.*

Whether this is good or bad, I don't know. It expands debate; it contributes to vivacity; but, I am, also, compelled to doubt whether it contributes to achievement. For, in the absence of a *built* public realm—that convergence of fantasy, idea, and myth—it may seem that consensus, the necessary basis of *any* achievement, is impossible. And, therefore, I think yet again about the problems of IBA.

IBA is being expected to do too much with too little. And, if IBA's proposals may frequently appear to be a little stretched and a little strained, this is the cause. It is the absence of the public realm. For, as a consequence of the pragmatic state of mind, and the double inheritance of war and Modern architecture, the concept of the public realm has disappeared. The idea became that of *Existenzminimum;* and, as a result, the *res publica* became reduced to little more than a retarded and unconvincing display of diminished Baroque and neo-Classical precedent. Which is to designate a universal problem and, more particularly, a problem of IBA, attempting to transform the *res privata* into something which it can never be. We have talked about kitchens and bathrooms; but have we *ever* talked—been *allowed* to talk—about the equivalent of the Brandenburg Gate? And to ask this question is to illustrate the greatest problem confronting Berlin 1984 (fig. 114, Diagram 13).

Notes

1. Werner Goerner, "Architecture as an Integral Part of the City," *The Cornell Journal of Architecture,* no. 1 (1981), 69.

2. The Tempodrom is an alternative organization for the performing arts housed within a marquee during summertime and located at the vacant site of the former Potsdam railway station.

The Vanished City

Speaking about the public and the private realm, Hannah
Arendt says:

> The public realm, as the common world, gathers us to-
> gether and yet prevents our falling over each other. . . .
> What makes mass society so difficult to bear is not the
> number of people involved, or at least not primarily, but
> the fact that the world between them has lost its power to
> gather them together, to relate and to separate them. The
> weirdness of this situation resembles a spiritualistic seance
> where a number of people gathered around a table might
> suddenly, by some magic trick, see the table vanish from
> their midst, so that two persons sitting opposite to each
> other were no longer separated but would be entirely unre-
> lated by anything concrete.[1]

244

Nowadays, wherever one travels, the table which has vanished has become the preeminent contemporary datum of life. "No longer separated, but entirely unrelated . . . by anything concrete," the vanished table is, of course, the vanished *res publica,* that public realm which, formerly, related and separated both objects and individuals, which simultaneously established community and illustrated identity. So, if not absolutely traumatic, the effective disappearance of the *res publica* is at least disturbing; and surely there is nowhere in the world where the presence of its absence is more acutely to be felt than in Berlin.

Le Corbusier's Table

It might be entertaining and instructive to consider Le Corbusier's version of Hannah Arendt's table; and, as might be expected, Corbu's table is infinitely more cluttered with physical detail than the pristine horizontal surface which is Arendt's image of the *res publica;* indeed Corbu's table is littered with all the acceptable debris of a meal.

Says Corbu:

> *Observez un jour . . . observez dans un petit casse-croute populaire, deux ou trois convives ayant pris leur café et causant. La table est couverte encore de verres, de bouteilles, d'assiettes, l'huilier, le sel, le poivre, la serviette, le rond de serviette, etc. Voyez l'ordre fatal qui met tous ces objets en rapport les un avec les autres; ils ont tout servi, ils ont été saisi par la main de l'un ou de l'autre des convives; les distances qui les séparent sont la mesure de la vie: C'est une composition mathématique agencée; il n'y a pas un lieu faux, un hiatus, une tromperie.*[2]

This is not to suggest that Le Corbusier's table in his popular eating house in any way diminished that table which Arendt presents as the ultimate theater of the public realm. For, with their alternative images of the table what they both specify is a *field for interaction.* The table (I think they both imply) promotes a convergence of interest; and, with the surrounding persons sufficiently primed (this is Corbu's contribution), it becomes apparent that the table, as a version of the *res publica,* is the great agent, perhaps the only agent, which is likely to produce political settlement, interesting dialogue, useful dialectic, and important debate.

The table, which, in both cases, is the evident field of interaction, is also, surely, that essential ground which is postulated by Gestalt psychology as the primary datum of experience. It is that ground in terms of which figure emerges into prominence, which serves as a framework in which figure is suspended, which 'relates' and 'separates', which not only supports figure but also qualifies it. So Arendt and Le Corbusier, with a comparable table, present us with two quite different grounds. Arendt's ground is mostly socio-political and her figures, I am sure, are mostly individuals; while Corbu's ground is mostly socio-aesthetic and his figures, one might guess, are mostly objects. So the one table is mostly about people and the other mostly about things; but, since they are both related to compatible arguments about freedom and order, private happiness and the more public structures which act to guarantee it, personally I find it immensely easy to place these two tables side by side in the same restaurant and to imagine a movement between them, listening to their different conversations and deriving invaluable impressions from both.

Since 1945, the so-called 'arts of peace' have proved just as lamentable in their influence as, before 1945, the so-called 'arts of war'; and I refer, of course, to that fatal tendency of Modern architecture never to imagine a coalition between buildings and space but always to attribute a figurative mission to building and to conceive of space as no more than a naturalistic extension. Berlin's urbanistic problem is in this case far from unique. Thus, if one assumes that a city is a built-up solid, it necessarily follows that its figurative elements must, most of them, be spatial. There may be a few presiding towers or domes; but, for the most part, figure can only be a matter of important and carefully considered voids; and with this in mind, now to contemplate the so-called Kulturforum.

The Vanished City

An indeterminate wasteland absurdly dignified with a Roman name, this is a part of the world which painfully discourages any possibility of convergence. For, contrary to any idea of an abstracted space embraced by extended continuities, the Kulturforum is an 'anti-space',[3] a breakdown of civil communications, a condition of undeclared war between compacted, self-centered solids which are independent of any concept of community, which are independent—to a ruthless extent—of any sustaining field.

Germanic Space-Talk

The Kulturforum should never be regarded as evidence of a cultural amnesia. It is not anything so unique. Following the expositions made by Schmarsow, circa 1894, and earlier by Hildebrand, space, as something other than negligible extension, became something of a primary topic of German art history; but, then, whatever influence did these themes exert upon the architect, whether German or otherwise? And the answer seems to be: apparently none. It provided him with a cultural alibi no doubt; but, in spite of all the Germanic space-talk (which, one thinks *should* have been enlightening), the architect, convinced of his 'modernity', continued in his habitual, conservative, imperturbable way. That is: the architect became increasingly driven to make object buildings, buildings which, of their nature, could only puncture space but could never enclose it.

It may have been in Paris, with Le Corbusier, and in Berlin, with Ludwig Hilberseimer and others, that the dissolution of the city—as continuous solid perforated by occasional voids—was first plotted or proposed; and the only too obvious advertisements of this excitement are Le Corbusier's Plan Voisin of 1925 and Hilberseimer's Friedrichstrasse project of 1927; and both of these were polemic. Corbu proposed the destruction of the Marais. Hilberseimer aggressively violated the continuities of Unter den Linden. In both cases, one imagines, the object was to irritate. In both cases it was a matter of *épater les bourgeois.* But, after 1945, with the bourgeoisie almost vanished, in that empty, devasted world, the irresponsible, avant-garde strategies of the 1920s came to be accepted as the inevitable program for the 1950s: the message had been delivered. It was logical, egalitarian, and hygienic; and this sort of thinking inevitably lead to such unfortunate specimens as the Lincoln Center in New York, the South Bank in London, and, in Berlin, the Kulturforum. From any intercourse with their immediate vicinity they are insulated by unbridgeable chasms.

But who does not know these places, the belated evidences of states of mind which could not tolerate heterogeneity, which still felt compelled to insist on the absolute segregation of function? And who, knowing these places, would not prefer to spend an evening at La Scala in Milan, at La Fenice in Venice, at the Opéra in Paris rather than to face the prospect of stepping outside such establishments as the Festival Hall in London and the Philharmonie in Berlin to experience, not the lights and traffic of a brilliant street, not Piccadilly or Kurfürstendamm, but only to be doomed to desolation in a quasi-surburban darkness?

No, the limpid and beautiful future which the reformation of the city was all about has not exactly been inaugurated; and, correspondingly, the mood is now more disingenuous than that of 1930 to 1960 would have been able to accept. Suddenly we have all become cynics. No longer a pure and a revolutionary idea, as simply a fact of life Modern architecture is increasingly revealed to have been a very shabby and a less than intelligent affair. The brave new world which was envisioned has become a more than sordid reality; and it is in this setting of disillusion, harsh but stimulating, that the activities of IBA must be placed.

Block or Street

IBA has proposed a return to the city of streets and controlling walls, and, in this connection, its preferred solution seems to be the perimeter block.

The perimeter block is a highly ambiguous construction which can only present the question: does one walk *along* the streets or *through* the courtyards? And I believe that the answer to this question is very simple. The preferred route will be via the courtyards. For the streets will remain residual, bald, and barely capable of arresting a focused attention.

But, if this is a criticism of the perimeter block as a *general proposition,* it must be noticed that, *as occasional strategy,* and embedded within a contrary fabric, it may sometimes be productive of the most satisfying results. For, in Munich what is the Hofgarten, in Paris what is the Palais Royal, in London what are the Inns of Court, in Oxford and Cambridge what are the colleges, unless they are examples of a highly specific use of perimeter block? However, all of these are places of restricted entry.[4] That is: they are under surveillance and, after darkness, they are apt to become essentially isolated little communities. Their security is elaborate. But can any such security be guaranteed for those abundantly many, open access courtyards which it seems are to be proliferated in Berlin? And this is a very serious question.

Immensely Large Blocks

By the standards of Paris, New York, London, and Rome, Berlin is a city of immensely large blocks; and, particularly, I think of those in southern Friedrichstadt. So could these be contracted (the persistent argument of Leon Krier), or could they be subdivided?

Many hybrid blocks both in Paris and Rome combine a quantity of *hôtels particuliers,* or *palazzi,* and often other items too. However these are, all of them, separate entities, often equipped with both court *and* garden; and, apart from their adjacency, there is apt to be no other communication between them. Their primary relationship is to the street; and, with regard to each other, relationship is little more than casual.

Perhaps this is a species of block which leaves room for a play of the imagination. It is not a place of passage for all and sundry. One may enter it but only to return the way in which one has already come; and the inevitable difficulties of deciphering it, as a whole, can only contribute unique community value to each of its parts.

As a proposed spatial experience, the huge perimeter blocks of southern Friedrichstadt render me apathetic; and, as a potential problem of security, they terrify me. It remains possible to imagine the subdivision of such blocks as these into minor entities, with spaces both multiplied and reduced, with the whole area rendered more private and, as such, subject to the supervision of its immediate residents who, in default of a concierge, will all have keys which open the street door.

An exclusive idea? Certainly. An idea of aristocratic *provenance?* Perhaps. But, then, I can see no reason why strategies, tried and true, should not be adapted for the purposes of *Existenzminimum.* So, apropos of IBA, a city of perimeter blocks must, of necessity, be better than a city of *Zeilenbauen,* but it is far from good enough. And preoccupation with blocks, in Berlin, is quite excessive. Everything is apportioned by block and never does it seem to be noticed that a street possesses, most usually, two sides. No, the street is always to be imagined as a battle between contending powers; and, about the organized street, I receive the impression that IBA has remained extremely passive. IBA proposes the reconstitution of the street and then doesn't follow through. Instead the street with IBA is a version of the Rhine, hopelessly flowing between France and Germany.

A Species of Architectural Zoo

We are at present threatened with a species of architectural zoo which, by that woman who calls herself Claire Obscure, has already been itemized—a Catalonian fort by Bohigas, an *esquisse* by Rossi, a *quadrillage ésotérique* by Eisenman, and a collection of Hanseatic warehouses from Lugano; all this is at the intersection of Kochstrasse and Friedrichstrasse.[5]

Then at present the Kulturforum is everything that I have described it as being; and particularly so at night. The Kulturforum could only begin to become redeemed and approach brilliance if the Nationalgalerie were willing to stay open very late! For try to imagine that Miesian *objet de luxe,* that glass box, that lantern of hospitality and Weimar 'illumination', as it was presumably supposed to appear. The transparent Nationalgalerie *ought* to become a beacon, a lighthouse of whatever values the city represents. But the basic problem remains that of the Zentraler Bereich, as it passes by the Potsdamer Tor. And, about this, both IBA and the city continue to be embarrassingly diffident.

In spite of the deficiencies which I have alleged, I am sure that IBA is still the best that exists. It is charged, I am sure, with an impossible mission. Its constitution is an evident conflict of interests. As far as I can see, no city can be made out of *Sozialewohnungsbauen* alone. The great city requires something in excess of *that.* It requires far more than the measuring mind of twentieth-century government and bureaucracy are willing to contribute. For the happiness and the *amour propre* of the people living within it, in order to make them proud, the great city requires the elaborate display of otherwise useless emblems—the *chevaux de Marly,* the screen at Hyde Park Corner, the Munich Propyläen, the Brandenburg Gate.

Several Suburbs in Search of a City

Ambitious to promote the *res publica,* for political reasons IBA has remained painfully trapped within the *res privata;* and this observation returns to my beginning. So far as I can see West Berlin (several suburbs in search of a city?) permits no consensus but only hostile examination of details . . . and about such a condition, I am reminded of a statement of Samuel Johnson's way back in the eighteenth century. Dr. Johnson said something like this: "If all possible objections must first be overcome then nothing can ever be accomplished."

Notes

1. Hannah Arendt, *The Human Condition* (Chicago: University of Chicago Press, 1958), 52.

2. Le Corbusier, *Précisions* (Paris: Crès, 1930), 9.

3. I derive this term from Steven Peterson.

4. An exception to this is now the Hofgarten, which has become so absurdly violated, like so much else in Munich, by the activities of highway engineers.

5. Claire Obscure is obviously exceptionally brilliant and sardonic and her remarks about IBA, written from the point of view of Maurice Culot and Leon Krier, make entertaining reading. They are to be found in *Archives d'Architecture Moderne,* no. 21 (1981), as "Lorsque la montagne accouche d'une souris." At the time of writing, 1984, I knew Claire Obscure to be living in Münster; but, since she was clearly well acquainted with Berlin, I felt her remarks on the Kochstrasse-Friedrichstrasse were abundantly worth attention.

A Student Project: Berlin

Raul de Carvalho and others (1983–1984)

In Berlin at the present day almost any proposal for a north-south axis, which was once considered so necessary, is still likely to be defeated by the memory of Adolf Hitler and the excessive determinations of Albert Speer. But, in spite of the frustrated endeavors of these not to be regretted individuals, there are also further reasons.

As already noticed, the collective mind of Berlin seems to understand only two strategies for the accommodation of vehicular movement: the Haussmannesque boulevard, derived from Second Empire Paris, and the *Autobahn,* or *let's get there quick.* So far as a foreigner is able to perceive, apparently it completely fails to understand that intermediate concept, a *corso,* related to a vehicular *passeggiata* or, in American terms, a parkway.

Moreover I was quick to learn that the mere mention of parkway was anathema to representatives of the Green Lobby; it would be injurious to the health of adjacent trees; and, compared with this, the argument that volumes of traffic pounding down a boulevard would be injurious to the health of adjacent residents was not an issue seriously to be considered.

And then to notice a prejudice of mapping to which reference has already been made. The plans and maps with which the *Experten* were equipped, all of them stressed east-west ligaments with, probably, the Landwehrkanal as a primary motif; and, in West Berlin, one might suggest that this style of mapping became more or less traditional (i.e., entirely not to be criticized) sometime in the mid-1950s.

However, in spite of bad memories and even in spite of the Green Lobby, a parkway is still there implicit as a strong possibility. Indeed with the abandoned railroad yards to the north of the Spree and the abandoned railroad yards to the south of the Landwehrkanal, it is a possibility which almost designs itself.

You just have to trace the outlines of the old railroad yards and allow for an extended corridor through the empty sites to the east of Scharoun's Staatsbibliothek and, at least, the extended park is there—whatever its functions might be assigned to it; and then, the specific career of the drive through the park might be left to the discriminations of sensibility. A solution which Schinkel might have applauded and a problem which might have stimulated Lenné? I tend to think so; and, therefore I quote *The Architectural Review* on the topic of this extended park system: "With Tiergarten [this] would form an extended *rus-in-urbe* of some 420 hectares which compares well with the great system of Royal Parks in London (485 hectares) and New York's Central Park (340 hectares)—the present area of Tiergarten is 105 hectares."

Myself cannot vouch for these figures, which—I would have thought—should have gratified the Greens; and all I wish to record is that the possibility of any very explicit, south-north communication is now very seriously attenuated. The decision to

115. Charlottenburger Chausee looking west from East Berlin over the Brandenburg Gate in Raul de Carvalho's thesis project. The proposed parkway route runs north-south across the Tiergarten.

A Student Project: Berlin

116. The northern part of the green axis: the area over the River Spree is envisioned as a sports park.

117. Volksgarten looking north. This people's park is suggested on disused railway land. It would create much-needed open space. The Tiergarten can be seen in the distance to the north.

A Student Project: Berlin

clutter up the Spreebogen (the arch of the Spree), adjacent to the Reichstag, with an accumulation of federal office buildings is fatally inhibitive to the success of any casually relaxed driveway leading from Tempelhof to Tegel.

However, at its inception, this was not what Raul de Carvalho's thesis was all about. Rather it belongs to the older east-west mapping of Berlin, emphasizing the line of the Landwehrkanal; and it began with a very special problem: between the Landwehrkanal and the southern face of the Tiergarten, between the Kulturforum and points west, within all this disparity, just how to assemble anything which might be considered almost reasonable?

It must be noticed that, as an urban park, the Tiegarten was always without effective enclosure. It was confronted by no walls of buildings like Central Park, New York, or like Hyde Park, London, along the Bayswater Road. To the west enclosure could scarcely be decisive; to the north there is no more than the river, with nothing much on the other side; to the east, apart from the Brandenburg Tor, there is little more than the walls of very grand back gardens; while, as one approaches the south face, it is only to find a very painful fragmentation of buildings, an area which, though ninety years ago it must have throbbed with opulence, must spatially have been almost as agonizing as it is today.

So this is the specific problem to which, in the beginning, this project addressed itself; and to which, I believe, it responded with great success. To quote *The Architectural Review:* "Southern Tiergarten is envisioned as being developed as a series of courtyards to structure fragmentary remains and modern development now existing. It would become a wall against the park. The lake is enlarged to clearly identify the northern boundary of the Kulturforum."

To this I can only add that one of the courtyards, supposedly derived from the Zwinger at Dresden, we called the Court of a Hundred Fountains (die Hof von ein hundert Brün-

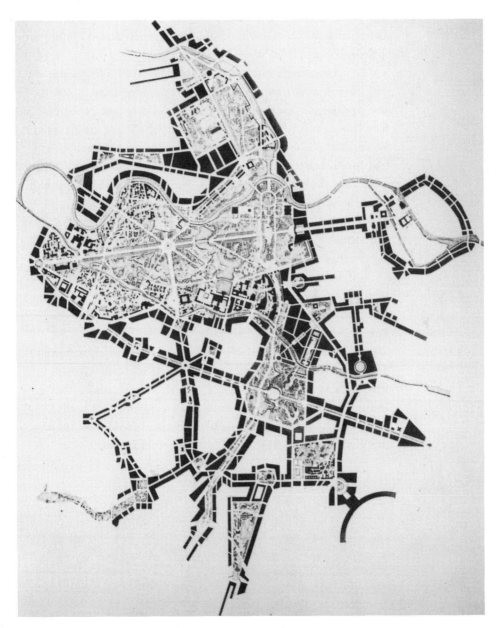

118. Master park plan.

A Student Project: Berlin

nen); and, privately, we put it forward as the only Platonic or Cartesian space available for public occupancy (theatrical or revolutionary events?) in West Berlin.

Apart from myself and Raul de Carvalho (from Rio de Janeiro and now living in Lisbon), we were quickly joined by the enthusiastic Esteban Senney (from Caracas and now living in San Juan, Puerto Rico); and then, somewhat later, by Douglas Fredericks, my former student at Maryland and Cornell, who had just spent several months with Matthias Ungers in Cologne, a brilliant draftsman who arrived determined to provide significant views from the air.

And, with all this, we became excited. If you like, the exuberance of discourse carried us away and off we went with suggestions in all directions.

But, though nowadays I would insist upon the elaboration of Carvalho's Südliche Tiergarten, I still think of this general plan as the logically inevitable result of the situation in Berlin circa 1984.

It is easier—and cheaper—to plant trees than to make buildings and, in this, I agree very much with the Greens; but, fifty years after the bombings, I still very much doubt that anything has been done about those abandoned railroad yards.

No, though the trees planted there could now be ravishingly mature, apparently this was not a viable possibility.

Urban Space

Of the brothers Krier, no doubt Leon is the more mercurial temperament and, perhaps, Robert the more serious architect; but, since Leon now seems to have retired—in a fit of pique?—to play the piano in Provence, who is to say? Anyway, I have long regarded them both as quasi-allies, and both the pieces which follow were written at their separate requests.

The piece for Robert was written in 1979 as an introduction to Stadtraum, *published in English as* Urban Space *(London: Academy Editions, 1979); and, though much of what is here said doesn't seem to have too very much to do with urban space, for the sake of convenience I have allowed it to retain that title. It was later republished, by Academy Editions, in* The New Classicism *(London, 1984); and it was this republication which encouraged me to break a rule which I had established for this collection—not to include prefaces and introductions. This because, though not exactly a pair of Siamese twins, Robert and Leon—both by similarities and by differences—evidently belong together.*

"The Revolt of the Senses," my piece for Leon, was written in 1984 when both he and I were at the University of Virginia; and therefore it is, perhaps intimately, related (since classical fantasies seem to come easy in the proximity of Thomas Jefferson) to my other Charlottesville essay "Classicism, Neo-Classicism, Neo-Neo-Classicism," which appears in volume two of this collection. It was first published in a number of Architectural Design *with the general title "Houses, Palaces, Cities" (London: Academy Editions, 1984).*

In the jungle-like politics of architectural self-advertisement it has become the misfortune of the late Emil Kaufmann's great achievement, inadvertently and considerably after his death, to have sponsored a highly edited and often mindless version of neo-Classicism. Was it *Von Ledoux bis Le Corbusier* or was it *Three Revolutionary Architects* which gave the cue? And it was probably the latter, with its so desirable connotations of dynamic and anti-academic insurrection. For, when the architectural Boy Scout camps of the 1920s (La Sarraz and all the rest) could be seen as equipped with a respectable, and still revolutionary, pedigree then the possibilities of annexation became endless. For, then, it became possible to be interested in the late eighteenth century without seeming to be desperately old hat, and for a series of hero figures to be observed. And so, and after certain strange leaps of the mind, Ledoux-Boullée was followed by the constellation of Saint-Simon, Comte, and Fourier and then, after the whole panoply of the French socialist tradition became exposed, by Karl Marx and the so curious notion that a William Morris society might be constructed out of French neo-Classical components; and one might abbreviate the process of argument by which all this may have come about.

With the nitty-gritty of the Welfare State and the appalling bureaucratic details of pseudo-Capitalist administration we will have nothing to do; instead we will simplify, abstract, and project to the degree of extravagance a highly restricted, private, and not very hospitable version of what the good society might be assumed to be; we will give a nod to Kaufmann; we will give three muted cheers for the Stalinallee; we will adore the manifesto pieces of Boullée; we will (mostly) refuse to observe the built work of Soane; instead we will unroll a few hundred yards of neutral Adolf Loos facade, build a lot of little towers and stand around on top of them a quantity of Ledoux villas, wave quietly but not too exuberantly to Louis Kahn (congratulations on the Trenton Bath House), insinuate a reference to the metaphysic of Giorgio de Chirico, display a conversance with Leonidov, become highly enthusiastic about the more evocative aspects of Art Deco, exhibit the intimidation of curtains waving in the wind, and, then, gently warm up the ensuing goulash in the *pastoso* of Morandi.

But, if here is displayed *the solution* (with all its atavistic seductions) fresh from Milano-Venezia, one might also be prompted to ask whether its Marxism is not a little too romantic and its presumptions a little too premature. Apropos of the so-called New York Five and their alleged intellectualistic involutions, Romaldo Giurgola spoke of *the discreet charm of the bourgeoisie,* and about this other context of gestures, postures, antics which has here been abruptly summarized, where social conscience, social agony, and high fashion are almost inextricably interrelated, just what is there more that needs to be said? That, although the stage set is almost completely changed from that of a few years ago, the form of the words which the players use is, in some way, distressingly familiar?

For, the idea that "art stopped short at the cultivated court of the Empress Josephine" has, in one form or another, been around for a considerable time; and, recently, though in a different framework of values, it has been given fresh currency. But, of course, even in 1881, W. S. Gilbert's endearing, philistine and distinctly inadequate satire of the miscellaneous aesthetes who populate the libretto of *Patience* disclosed a quasi-critical orientation which was in no way new.

Something went wrong in 1714, or 1750, or 1789, or 1804, with the beginning of the Georgian era or at its end, with the death of Queen Anne or the accession of Queen Victoria, with Andrew Jackson, with Ulysses S. Grant, with the discovery of Pompeii, with the emergence of the Roman Empire, with the collapse of the Roman Empire, with the decline of the Middle Ages, with the appearance of Brunelleschi, or Michelangelo, or Inigo Jones, or Borromini. One can rearrange the dates, rename the style phases, re-identify the personalities which decorate this scenario, but the basic structure of what, after all, must still be historical myth will remain surprisingly consistent and intact. At some moment in time there occurred a cessation of meaningful artistic production and a catastrophic decline in all sense of value. Standards of craftsmanship were abruptly terminated. Collective endeavor declined. Society became atomised and the individual alienated. Dissociation of sensibility ensued and a tragic schism between feeling and thinking was the inevitable result. But, now, *nous avons changé tout cela*. For we, the protagonists of the new, have scrutinized and discriminated. *We* know the evil, *we* have the remedy, ours is the prescription; and, as for *you,* just you take a good look and a good listen.

Such, in its time, was one of the primary messages of Modern architecture—a primary message of Walter Gropius, Sigfried Giedion, Le Corbusier, and Nikolaus Pevsner. Only believe in this; and if you will but do so, the world will become reintegrated and the wounds of society healed. But if, contributing to the litany of this myth, there have been many of the would-be self-consciously critical names of recent Western civilization, it must still remain a particularly savage irony that Modern architecture's polemic has now been enlisted against Modern architecture itself. For the locus of the historical rift valley is now shifted; the bad date is now 1923—or thereabouts; the bad gestures/propositions are those of CIAM; and the really evil guys (the Pied Pipers who lead the children in the wrong direction and finally deposited them in a Carpathian wilderness, terribly dangerous and ever so far from home) are rapidly coming to be the bearers of those names which, only the other day, seemed to be so highly respectable and so firmly established in the architectural hall of fame.

So, perhaps, we now inhabit a somewhat desperate Transylvanian landscape of the mind, lugubriously furnished with the wreckage of reputations and the debris of good intentions. Hamelin town is far away ("in Brunswick near famous Hanover City"); but, having been brought to our present destitution by the most charming of music, the most interesting of leaders, the most curious of subterranean routes, we can only feel disquieted, abused, disturbed, and, being unable to forget the Hansel and Gretel toy town out of which we were seduced, we can now only suspect the instrument of our temptation—the notion of an impeccable and 'scientific' solution through instant 'total' design—was itself no more than a species of late Biedermeier ornamental gingerbread. For, apparently, nobody—ever—was really very good, and nothing was really very true and, in the twentieth century, even those few who approached goodness, almost embodied truth, were invariably debauched by the flagrant influence of a local grandee—a capitalist Dracula, monstrous, sadic, and perverse—who distorted the message and rendered its results utterly vain.

Or, at least, something like this seems to be among the many inherently inconsistent diagnoses of Modern architecture's impending collapse; and, up to a point, this diagnosis is almost believable. But, it is surely not so much the credibility as it is the wholly conventional character of such argument which deserves attention. For if in their implication that most cities of the world have been approximately wrecked via the agency of Modern architecture, the proponents of *architettura razionale* can only be entirely correct, then should it not seem to be strange that the style of argument in which these judgements are delivered—bourgeois angst, apocalyptic threat, incipient world-transforming event, holistic deliverance—is representative of a critical strategy of which Modern architecture should have made us only too skeptical? For, again, the decorations of the stage infer something significantly avant-garde, while the libretto of the opera comes over as a standardized and entirely to be anticipated plot. To repeat: the bad date is now 1923, the good date is 1974, or '75, or '76; and it is the persistence of an old argument, transferred from context to visual context and still presented as novelty, which is here the profoundly disquieting factor. For what we are here presented with is something professing to be radical chic, elegant *fa figura,* social concern; and if, in terms of the visuals, what we receive is an engaging archaeology of the future, then in terms of the verbals, the situation is much the same.

The verbals are antique; and the problem of the symbiosis of antiquity and the would-be-way-out, though not insuperable, is certainly considerable. For avant-garde protestation (hey, look at our acrobatics!) and the eternal creakings of old verbal machinery are, in the end, not the best of all possible bedfellows; and, simply, the combination is less than respectably athletic.

Until recently when Modern architecture, in spite of its longevity, was still, universally proclaimed as 'new', almost any architect under the age of sixty (with appropriate achievements to his credit) was likely to be saluted and advertised as 'young' and the question "But just how old does one have to be in order to become a young architect(?)" was scarcely ever propounded. For the legend of uncorrupted, incorruptible architectural youth (youth synonymous with the only quest worthwhile—the ongoing quest for the new and agile) persisted as one of the most fundamental of fictions; and, indeed, the collusion between Peter Pan, Jugendstil, the Boy Scouts, and the early Fascist *giovinezza, giovinezza* is likely to remain among the more observable phenomena of the early twentieth century culture—perhaps part of the inevitable heritage of the Art Nouveau.

So it was an important idea—and a dangerous one; and, like many important—and dangerous—ideas, it has become fossilized and survives as no more than unexamined and tedious tradition; let us rather be potential than productive; let us be dynamic rather than introspective; let us prefer animation to reflection; let us condemn the unjust sophistications and specious moral codes of established society; since Rousseau's noble savage (primordial energy uncontaminated by culture) is almost the same as Peter Pan (who is almost the same as the statue of Eros in Piccadilly Circus), then, in order to make *tabula rasa,* in order to disclose a *primitive* house and to engender a future society—redeemed, and of renewed aboriginal purity—let us proceed to mock, to injure, and to destroy the existing.

Now the fiesta of destruction (one imagines broken bottles on a New Year's Eve in Naples) which has continued since the Enlightenment surely deserves to be applauded. For the most part it has been exhilarating; also it has resulted in previously undreamed of blessings; and, as one attempts to imagine the condition of provincial society, circa 1770, in almost any small city in the world, then one can only say: Thank God for the ventilations which, over the last two hundred years, have been made!

But, at least for the impatient, the route of what might be conceived to be a progress has still taken an extremely long time; and, of course, one of the major roadblocks to emancipation has now become the fantasies which the architect entertains about himself, fantasies now little more than the platitudes of criticism, but, still, fantasies which, in their own day—now a very good many years ago—were conceived of as dazzling illuminations which were forever to make visible the surface of a glorious *autostrada* leading to a crystalline social condition of limpid authenticity.

> And I, John, saw the Holy City, New Jerusalem, coming down from God out of heaven . . . and the City lieth foursquare, and the length is as large as the breadth . . . and the City was pure gold like unto clear glass . . . and the street of the City was *pure gold,* as it were transparent glass . . . and the City had no need of the sun, neither of the moon to shine in it: for the glory of God did lighten it . . . and there shall in no wise enter into it anything that defileth, neither whatsoever worketh abomination or *maketh* a lie: but they which are written in the Lamb's Book of Life.[1]

The vision of Final Judgement and Deliverance, of the Great Hallelujah, when equipped with a technological gloss, is, of course, immensely like in kind to the vision of the *ville radieuse* to be later experienced by Le Corbusier; and, if this later vision, of a world redeemed by architecture, is now severely discredited, it is still not too unreasonable to suggest that some eschatological framework of this kind still survives as the psychological underpinning of much currently fashionable architectural polemic—particularly that of Italian origin. For this is a polemic which, professing to be coolly critical, is still, more often than not, evidently inflamed by notions of that glaring turbulent upsurge which will forever release us from the stinking limitations of bourgeois culture and effectively initiate the millennial establishment.

And this (though, to a degree, charming and of a period) is surely something of a pity. For, if the advocates of *architettura razionale* (who are in great danger of flooding the market and inspiring a counter-wave of disgust) are able to make a highly apt critique of Modern architecture's urbanistic failure and if this is of immense value, it does not automatically follow that *all* of the physical achievements of Modern architecture are to be condemned and that we are entirely obliged to return to a simplified and innocent world, à la Laugier, a species of antediluvian (and Marxist) *belle époque,* reminiscent more of Knossos than New York, in which strangely deserted piazzas, seemingly prepared for not yet to be anticipated rituals, in the meantime support a somewhat scanty population of mildly desperate hippies.

Indeed, it may be a rather curious commentary upon a contemporary failure of nerve that a merely abbreviated reconstitution of the nineteenth century city, enticingly equipped with surrealistic overtones, is now so widely received as the most pregnant and potent of disclosures. For, though such a reconstitution is, in many ways, what is required, there are still inhibitions about the tricking out of Beaux-Arts plans with neo-primitive facades ("a poor thing but Minoan," as Sir Arthur Evans almost certainly did *not* say about his Cretan restorations) and there are still reserves of feeling (oddly Futurist and strangely technophile?) which will operate to prevent any such, immediate, dispensation.

So much could seem to be a highly negative series of remarks to open an introduction to the English edition of Rob Krier's

Stadtraum; but they are not intended to be so interpreted. An implicit theme of Krier's book is a *rappel à l'ordre.* It is an evident critique of 'planning', highway engineering, the urbanistic propositions of CIAM, of science fiction cities, populist do-it-yourself, and townscape; and, if as such it is a book which one can only receive with sympathy and happiness, then the purpose of all the foregoing rather protracted observations is to suggest, not apropos of Rob Krier but apropos of the context to which, ostensibly, he has been assigned—the context of *architettura razionale,* Postmodernism and all the rest—that a recall to order need not directly involve the flushing out of both the baby and the bathwater, that we do not only revolve but also evolve, that if a reasonable object of criticism is certainly the cutting of Modern architecture down to size, then it is slightly preposterous to attempt any such undertaking while still assenting to a particular mystique—the mystique of the critical date, of *giovinezza,* of the *Zeitgeist,* of building as a version of physics, etc., etc.

Indeed to attempt a critique of the Modern movement, damming its physical embodiments while still concerned with the endorsement of its psychological virulence, one must finally say is a procedure so extravagantly half-witted as to defeat comprehension. At which stage, and mercifully, the time has come to reverse the argument. For we are confronted with a book, equipped with lots of visuals and not really too many words; and, if some of the visuals and some of the words display an affiliation, this book both impresses and invites and there are many specific things to be said about it. So like what to say?

That Rob Krier somehow doesn't fit, that he cannot be relegated to a category, might quite well be a first observation. For, if one can sense in this book a romantically Marxian and Italian connection, and if by many of its readers it will be placed in something very like the context of ideas which has already been noticed, this can seem to be only a very small part of the whole. For Krier has produced a highly eclectic book which is evidently charged with conviction and a highly radical book which is eminently conservative in its tone. It is, perhaps, not a very highly self-conscious book. Its author is, maybe, a little too sure of his principles and a little too unconcerned in protecting himself against flank attacks, possibly a little more equivocal than he is aware. He dedicates his performance, rather surprisingly, to Sitte; he seems to owe a great deal to Stübben; he certainly owes very much to the urbanistic contributions of Matthias Ungers; his graphics oscillate between late nineteenth century Old Fashioned and strip cartoon Pop; but, clearly, this is a book which has been put together with a controlled indignation and it is a quality of Rob Krier's quiet indignation, issuing in an exhaustive encyclopedia of urban spaces, that one feels compelled and happy to salute.

Notes

1. Bible, Revelation chapter 5.

The Revolt of the Senses

Leon Krier is a master of publicity. Both graphically and verbally he promises to become almost the Le Corbusier of our day; and, like Le Corbusier, he is already beginning to think of himself in the third person.

Now to attract the attention of even a small public requires the exercise of a relentless simplification. The message must be direct and elementary. It should involve much reiteration and a minimum of fastidious reservation. Indeed it should be little more than a caricature of logical argument; and, correspondingly, the message must also be quite a little wild.

A large simplicity of posture and an apparent inflexibility of disposition are, therefore, among the basic instruments of any successful campaign. Its author must appear as something of a *naïf*, any inherent sophistication he must dissimulate; but, while such advertisement, if protractedly sustained, will—in the end—almost certainly persuade the majority, for an intermediate time it may warp and distort a just appraisal of its promoter's intentions. It was thus with Le Corbusier; and, today, it is thus with Leon Krier. For, nowadays, when the Platonic triad of goodness, truth, and beauty is no longer a self-evident proposition, when the claims of ugliness have become so highly pre-eminent, then it can only follow that the beautiful performance of this architectural mini-Mozart will, often, be conceived as too good to be true.

And so there is an argument which follows and which I regard as vindictive. Krier *must* be irresponsible; he *must* be self-indulgent; at the expense of the world he *must* be engaged in a private joke. And, if this is demonstrable, then *must* we not regard Krier as no more than a puppet in an entertaining children's theater, as part of an architectural Punch and Judy show which, for adult purposes, will remain yet another twentieth century theater of the absurd?

This species of dismissive, patronizing opinion I have heard expressed in New York, Boston, Toronto, and Berlin; and, no doubt, it must abound elsewhere. But, all the same, I continue to be astonished by the cultural ingenuousness of its proponents. For, in the end, are not these persons of ingrained mental habit, the conservatives of Modernism who, in despite of horrid evidence, still assume the impregnability of their own scarcely equipped intellectual Bastille?

In any case I have lately begun to receive little postcard communications from Leon—to which I am not expected to reply. So far they are always of landscapes by Claude; and, so far, the words on the back are equally predictable: "This is the world that we deserved: it is after all quite a simple proposition compared to the efforts our contemporaries go into in order to destroy all possibility of having it again. I am sad . . ."

So Leon makes some assumption of an alliance of sentiment; and, on the whole, I am prepared to accept this assumption. However, until comparatively recently my own relationship with him was never the very easiest. In the first case he was an irrepressible *enfant terrible* working for Stirling, with results of which he has made everyone aware; and then, after that, he became a fashionable reputation with slightly Marxian and quite gratuitously anti-Catholic undertones. This was the time of the first demonstrations of *architettura razionale* in the early seventies when, recognizing a capacity which I loved, I found myself offended that it should become associated with a program which, to me, could only appear misguided, intellectualistic, and absurdly abstruse. Slightly later, two persons intimately known to me will vividly remember Leon in this particular phase, which was fairly protracted and often painful.

The occasion was at Harvard in, so I think, November '77 and Leon was giving a little lecture about his own contribution to the "Roma Interrotta" exhibition to open in the following April. Therefore and inevitably, he displayed those elegant drawings in which he had wittily mutilated the Campidoglio and its palaces; and then he said words something like these: "You see I intend to give Michelangelo a lesson."

Now Leon is so effervescent and, fundamentally, so self-depreciating that a remark of this kind (obviously one of many) could only be attributed to innocence rather than to arrogance; but, on this occasion, Fred Koetter, Rodolfo Machado, and myself just were not able to cope with it. We were all sitting together and we all communicated our embarrassment: Leon is intending to give Michelangelo a lesson. But why not give a lesson to God?

All the same we didn't publicly divulge our reservations until much later at the Machado-Silvetti house in Marlborough Street; and then, probably, we yelled a bit. "But Leon," we probably said, "just *don't* be so impossibly provincial" (this was, maybe, Rodolfo); "and *don't* you recognize," we probably said, "that the compounding of walls and columns is the supremely important motif which the Capitoline palaces represent?" (this was, maybe, Fred); and what we also probably said was something like this: "But, dearest Leon, genuinely, what is so very, *very* great about the Abbé Laugier and his excruciating, dreary primitive hut?" (and, almost certainly, this was me).

However, I don't remember that any of this did any good, or even clarified our objections. Simply we were blissfully ignored.

The Revolt of the Senses

It was shortly afterwards that he sat down with Jorge Silvetti to play Schubert and Beethoven duets. And it was then that this drawing room of a Back Bay apartment became transformed. Quite suddenly (in a way I think scarcely possible in London), it belonged to the Biedermeier Vienna of the age of Metternich.

I have experienced this kind of musical transformation before, mostly in Jewish houses in New York; and, of course, it alters an understanding, it manipulates an understanding—both of ideas and the world. But, this apart, it was now that I first experienced the full volume of Leon's incredibly felicitous talent. He sat down to play with Jorge, an infant piano prodigy in Argentina before he gave up music for architecture; and, to my always uninstructed ears, there was little difference between their execution. Simply the room was filled with enviable Romantic sound; and I came to perceive that, if you give Leon a grand piano, he will remain a rewardingly noisy and utterly self-absorbed guest.

But this was no more than a prelude. For observation of the notorious architectural 'failure' who draws like an angel and who alleges that he prefers not to build: this is a little introductory maneuver, and it will now be useful to set down a series of fairly obvious propositions.

First, that Leon Krier has made a deliberate attempt to place himself completely outside what, for better or worse, may be called the culture of Modern architecture. Second, that Leon Krier, with a complete absence of Postmodern clichés, has made the most complete and consistent rejection of Modern architecture which is yet available. Third, that Leon Krier has not only repudiated the preferred formal dispositions of Modern architecture but that, even further, he has refused to accept the functional and technological hypotheses which were among the more spectacular and ruthless of its premises. Finally, that, with all this, in terms of his inferred sociology, the obvious socialist content of so many of his projects, Leon Krier, more visibly than anyone else, has sustained and, maybe, amplified a strand of Modern architecture's pedigree which for a long time has been in frightful danger of getting lost.

This is a rough laundry list of formal and ideological choices; and now to place these choices in a more expanded critical context.

First, the culture of Modernism (as regards architecture) increasingly reveals itself to have been a highly dubious confection. Mostly it was surely an affair of what Denise Scott Brown has called "physics envy" (belated positivism) and what David Watkin has called "*Zeitgeist* worship" (the notion of the architect as a sensitive antenna simply registering the assumed demands of an Hegelian abstraction); and, since this culture almost defeats common sense, its rejection should be no occasion for either surprise or shock.

Then, in terms of how buildings look and how they are put together, of course there are others who have also separated the genealogical threads which are said to have led to the formulation of Modern architecture; and one may think of those who have done it: James Stirling, Aldo Rossi, Robert Venturi, Michael Graves. However, so far as I am able to see, none of these ways has approached the conclusiveness of Krier's. With varying degrees of success, all have maintained much more of a liaison with the morphological components of Modern architecture. Neo-technological, neo-avant-garde, neo–Art Deco, neo–Belle Epoque; whatever the surface trim, all alike have been unwilling to cut the umbilical cord and to make the ultimate separation. Almost all alike make willful complexity or willful simplicity. Almost all alike survive on irony, private meaning, and double entendre; and it is in this situation that Leon Krier makes his great point. For what he has done (admittedly in the form of drawings rather than buildings) rises above the absurdity of mere particulars to become general. Rather than involuted, it is deadpan direct. Without jokes, it is poetically persuasive. For Leon Krier, with his genuine simplicity, has accomplished the unlikely act of restoring Utopia. No doubt a very miniature and limited Utopia it is. It makes no claims to big city grandeur; but, all the same, its mere existence—as an ethical frame of reference—sharply distinguishes its author from all the others, including all those practitioners of *architettura razionale,* who (whatever their professed urbanistic interest), in Venice, Lugano, or elsewhere, still continue to see the city as an empty, inscrutably enigmatic Giorgio de Chirico stage set. Instead Leon Krier's little city is without metaphysical pretension.

All the same, about this elementary, highly literal Utopia, which discloses a profound conviction and which, by now, has almost obliterated the influence of the *ville radieuse,* there is a familiar question which invariably introduces itself—*How, in this day and age, is it possible that a William Morris world curiously contrived out of Ledoux/Schinkel bits and pieces, with a dash of Poussin and a large tribute to Claude, can ever be considered a useful or a viable endeavor?*

Now, inherently, this question must be related to stylistic rather than to functional and technological criteria. And its simple impact may be made less devastating by pointing out that, had Krier selected to operate within a less polemical, less restricted format, such scandal as this question seems intended to elicit would be entirely without any value or shock. No, it can scarcely be Krier's divorce from the more exacting demands of function and technology which excites the potential hunter of heresy; but, rather, it must be his loud advertisement of this divorce and the high style enthusiasm with which he has proclaimed his embrace of Classicism that has made it apparent that this goddess (with all her arms and legs complete) is now the sole lawful object of his attention. For, if casual and intermittent relations with a somewhat disabled Classicism will titillate the world and cause no raising of critical eyebrows, apparently the idea of a thoroughgoing, monogamous attachment (until death us do part) is still to be thought of as a disturbingly quixotic ambition.

In other words, as it is brought into focus, the question now seems to revolve around doubts as to Classicism's fecundity. Because, always bowing herself off-stage in a sunset glow and always returning for yet another performance, how can it be possible that this ancient prima donna will prove adaptable to the stringencies of a theater of which she has no experience? Which means that, without knowing it, Krier has produced the predicament of Classicism as though *he* were a prince and *she* were a royal bride. And the situation is that of a late nineteenth-century court, alive with rumor: but, after all, she's just *eine kleine Prinzessin;* and isn't she getting on in years and isn't she well known to be frigid? In Mecklenburg, perhaps . . . but she is very ingenuous, isn't she; and, apart from a small *Residenzstadt* which is all her experience, just how can we expect her to perform in our much more sophisticated metropolis?

So this is to elaborate reservations in terms of a slightly laborious metaphor; and to some of these reservations (though to very few) I confess assent. Leon is a Luxembourgeois (*toutes proportions gardées*); and his world, because of Luxemburg and partly because of Belsize Park, is small town. It is a Biedermeier world of fiercely independent cantons. It is Switzerland or New England of a certain period; and it has little to do with the world of heavy industry, of the oil rich, of the stock exchange, and of multi-national corporations. Leon, as everybody should be, is concerned with the *Geist* of the canton, with the comprehensible community which has been, effectively, destroyed by the agency of all those institutions which I have just listed.

Therefore, as a defense of Leon, does one first postulate what could be called a *revolt of the senses?* And might a contracted argument here be something like this? That, from circa 1900, certain ideas came to be influentially entertained, as for instance: the disintegration of centrality by logical atomism, the spontaneous generation of structures without centrality, the principle of decomposition, and the realization that ideas must be replaced by constructions wherever possible. For, evidently, around 1900 such notions were very much in the air; and, if an entirely trivial reading of Russell and Wittgenstein will reveal their presence, an equally trivial survey of the visual world will disclose their important influence. And, of course, as these attitudes of mind became increasingly active and popular, a disintegration or decomposition, or a 'deconstruction' of the city began. The public realm (always concerned with centrality of some sort) became progressively attenuated; and then, as capitalist greed—or indiscretion—found it agreeable to become associated with the intellectual formulations of early Modernism, and as these ideas became embodied in legislation and bureaucratic code, there came into existence that mishmash world compounded of convenience, sheer incapacity, and unspeakable inattention which is *today*. And is it not by this world, now to be augmented by a glass pyramid in the courtyard of the Louvre, that the revolt of the senses is abundantly to be explained? For, after all, do not the senses require some perceptible field in which the pleasure that they sponsor may be allowed to surface as an important contribution to the good of all?

This is scarcely to suggest that the documents of early Modernism do not remain immaculate, provocative, and pristine. It is simply to underscore the obvious: that, in the last thirty years or so, we have witnessed environmental nightmares of which, in the liberal world of 1900, it was impossible to conceive. That admirable slightly bourgeois and slightly Jewish *ambiente* which initiated Modernism has forever gone away. We are entirely separated from its ethos. Instead we live in a hedonistic condition of vulgar debauch, satisfying to neither sense nor mind. All standards are diminished by an horrendous laissez-faire; and it is in this predicament that a concern such as Leon's deserves respect. For might it not, just possibly, introduce both ventilation and decency?

Perhaps not very likely. Perhaps *reasonable* prototype for *bad* imitation. However, if the reconstruction of the city must today be a primary obligation, it will now be useful to approach details of Leon's little Utopia.

On the whole it is surprising that Louis Kahn's Trenton Bath House—a hipped roof with four over-large piers to support it—has enjoyed such an extensive circulation. I have never checked out its offspring, but, if its American descendants are scarcely any, then, outside the United States (in Japan and Ticino?) one might guess that they abound. Indeed, one might suggest that, to many, it has proved a lifesaver. A respectable tetrastyle, always available to fill in a gap or to promote stability, dare one suggest that, much enlarged, it is overemployed in the Utopia under observation? For, from La Villette, to Bremen, to the Corso, with the piers grown to become small towers of studios, it has been reproduced so many times as to become something of an obsession. What it means I do not know; but, iconography apart, I do know that I would be entirely unhappy to be located within it. Surely a drafty and lugubrious place which would repel rather than stimulate convergence. And now to direct attention to the condition of extremely small blocks with buildings four floors high.

Perhaps in the mid-seventies some people, including myself, became extremely infatuated with that area of Naples going up the hill towards Castel Sant'Elmo; and, in terms of plan, these seventeenth-century Neapolitan blocks make something very pretty. They are a highly legible and a very enticing insert; but, imagined as a universal strategy, can they ever be completely believable? For, with so slight a population, just *who* is to occupy all the streets which result? And just *how* many shopkeepers will consent to set up in what threatens to become ever so many boutiques, all of them to be envisaged as selling costume jewelry and sandals?

Which may now lead to the notice that the miniature block, much smaller than the typical block of New York, London, Paris, Berlin, has, incidentally, provided Leon with a highly interesting resource. For the miniature block permits and promotes a composition of jerkiness, syncopation, and high staccato. It discourages and disallows the deployment of protracted continuities; and its usage is, therefore, a means by which the architect can escape the massive problems of extended and 'smooth' orchestration. Not for him the necessity of dredging up all the accumulated apparatus of a Cumberland or a Carlton House Terrace. No, with the miniature block, the need for complicated gradations of interest is made to disappear; and, as a result, each independent composition is able to emerge as an engaging dollhouse, a very innocent, somewhat nursery gesture. In other words, by sponsoring a classical primitiveness, sometimes the miniature block may serve as the agent of a charming though somewhat inadvertent modernity.

The Revolt of the Senses

These notes, related to Louis Kahn and the little block, comprise almost the total of my reservations with reference to *Stadt Krier;* but casual remarks about syncopation and staccato deserve to be enlarged because, in his use of staccato, I believe that Leon has made contributions which are not yet sufficiently recognized. And I am thinking particularly of the project for the school at St.-Quentin-en-Yvelines and, to a lesser extent, of the Pliny's Villa extravaganza, which both represent the rediscovery of a territory long abandoned.

So the demonstration relates to the values of jerkiness; and, if the site of St.-Quentin is flat as a pancake and Pliny's Laurentine villa occupies a site which, as a rocky promontory, is never to be found between Ostia and Anzio, they both of them still employ comparable strategies. St.-Quentin is a primitive Roman *castrum.* If you like, it is the Palace of Diocletian at Spalato without the enclosing walls. Of, if you like, it displays something of the same format as the monastic buildings at St. Gall. In any case it makes a great play of a somewhat banal grid, a neutral scaffold within which enclosed spaces and objects of very high individuality are then to be discovered. Also, it is a chess board within which these individuated pieces, all retaining their particularity, are then to be moved about. For, seen as discrete but highly organized pieces, necessarily these are juxtaposable; and, if need be, they may be shifted from the regularities of the *castrum* into completely different constellations— as at the Laurentine villa. But in each case, the strategies will remain the same: the pieces very assertive, the ensemble seemingly very casual. So were these the strategies of Schinkel at Glienecke and Charlottenhof, where he crammed and jammed and crashed his ideal fragments into the most aggressive proximity? Maybe, but no great matter since the Krier message appears to be very simple: a Roman *castrum* is surely, for all practical purposes, good enough; but, if we can approach the irregularities of the Hadrianic picturesque (with *exactly* the same details), then why not try?

Leon Krier's attack upon the traditions of Positivist planning has, perhaps, been more a matter of heart than head; but none the worse for that. He hates the Positivists, who are incapable of considering any question of their now tottering doctrine. In any case he knows that they are wrong; and, therefore, after a cursory survey of the field of battle, he charges—with lots of panache. But if Leon belongs to the ranks of good, adventurous, speculative, stylish light cavalry, his ultimate objective is very simple, pragmatic, and paradigmatic. Fundamentally he wishes to make something easily buildable and immensely memorable, something of the order of an early nineteenth-century British barracks in Barbados or Bombay, perhaps with a few trimmings from late eighteenth-century Calcutta. In other words, something not too unlike Thomas Jefferson's University of Virginia (where most of this essay was written).

At the same time he seems to be moving, ever so gradually, from Claude/Schinkel to Serlio/Poussin; and Rita Wolff, who should be acclaimed, has made the point. For, with her beautiful rendering of the proposed piazza at Filadelfia di Calabria, Rita has perfectly illustrated the direction. An astonishing conflation, this square is simultaneously Poussin's *The Plague at Ashdod* and *The Rape of the Sabines.* And the sources emphasize both the seriousness and the poetical intensity of the person who, utterly estranged from the present day, is still one of our greatest teachers.

But, at a period when adulteration of all achievement is extremely rapid, should we not also be thinking about those lines from Pope's Epistle to Lord Burlington?

> *Yet shall, my lord, your just, your noble rules,*
> *Fill half the land with imitating fools.*

I think that we should be thinking about these lines and also be prepared to revise them. No longer "half the land," the revision of Pope should read "all the world." For, in our day and age Classicism and the *Geist* of the canton which, correctly I think, Leon professes, can quickly be reduced to kitsch. Poussin and Serlio in Japan? Indeed one can see it already.

About all this I can say no more.

The Revolt of the Senses

119. Nicolas Poussin, *The Plague at Ashdod.*

120. Rita Wolff, proposal for Filadelfia di Calabria.

The Revolt of the Senses

"I Stood in Venice on the Bridge of Sighs"

A contribution to a symposium on the Minneapolis Skyway sponsored by the Walker Art Center, Minneapolis, 1985, and published in Design Quarterly, *no. 129, as part of the record of that symposium.*

From a journalistic source I subsequently learned that, on the occasion of what I had to say, myself was looking "rather like an unmade bed." And I am not a bit surprised.

Examining a newspaper image of a section of the Minneapolis skyway, I was strongly reminded of the opening of the fourth canto of Byron's *Childe Harold:* "I stood in Venice on the Bridge of Sighs, A palace and a prison on each hand." And proceeded to fabricate a parallel: "In Minneapolis I scampered across a section of the local skyway, the ladies' lingerie section of a department store behind me and an upper-level foyer of the Amfac Hotel in front." And, of course, I concluded that the two experiences could never be strictly comparable.

Byron on the Bridge of Sighs (fig. 121) is in the position of the cultivated nineteenth-century tourist for whom Karl Baedeker was to write his many guidebooks. Whereas the hypothetical version of myself was much more in the position of one of those mid-twentieth-century tourists to whom the guides of Fielding have proved so useful.

I am proposing here not only the affiliation of Fielding to Baedeker, but also a decline in the sense of value represented by the two men. While Baedeker assumes the primacy of culture and prefers to inform his readers about churches, palaces, and museums, Fielding's interests are wide apart. To culture Fielding prefers consumption. Accordingly, his purpose is to tell his readers about eating, drinking, and shopping; what to order at Harry's Bar or Alfredo's, or where to buy Gucci, Valentino, and Armani.

I am assuming, in other words, the superiority of Baedeker's city and the Bridge of Sighs to Fielding's places of comment and the Minneapolis imagery of the local skyway. And my apprehensions are general, but based on experience. Thus, in Cincinnati's skyway, I found myself dreadfully disoriented and the streets below painfully degraded. While in Charlotte, North Carolina, where they have another skyway, the small, upstairs bourgeois boutiquesville appeared to be simply an added agent of ethnic discrimination. The blacks were on the streets and the whites were in the skyway. But, for all that, can there be an intrinsic objection to climate-controlled, upstairs environments or to bridges over streets? Or is the question a matter of how well, or how poorly, these multi-level maneuvers are effected? Let us survey the quality of skyway precedents.

The first reasons for upper-level communication leaping over streets must have been secret and political rather than public and climatic. In the fifteenth century, a judicious prince was advised to build a convenient bridge which, if necessary, would lead him to a place of refuge; and, while private passages for princes seem distant from the skyway context, we might still pause to reflect on the concepts of escape and refuge.

121. Ponte dei Sospiri (Bridge of Sighs), Venice.

"I Stood in Venice on the Bridge of Sighs"

One of the earliest of these elevated passages was that leading from the Vatican to the Castel Sant'Angelo. It was over this structure, unprotected from rain or sun, that Pope Clement VII scurried, in May 1527, in order to save himself from that strange international army which was about to sack the city.

About thirty years later, Cosimo de' Medici, first Grand Duke of Tuscany, felt the need for an equivalent *corridoio,* in this case, from the Palazzo Vecchio to the Palazzo Pitti (fig. 122). Cosimo's passage is the most famous of all these private bridges. Beginning at Palazzo Vecchio; traveling through the Uffizi, it forms the upper level of an arcade along the river, traverses the Ponte Vecchio, penetrates a number of houses, becomes the facade of the church of Santa Felicità, and finally terminates at Palazzo Pitti, from where further escape to the Fortezza del Belvedere was always available.

Cosimo's Corridoio Vasariano always dissimulates its presence, however; and, we must note that these early skyways are, primarily, advertisements of subterfuge. Secrecy and privacy are their controlling ideas. They lead from specific points of origin to specific points of destination, barring all other points of entrance or exit.

But there are many of these upper-level passages. Thus, towards the northern edge of the formal Papal States the small town of Farnese displays, at appropriately miniature scale, much the same strategies as those employed in the *corridoio;* then, at Innsbruck and Munich, one understands that there were further versions of this upper-level communication; and, of course, in Paris this theme became monumentalized as the Grande Galerie of the Louvre (fig. 123), built to secure a private route between the closely adjacent palaces of the Louvre and the Tuileries—a purpose now long forgotten but which was available for the Empress Eugénie when, in 1870, a mob attacked the Tuileries and she used the Grande Galerie as a means of escape, not, like Clement VII, to a Castel Sant'Angelo, but instead to the home of her American dentist. Or, in other words and four hundred years after it had first been proposed by Filarete, the princely skyway was still in full working order. The mob may have

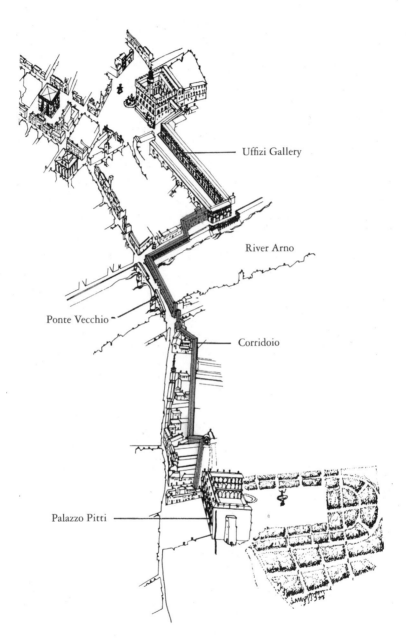

122. **Corridoio from Palazzo Vecchio to Palazzo Pitti, Florence.**

"I Stood in Venice on the Bridge of Sighs"

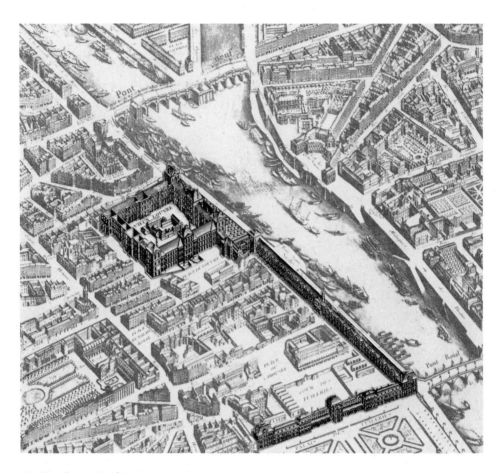

123. Grande Galerie of the Louvre, Paris, showing connections to Vieux Louvre and
Palais des Tuileries.

assembled to attack the prince; but, meanwhile, he—or she—is just not there.

However, the skyway theme envisages not only elevated, but also multi-level circulation; and, for these precedents, we must descend from the princely skyway to what might have been the city that, in the 1490s, existed in the mind of Leonardo da Vinci. In the last of his years in Milan, Leonardo was preoccupied with a city of great complexity: canals, subterranean service streets, and upper-level *strade nobili.* All this may be represented by a model in the Museo della Scienza e della Tecnica in Milan (fig. 124). The vision is an entirely arbitrary grouping of Leonardo-like propositions. Still, it may represent a state of mind which was not to be recovered, in any important way, until the present century.

Certainly, Robert Adam's Adelphi, circa 1770, might be considered a premonition of what was to come; it was just the Piranesian performance that Adam admired and Leonardo would have understood. The lower level was rough and servile, and above, in the world of the *signore,* a slightly febrile elegance prevailed. Communications between levels were not many and the social segregations were extreme.

So it was to be in New York, 1903–1913, that long-standing fragmentary suggestions were accumulated into an heroic synthesis: Warren & Wetmore's Grand Central Station. Although no longer sufficiently appreciated, the impact of this immense undertaking does live, I think, in the pages of Scott Fitzgerald and also in the excitement of Le Corbusier.

A shift of the terminus from 34th to 42nd Street, a deck over the New York Central tracks from 96th Street south, and the creation of a major residential avenue were all part of the comprehensive operation, unmatched in London, Paris, or elsewhere. The project was the complement to the big ships in the docks that signified the Atlantic; equally, it was the monumental response to the tribute of an entire continent.

Arriving on one of the great trains (the Twentieth Century Limited, perhaps), plunging underground at 96th Street, and surfac-

"I Stood in Venice on the Bridge of Sighs"

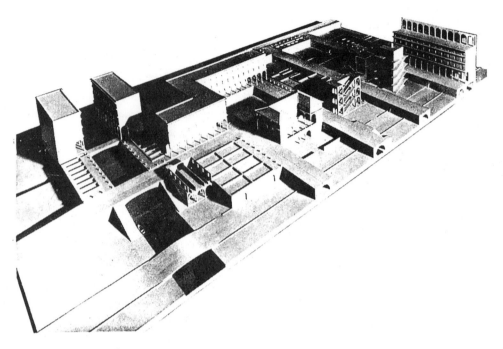

124. Idealized City, 1490. Leonardo da Vinci. Contemporary model at the Museo della Scienza e della Tecnica, Milan.

ing to enter the great concourse hall, perhaps from the Baths of Caracalla (nothing less being worthy of New York's mission), one then had the choice of a taxi or hotel. If a hotel were desired, without having to leave this crypto-city one could walk to the Biltmore, the Roosevelt, or the Commodore. Although the station has long since languished, the city progression it celebrated lingers.

Meanwhile, one should notice how demure is the outside of Grand Central. Somewhat like an enlarged version of one of Sanmicheli's gates at Verona, reworked by a Frenchman of conservative taste, and disclosing none of the intricacy of section and organization that lies behind, it nonetheless became a cult object to the Futurists in Milan. Simultaneously an exhibition of aggressive American dynamism and enfeebled American reluctance to go ahead, the station became the object of Futurist ambition to strip away the classical and American decorum and turn it inside out.

Without doubt, many of our current afflictions descend from this ambitious 1910 paradigm. If one chooses to go to Montreal and negotiate the crypts of Place Bonaventure, just possibly one may find a similar message. But while at Grand Central the message is mostly condensed and laconic, at Montreal one's clues are indecipherable and dissipated. In the winter, subterranean Montreal provides relief from shocking cold; but, otherwise, it deprives the streets above of animation.

Clearly, a crypto-city must be created only in a very special situation. At Grand Central, quite dramatically, it was justified. Grand Central is the *beau idéal* of Leonardo's crypto-city. It related to great entrance and great exit; without these, with what are we left? Simply, I think, we are left with a crazy labyrinth.

A famous New York fantasy of 1908, called *King's Dream of New York,* shows the same preoccupation with multi-level circulation as Grand Central (fig. 125). At bottom level is a street with an elevated railroad running along it and miscellaneous low-level bridges. Above the street is a high-level bridge with a train running across it. Then, infinitely elevated, there is a variety of curved approaches (railroads or primitive *autostrade*). And, finally, not so far above, but in the sky, a frightening, disorderly collection of peculiar old airplanes is flying around. A document of this order must have been God's gift to Milan, where the excited Futurists felt themselves to be on "the promontory of the centuries," on the cutting edge of history. To the Futurist imagination, this cosmopolis offered something far better than Grand Central. The vision of the city of Sant'Elia in 1914 by Mario Chiattone (fig. 126) may be regarded as an organized reply. A city of towers, rather abruptly penetrated by what appear to be railroad viaducts, Chiattone's project presents the received myths of New York, but crisscrossed with ideas from Vienna. The infrastructure is from the world of Jules Verne, and the superstructure is from the repertory of late Habsburg Jugendstil.

Looking at the protracted tubes that carry the railroads, one might feel compelled to conclude that the origins of the Minneapolis skyway are in such Futurist manifesto pieces as this. But we

"I Stood in Venice on the Bridge of Sighs"

125. Moses King, *King's Dream of New York* (1908), frontispiece.

126. City of Antonio Sant'Elia and Mario Chiattone, 1914.

"I Stood in Venice on the Bridge of Sighs"

must learn to approach the topic of bridges, which may be something more than tubes; and bridges are likely to become the preferred connective tissue in a relatively closed aggregation of spaces such as downtown Minneapolis.

Now, a bridge has two primary exposures: the entrance for the people and vehicles crossing it, and the entry surface for the people and vehicles penetrating beneath it; and both these movements should be appropriately celebrated. The traffic above should not degrade the traffic below; but, likewise, the traffic above must be alerted that a crossing and a bridge are imminent. Consequently, a bridge can be only a highly analyzed structure. Below, however modified, a bridge presents some version of triumphal arch; and above, it behaves as a distinctly articulated gallery, as an Aristotelian distribution with a beginning, middle, and end.

Palladio's proposal for a bridge at the Rialto (fig. 127) may illustrate the argument. Undoubtedly, had it been built as originally presented, this bridge would have been an unmitigated catastrophe; but this is scarcely an issue. Palladio was presenting a *theory* of the bridge, presumably true for all times and places and almost certainly to be modified in execution. It is a *theoretical* bridge conceding ceremonious passage to both pedestrians and boats. By detaching itself from the more random, immediate physical environment the bridge further advertises the proposition that, in addition to being a transition between places, a bridge may be considered *a place in itself*. Great bridges such as the Ponte Vecchio in Florence, Old London Bridge, the Pont Neuf in Paris, and the covered bridges of New England and upstate New York have always been places in themselves. And, to this inventory, there may now be added the connection in Cambridge, Massachusetts, proposed by James Stirling, between Harvard's Fogg Museum and his own extension to it, the Sackler (fig. 128). Although controversial, I would almost like to see this bridge built, among other reasons, as a possible model for Minneapolis. Unlike the abstract tubes of the existing Minneapolis skyway system, the Fogg Museum bridge is a crossing equipped with character and personality. It is conceived as an articulated gal-

127. Canaletto, after Andrea Palladio, *Rialto Bridge.*

"I Stood in Venice on the Bridge of Sighs"

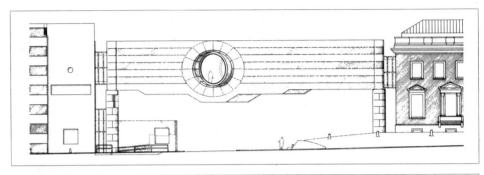

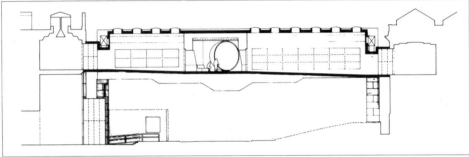

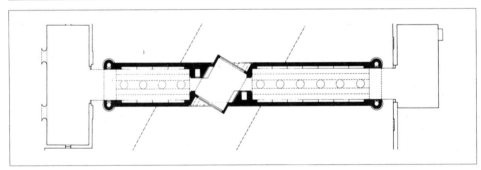

128. Arthur M. Sackler Museum, Harvard University, drawing showing proposed connecting bridge to the Fogg Museum. James Stirling. Drawings of the elevation, section, and plan of the bridge over Broadway that might contain a gallery space, a function appropriate to the link between two Harvard University museums.

lery with a particular room in the middle, the room with the circular windows, from which the street becomes dramatically visible. But also, and even more important for Minneapolis, this bridge distinguishes itself as an independent structural and spatial performance, actively disengaged from the buildings at either end. The Minneapolis skyways rely all too exclusively on the deployment of glazed *tubes as transition.* But, by now, in selected locations, Minneapolis should envisage the alternative strategy of the relatively opaque *bridge as place.* Vierendeel trusses, of course, will suffice—on most occasions; but their universal, utilitarian proliferation can only engender a movement without apparent destination, likely to defy the capacity of both the memory and the mind.

A number of elaborate and highly specific bridges might be seen as a corollary and counterpoint to the prevailing system. As such, one could conceive them acting as spatial magnets, in an otherwise somewhat labyrinthine confusion. As centers of convergence, they might indicate those approaches to the skyway which are now scarcely visible; and, incidentally, they would surely present an exceptional air-rights proposition to the city. For the elaborated bridge could contain an enormous number of facilities, and its volume might be sustained for several floor levels. Indeed, one might even envision such a bridge acting as a major skyway plaza above a four-point intersection below!

"I Stood in Venice on the Bridge of Sighs"

Bibliotheca Alexandrina: An Also-Ran?

Related to the competition of 1988. Written 1991. Published, with the significant omission of the Postscript and related illustrations, in ANY, *no. 7–8 (1994).*

But the Postscript just happens to be the "Also-Ran" of my title.

> Beware of the prestigious international architectural competition. Try and ascertain beforehand if the final choice is going to be made by the national leader and not by the architectural judges—particularly important if you are not from the country of origin.
>
> James Stirling[1]

Among the congenitally sceptical the announcement, made in 1988, that the Egyptian government and UNESCO were proposing a reestablishment of the library of Alexandria was received with a degree of irony and amusement. For, nowadays, how could any such institution, even remotely, begin to compete with the great collections of Europe and North America, with those in the British Museum, the Bibliothèque Nationale, the Library of Congress, the New York Public Library? And this is not to mention the collections of Yale, Harvard, Oxford, Cambridge, et al.

Nevertheless, it was an enticing idea; and, as it was patently addressed to the Third World, it seems to have commanded the support of the ubiquitous President Mitterrand and the, no doubt, charming Mrs. Mubarak. For here was proposed the superlibrary, no doubt immensely endearing to the aspirations of cultural imperialism in the French style (a case of more *retour d'Egypte?*) And, if its financial resources were completely unknown, since its provenance was impeccable and its ambitions were enormous, it was—correspondingly—to be hoped that, by the end of the century, it was instantly to compete with the great libraries of the world.

An impossible idea this bonanza for rare book dealers? Though it is a joy to imagine these scholarly, and slightly mercenary, persons dreaming up their little catalogues in Florence, Paris, New York, Geneva, Amsterdam, and London; an almost impossible idea because, evidently, its realization must depend on a massive deployment of money, reluctant money, presumably from the United States, upon the implicit assumption that the U.S. will always pay even for the eight million books which are here talked about. And not a meager amount of money this. For, even if one assumes the unduly modest average of $100 per book, it is a proposal which seems to envisage (apart from the cost of the building itself) a fairly quick expenditure of something like $800,000,000!

All the same, not entirely unrealistic this bibliophiliac extravaganza intended to return Alexandria to the cultural map of the world after a lapse of rather longer than one cares to think about. For do not we, in the so-called 'West,' owe so much to the Moslemic presence particularly in Spain? Averroes, the rediscovery of

303

Aristotle, and, hence, the philosophy of St. Thomas Aquinas? The pointed arch and, hence, the articulation of 'Gothic' architecture? Quantities of medical and optical 'borrowings'? Algebra and even the word *alcohol*? But of course; and, more importantly (though perhaps originating in India), the propagation of the *zero* from which was derived a far more efficient numerical system than any which prevailed in Greco-Roman antiquity?

No, the debts of the 'West' to Moslemic scholarship are very prominent; and, even though the countries of the Middle East[2] have lately shown a preference for terrorism, armaments, and religious fundamentalism rather than for science, arts, and learning, a suspension of disbelief on the part of the sceptical might suggest that the proposed library, as a focus of study, could plausibly serve as an instrument to cool passions and to pacify, to bring the desert into the orbit of the Mediterranean. In which case, surely cheap at the price? And, in any case, surely infinitely cheaper than the costs of the recent war over Kuwait!

After which perfunctory remarks, related mostly to money and to politics, it must now be time to approach the terms of the architectural competition itself which were published in 1988.

It was a highly alluring document. The program was exacting; both topographically and historically the site possesses dimensions which approach the spectacular (fig. 129); and the jury was, adequately, illustrious. In other words, the prospects for the winner appeared to promise instant international *réclame*: and, therefore, there should be no surprise that, a year later, 524 participants sent in their entries—presumably few of them willing to "beware of the prestigious international competition" which Stirling appeared to consider a major menace.

Now, to imagine the chagrin of the unsuccessful, of those eager, ambitious, often talented individuals who sweated out their projects (and constitute the debris—or the fallout—of *any* architectural competition) is a terrible misery—all the same, it is no less misery making to turn over the pages of the book which has been produced as a record of the transactions of the competition jury.

Bibliotheca Alexandrina: An Also-Ran?

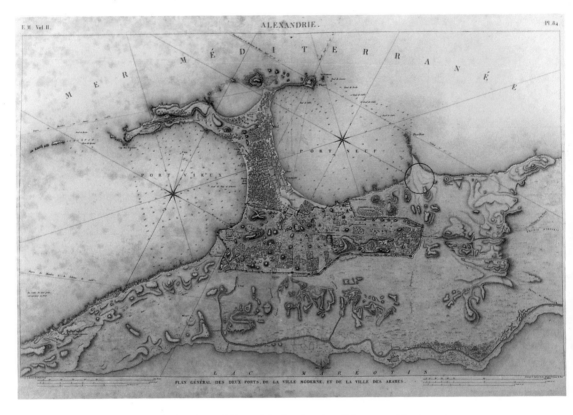

129. New Port of Alexandria showing site of the competition.

And this is a book, *Bibliotheca Alexandrina, International Architectural Competition,* which will go far to reinforce the reservations of the congenitally skeptical—not about what seems to be Stirling's greatest horror, the over-riding dictates of some 'strong man' politico. For here, at Alexandria, there is absolutely no trace of his chauvinist and dreadful presence. No, that big bogeyman can scarcely be introduced; and, instead one is obliged to direct attention to the activities—and the acuities—of the professional jury itself.

Therefore, in order to discover something of the jury's mental orientation, one may quote several passages from *Bibliotheca Alexandrina.* For instance, in the case of this library, "we are again confronted with the very issue of defining the identity of the present time";[3] and, by implication, one thus learns that the library must be expressive of some absolutely contemporary *Zeitgeist.* But, though one may wonder *how* (and, for that matter, *why*) this *can* (or *should*) be the case, by what act of clairvoyance this condition is to be discerned, one must continue.

> A building like the New Alexandria Library calls for *modern monumentality.* It must be modern to identify with our time, but must also possess publicness. . . . Monuments, whatever they are, are to provide lasting impressions to beholders. . . . In this respect architectural creation is not invention but discovery, it is not the pursuit of something beyond the imagination but the externalization of the collective imagination of an age. . . . Whether in the East or the West, or in the past or the present, all buildings worthy of being called monuments have had that quality. They become a testimony of the time.[4]

A resounding accumulation of more than fatigued platitudes? A collection of highly disputable inferences almost presented as revelation from 'on high'? But of course. Nevertheless, these are the words of Fumihiko Maki, vice president of the jury; and they deserve our attention, particularly so after having received almost the imprimatur of the United Nations Educational, Scientific, and Cultural Organization. For just to think about this bland iteration of pseudo-Hegelian dogma, this notion that true authenticity requires the presence of two unknowable and indefinable imperatives, *Zeitgeist* and *Volksgeist,* is to make comment enough upon a quite painful intellectual naïveté.

By comparison, the president of the jury, John Carl Warnecke (Rose Bowl to J.F.K.), without any apparent traces of cultural pretension, is much more down to earth; and he contents himself largely with praising the winning design, a circular building which seems mostly to be sunken underground (fig. 130).

> The design of the Library is in the form of a circle, which becomes its predominant symbol.
>
> The circle is not only one of man's earliest symbols, it also expresses a basic continuity to man's existence.
>
> The sun is a circle.
>
> The moon is often an emerging circle.
>
> The site of the Library looks out on the ancient harbor of Alexandria, which is in the form of a circle.
>
> The circular plan of the Library thus relates to all these elements.
>
> The circle is a symbol of the unity and continuity that embraces the past, present and future.
>
> In this winning design the Library is in the form of a tilted cylinder, whose circular roof slants subtly toward the sea and the harbor, and points toward the sky, the sun and the moon. A large portion of the Library itself is below ground. And from the ground level it appears as a strong, cylindrical masonry form emerging from the earth. It is like a new moon that will grow to a full moon. It emerges from this particular site like the rebirth of an earlier form.

And, after all this neo-atavistic rapture, finally from Warnecke: "In modern times and in recent international competitions, the design

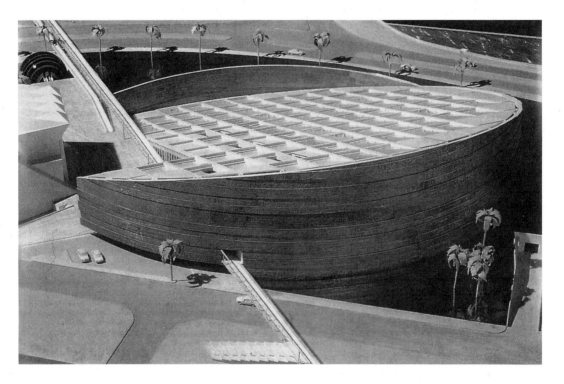

130. The winning entry. Snøhetta.

Bibliotheca Alexandrina: An Also-Ran?

of the Sydney Opera House and the Arch of La Défense in Paris leave an unforgettable impression on those who have seen these buildings once."[5]

Perhaps so, but, in the case of the Arch of La Défense, could not this tribute to We Know Whom be also an impression which the observer might gladly be only too willing to forget?

But now to annex the Aswan Declaration on the Bibliotheca Alexandrina: "On the site of the palace of the Ptolemies, the new Alexandrina will give modern expression to an ancient endeavor. A splendid contemporary design for the Library has already been adopted through an international competition."[6]

Signed, among others, by President Mitterrand and Mrs. Mubarak, the terms of this declaration might complete a brief examination of the psycho-intellectual climate which has encompassed both preconceptions of the library and adjudications of the competition. For, given the mood of the jury (Maki's somewhat retarded embrace of the tenets of historical determinism and Warnecke's enthusiasm for the Arch of La Défense), given the *délire de grandeur* of President Mitterrand (it must be far more extreme than that of the late Nelson Rockefeller), given Mrs. Mubarak's perhaps slightly ingenuous enthusiasm, in this quaintly charged climate of opinion it must be apparent that 'accepted' procedures of analysis and synthesis can scarcely be expected as likely to flourish and to prosper. Indeed, to state the situation crudely, may it not be suggested that their survival factor is just about as tough as the predicament of a snowball in hell?

As a guide to navigation the Pharos of Alexandria was one of the seven wonders of the ancient world and, also, the most significant object in the scenery of Alexandria's eastern harbor. Then, on the other side of the harbor entrance but somewhat removed, it possessed a pendent in the long since vanished palace of the Ptolemies, its gardens, and its various dependencies.

Through the process of ruin and decay—abrupt or gradual—and the process of random reconstruction, the site of the

Pharos and parts of the Pharos itself became incorporated in the present Fort Kaid Bey, the Château de Phare of French nineteenth century illustrations; and it is now proposed that, on the approximate site of the Ptolemaic palace, there should be established a major library which, just as the Pharos operated as a notice to sailors, will itself serve as an intellectual beacon, an advertisement of rebirth addressed to both the present and the future. Analogically the library is to become what the Pharos used to be!

Such a dramatic confrontation or dialogue seems to have been a major idea, perhaps the *major* idea, of the promoters of this competition; and it *grabs* the imagination. For by all the standards of poetry, it can only be a supremely apposite idea: the eastern harbor of Alexandria to be approached via a great portal to be flanked, on the right, by memories of the lighthouse and, on the left, by the new reality of the Alexandrina and all of the enlightened possibilities intrinsic to its establishment. An overwhelmingly simple iconography and a case of time discovering truth?

But between poetry and prose, between dream and reality, between the Platonic idea and its partial embodiment, between a vision of almost Hellenistic splendor and a McDonald's hamburger stand, inevitably there is something which intervenes. In this case, I think, not the state of mind of those who envisioned this competition but of those who put together its program.

And in this case it is possible that the published exigencies of the program and what one might assume to be the exigencies of the site are more than slightly contradictory.

We are talking, after all, about a collection of books maybe worth $800,000,000 and about a building to house them which can scarcely be inexpensive. We are talking about what is proposed to be an illustrious institution and a comparably illustrious 'monument' to enclose it. So how much might this 'monument' be expected to cost? Hard to say? What with graft, kickbacks, and all the rest, perhaps another $200,000,000? In any case a total sum likely to reduce any reasonably cautious minister of finance (secretary of the treasury, chancellor of the exchequer) to a quivering jelly.

Bibliotheca Alexandrina: An Also-Ran?

However, if this is no matter, if this money can easily be af-
forded—from *some* source or other—this is not to the point; and
much more important it is to notice that, until quite recently, it
was commonly accepted that a major building *did,* and *should,* possess around itself an orbit of influence, or as it used to be called an
entourage. Simply, a major building *could* not be reduced to the condition of a casual episode. The building *could* not be conceived of as a
complex in itself, complete within its own walls. It produced rever-
berations. *Around itself it involved the extended intimations of its presence.*

An anachronistic strategy which the relentlessness of a contemporary *Zeitgeist* has rendered invisible or only deserving of a perfunctory observation? Something like this seems to have been the
bias of the program; and I am sure that, apart from myself, many
persons who sent in their projects to this competition must have
wondered why. For the program excluded any consideration of the
peninsula which the site of the library so closely adjoins.

The eastern harbor of Alexandria is separated from the sea
by a series of breakwaters extending from Fort Kaid Bey to the
north and completed by the peninsula of Selselah to the south.
Then, from the south of the harbor and prolonged almost ad infini-
tum to the east, along this north-facing coastline there travels a marine driveway, backed up by mostly six-story apartment houses. It is
known—with obvious reference to Napoleonic highways behind
Monaco and Nice—as the Corniche; and, in his introductory essay,
published only in French, Franco Zagari describes this general spectacle of harbor, fort, peninsula, and marine drive as: "le scénario,
stratégique, le coeur psychologique des Alexandrins, où tout passe,
tout se passe. Le jour, vie et traffic très intenses, la nuit, les mir-
acles. . . . Dans cet espace magique la Bibliothèque vient se situer
sur le bord à droite, dans la continuation de l'Université étendue
vers la peninsule de Selselah, joyau spéctaculaire de Kait Bey."[7]

So, in this strategic scenario, in this psychological heart, in
this jewel-like setting with all its intense traffic and nocturnal mir-
acles, when all this 'magic' is so romantically envisaged, why was so
little proposed to build up the *coup de théâtre,* the climactic statement which is so obviously invoked?

One might suggest that, apart from the difficulty experienced by the authors of the program in addressing themselves to a larger than on-site context, there were at least two arguments involved.

1. The peninsula of Selselah is, at present, a military reservation and, hence, there in the center of it all, and for all its potential as a public park, it is untouchable.
2. The Corniche, with all its heavy traffic, is admittedly an impediment to pedestrian access to the water and such beaches as may occur; but what of it? Pedestrian bridges can always be supplied as necessary; and isn't this the cheapest solution anyway?

But, against these arguments, there may always be cited Le Corbusier's "eyes that do not see," transposable if necessary as minds that do not think.

Thus, although it is notoriously difficult to dislodge the military, who are often to be found fighting the last war but one, at least they might be given a suggestive push; and, in this connection, a little smile from Mrs. Mubarak might have helped a lot. For it is surely inconceivable that a centrally located position, immediately adjacent to a highly expensive building and what is hoped to be a magnetic one, should forever remain a negative site, a *terra incognita,* a place of restricted access.

Rather, the peninsula of Selselah is, potentially, the most positive site in the whole scenic constellation of the eastern harbor. Equipped with avenues and pavilions, an extension of the university and the library precincts, in the daytime it might and should serve as an academic grove and in the cool of the evening as a place—like so many Italian places—*per fare la passeggiata* after a day which has been rather too hot.

But the Italian reference (and, after all, they did do this sort of thing rather well in nineteenth century Italy) may allow attention to be directed to the behavior of the Corniche as it passes between the peninsula and the yet-to-be-built library. So just what about the pedestrian crossing of the Corniche? And is it not degrading to the pedestrian, in so prominent a position, to oblige this person to climb and then to descend? And would it not have been perfectly possible, in the vicinity of the library, to oblige the automobile to descend and then to climb? It is surely not beyond the mind of humanity to think about it (after all we do this kind of job almost every day) and not beyond the resources of an opulent society to bring it about. And is not the automobile tunnel a slightly more elegant and sociologically useful solution than the exiguous *passerelle,* furniture of the wasteland, which leads—for the most part—from nowhere to nowhere?

And the making of the tunnel, producing above itself some plaza or *piazzale,* would possess the merit of putting the library into direct communication with the harbor; and, from hence, all sorts of benefits might accrue. For instance: a place where citizens and students might converge; a place serviced by two *embarcaderos* at which little motor boats would arrive from east and west loaded with eager people who, as they moved in, would find, on the one hand, the floodlit facade of the library, a beacon of knowledge addressed to the city, and, on the other, the gates to the Garden of Selselah, beyond which for a few hours—and one imagines the scene at night—there would be mysterious lighting, music, the consumption of refreshments, and the occasional display of fireworks over water.

Too lurid and too much of an Italian souvenir this image of pleasure? In any case the authors of the program, whom one might conceive to be protestant, puritan, positivist, and blond, never conceived of such a hybrid focus of animation; and, since the jury seems to have voted *hors de concours* all those solutions which involved more than the slightest transgressions of the program and all but the most minor concessions to the Corniche, as a result we are left with the anomaly of the winning solution—the glass-roofed quasi-cylinder saluting the sun and moon of John Carl Warnecke.

It might be better if it saluted the harbor or made any but the most imperceptible impact upon the Corniche; but, being in great part sunk underground, from the harbor it can scarcely be visible and, in close proximity to the Corniche, it seems scarcely to rise above the level of the highway. In the wall of six-story apartment houses, instead of a climax it will be a decrescendo (surely very disastrous as seen from the harbor?); and the driver, going either way, will barely be in the position to notice it. Going east it will be a very low wall. Going west it will just not be seen!

Strange fate for a hoped-to-be illustrious institution for which all responsible nations are expected to provide their support! But stranger still are certain further features of the winning project. A glass-roofed library is surely nearly always an absurdity since, unless the glass is screened, the books will fade. But a glass-roofed library in a southern latitude is evidently a double absurdity since it can only produce immense air-conditioning expenses; and this at a time when energy conservation is one of the great themes of the ecologically self-conscious. And, finally, while the Corniche is maintained at its present level, no tunnel permissible—*the library itself is sunk*—one would think a more expensive, perverse, and less justifiable undertaking than the sinking of the highway!

With all this said, it is probably safe to add that, if the library is to be built in this form, scarcely apprehensible except from the air, then surely its building will add nothing to the repertory of postcards—Santa Maria della Salute, the Stockholm City Hall, lower Manhattan as it used to be, even a little Apulian-Adriatic town like Trani—those great land-water confrontations which conscientious student tourists have been accustomed to send back to their ever-so-concerned families.

Samuel Johnson said about the death of David Garrick that his "decease had extinguished the gaiety of nations"; and, following his example, might one say that the proposed Alexandrina is likely to extinguish both the enjoyment and the support of those political societies most willing to subscribe to its general idea. The President of the French Republic, among his other concerns, may be overjoyed by the *dénouement* of this competition; but there are others who might doubt both his judgement and his discernment.

Bibliotheca Alexandrina: An Also-Ran?

Postscript

Against the advice of Jim Stirling (specially repeated in her case), my friend Judith DiMaio, teaching at Yale, was determined to enter this competition, which she did in collaboration with William Palmore from Texas, and assisted by Matthew Bell, Myriam Bella-zoug, Sally Gilliland, Sophie Harvey, Daniel Lawler, Amy Lelyveld, Kent MacDonald, Cheryl O'Neil, and William Smith. And, as was to be expected, needless to say, they did *not* win.

By my own standards the DiMaio-Palmore project (figs. 131–133) has many virtues—it does not hide itself; it makes a major contribution to the urban scenery of Alexandria; and it displays only one glaring defect—communication between bookstacks and reading room is, to say the least, exiguous and tortured. However, it is very evident that, with a willingness to surrender the simplistic charms of pristine *dégagement,* to reconsider the problems of a very tenuous joint, arrival of books in the reading room could be accomplished without undue frustration to readers. No, it was for no such relatively banal reason that this project was presumably declared *hors de concours.* Rather it was because (and probably like so many others) it proposed an eviction of the military presence from the peninsula of Selselah—as though this peninsula had been, in any way, vital to the maritime defenses of Alexandria at any time during the last one hundred years!

So that is most of the story. Professor DiMaio was convinced that the editors of *Perspecta* might like to ventilate issues related to Bibliotheca Alexandrina in their pages; and, accordingly, I wrote this piece—for *Perspecta.*

Then, as to what else happened, I can have no idea except that, unlike Stirling and myself, the editors at Yale were, probably, not to be persuaded that the conditions of this competition—to quote Neville Chamberlain, "in a faraway country of which we know nothing"—were not too hopelessly irrelevant to deserve a privileged discussion.

And, if this is what they thought, then perhaps they were right. Or, maybe, they were not quite so right as they supposed.

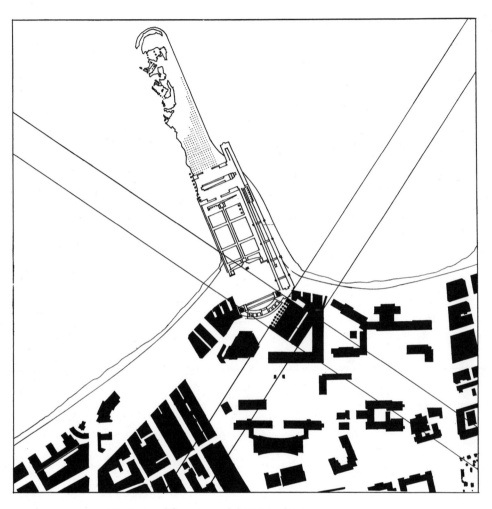

131. Proposed figure/ground. DiMaio and Palmore.

Bibliotheca Alexandrina: An Also-Ran?

132. View of model. DiMaio and Palmore.

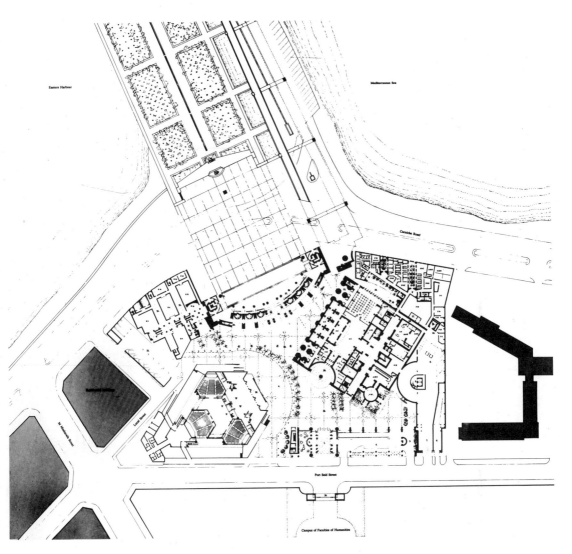

133. Ground plan and peninsular garden. DiMaio and Palmore.

Bibliotheca Alexandrina: An Also-Ran?

Notes

1. James Stirling, "Architecture and Politics," *RIBA Journal* 38, no. 6 (June 1991): 43.

2. Of course the term Middle East is now 'politically incorrect'; regrettably Euro- and Americano-centric. Instead this whole part of the world is now to be designated Southwest Asia, and Egypt, which everyone knows is part of Africa, is now, 'correctly', to be spoken of as, in some way, Asiatic!

3. Fumihiko Maki, "The Modern Monument," in *Bibliotheca Alexandrina, International Architectural Competition,* ed. Franco Zagari (Paris: UNESCO, 1990), 35.

4. Ibid.

5. John Carl Warnecke, "The International Architectural Competition of the Ancient Library of Alexandria," in *Bibliotheca Alexandrina,* 30.

6. "Aswan Declaration on the Bibliotheca Alexandrina," in *Bibliotheca Alexandrina,* 243.

7. Franco Zagari, "Alexandria Turning Point," in *Bibliotheca Alexandrina,* 41.

Interview: *Design Book Review*

An interview with Richard Ingersoll in Rome, published in Design Book Review *in 1989.*

Design Book Review: During the past ten years a trend that could be called Postmodern Urbanism has been put into practice in many significant urban projects both in the centers of existing cities and at their outskirts. As a revival or reinterpretation of traditional urban forms and a return to enclosed figural space, this trend emphatically rejects postwar models of freestanding towers and vast parking lots. Since the early 1970s you have argued eloquently against both the formal consequences and the Utopian premises of postwar architecture; are you satisfied with the Postmodern alternative?

320

Colin Rowe: With the designation Postmodern I run into trouble right away because it presumes an avant-garde movement and thus psychologically belongs to the mental set that produced Modernist architecture itself. Like other avant-gardes it places an extremely high valuation on novelty. It's obviously different, but whether it's better I do not know. If you compare it with the social housing of the 1920s, such as that of Bruno Taut in Berlin, it doesn't get anywhere near that quality. Let's take the IBA (Internationale Bauausstellung, 1981–1987) proposals in Berlin: the problem was that sites were assigned block by block, so that no single architect could deal with both sides of the street. You don't get a balanced street or complete square but instead a collection of signature buildings. As one critic complained, "Here a Catalonian fort, there an *esquisse* by Rossi, a *quadrillage ésotérique* by Eiseman, and a collection of Hanseatic warehouses from Ticino." You might say that this heterogeneity is an accurate portrayal of our times, but I'm not really interested in our times—that would presuppose some Hegelian point of view about history by which the object is supposedly transcribing the spirit of our times. Another problem specifically with IBA is that other than social housing they did not have money for the kind of things that a great city needs. In West Berlin there is simply no *place* anywhere (the so-called Kulturforum included); it is a-spatial. The grand spaces and the cultural apparatus that go with a big city are all in East Berlin.

When you look at another project like Bofill's Antigone in Montpellier and that huge plaza drawn in the shape of the plan of St. Peter's—a few years ago most people would have said that that was completely unjustified and I still think of myself as probably agreeing. They thought that to go beyond an accumulation of *Zeilenbau* buildings was intolerable because it distorted the real facts of the program. My argument against Bofill's scheme is that there can never be a center until there is enough pressure on it by the surroundings to make it central. Despite its attempt to make shapes, there are too many gaps. And you don't enter St. Peter's on the apse, do you? Antigone is actually based on the plan of Nancy, with the

134. Antigone Project, Montpellier, 1979–, aerial view. Ricardo Bofill.

three linked squares, but they are not stitched together well at all. Compared to the eighteenth century Promenade du Peyrou in the historic center, which has perfect proportions and is discreet, Bofill's work is grossly overscaled and it's kitsch. Still it aspires to make shapes like those you got in late eighteenth and early nineteenth century Edinburgh, a network that seemed to be arbitrary but after a lapse of time everybody accepted as genuine. And that I suppose would be true for the Disneyworld type of city: It's arbitrary and it's vague until the passing of time. (Of course I've never been to Disneyland and I don't intend to go either!) All that I'm saying is that it's relatively easy to provoke what Coleridge called the "willing suspension of disbelief"—this could have been the case with Edinburgh, but for Modernists this was absolutely unthinkable in terms of ideas of equality, light, aspect, prospect, and all that.

DBR: One of the major justifications of the postwar city is that it is functional for a mass society; it is well suited to the mobility-oriented technologies of our times. The postwar city looks bad but is Modern architecture really at fault?

CR: It's very hard to know; when you look at someone like Bruno Taut in Berlin or a place like Siemensstadt by Gropius and Scharoun, or Ernst May's beautifully planned public housing estates in Frankfurt, these are very distinguished layouts—you cannot say that Modern architecture was all that bad if it could produce things of this quality. I think that one has to recognize that a period from the late 1800s to somewhere in the mid-1930s was a period which possessed a high sense of order. This is evidenced in the U.S. by the Chicago Columbian Exposition of 1893 and the City Beautiful Movement and lots of American campuses. You saw it on Park Avenue after they removed the train tracks—but when they took away the "L" on Third Avenue in the 1950s, that produced nothing at all! Why was it after 1945 that the street suddenly disappeared? You see it in the U.S. and in Europe. The continuous built-up street was abandoned even in a place like Rome. It was not just the auto-

135. Central Edinburgh, New Town development, 1827.

Interview: *Design Book Review*

mobile. In Florence if you take Via Borgicino, this area was bombed in World War II, and the difference from its late nineteenth century continuous fabric and the completely disjointed pattern of the post-war buildings is quite clear—this was not the result of the automobile. You've got to attribute something to the object fixation which was endemic in Modern architecture. If you take Hilberseimer's scheme in the 1920s for Unter den Linden in Berlin, he placed a dreadful series of *Zeilenbauen* perpendicular to the great axis—an attack on the line of Unter den Linden as a theater of bad memories. The attack on the street I think is long previous to the dissemination of the automobile in these early Modernist schemes of the 1920s.

It's particularly after World War II that the object building took over. In terms of campus design one may suspect that it began at MIT around 1950 with the Aalto dorms and Saarinen's Kresge Auditorium and chapel, and after that every campus from coast to coast decided it had to turn itself into an exhibition of unrelated works by what were thought to be prominent architects. This really did happen—and it could have happened earlier.

If one took all of the masterpieces of Modern architecture, the Tugendhat House, Garches, the Schroeder House in Utrecht, and set them down on the usual American commercial strip, they wouldn't add up to anything, they'd be lost. As objects they would devalue each other by their proximity. Then, if you've driven the *autostrada* north of Milan, where Le Corbusier planned his building for Olivetti, you'll note that it is a continuous pile of junk; the Corbu project on that strip would just look like a heap of junk like everything else. Liberal policy is to blame for all these strips—deliberate acts of policy created these linear jumbles . . . a linear city they dreamed of, all the way from Florence to Los Angeles.

DBT: Often in the enthusiasm for a return to city fabric, the city is treated as if post-industrial times were post-automobile times. Isn't the problem of the automobile, even if it was not the origin of the formal solutions of Modernism, still central in a current urban scheme?

CR: I keep thinking that it would be perfectly easy to assume a little city which is jacked up and on the floor below a big sort of pedestrian level. I would, for instance, love to live above a shopping mall. You can drive into it easily, and sometimes you need never leave the complex, you can just go below and buy things. The only really successful twentieth century urban project that I can think of, which helps me assume that the problem of the automobile can be solved, is Rockefeller Center. It's a miracle: the right size, you're not overwhelmed by height, and it's just at that moment when there's a Beaux-Arts residue in the details that adds quality. I wasn't thinking of it as a model for historic centers, such as what occurred in London at the Barbican Centre, but more along the lines of the outer suburbs of Washington, D.C., where you get all these terrible jumbles of garden apartments, over-designed and without the sort of shopping and services that should go with them. There you must get into your car and drive twenty minutes to the supermarket— but to live *above* the supermarket, then you'd have it all. I must say that here in Rome there are times, in fact every day, when I would prefer to get into an automobile and go shopping in a supermarket than go shopping around in all these little stores. The ideal thing would be to have a good American suburb adjacent to a very concentrated Italian town, then you'd have the best of both worlds.

It wouldn't be impossible to build a grand apartment scene above a shopping center, and instead of the usual jumble have something like the Vieux Carré in New Orleans, a regular little city built up there. The shopping mall doesn't need an exterior, except perhaps a representational facade, and above it there is a fabulous site for building which is never exploited.

DBR: If one proposes all kinds of nice public spaces, connected streets and figured *piazze,* will there still be an audience in a highly technological society for their use? In other words is the return to traditional urban space a guarantee of a certain kind of social life?

CR: The steps of the Metropolitan and the steps of the library at Columbia University were obviously intended for walking up, and though they make for a rather tedious climb they quite obviously serve better for sitting on and having lunch, on a fine day; they are spaces for socializing. Whether this is a social phenomenon that can only happen in dense cities such as New York and San Francisco, I don't know; steps in Houston certainly wouldn't generate this kind of activity. The U.S. inevitably suffers from lateral spread, but then again people like that, don't they? Having spent three years in Texas, I often think of the small Texas town with the courthouse in the square. You never have churches as far as I know—that's a private matter that fits with the U.S. constitution and all. When the courthouse square disappears, I don't see how the *res publica* can survive. If the courthouse were placed outside of town and surrounded by parking, then the idea of law supporting the institutions of society is no longer present.

I'm always impressed by the decorum of the small nineteenth century American town with its Main Street which is a bit rough and then all those elm-lined streets with white-painted houses. I never get tired of looking at them. It's basically a grid with a matrix of trees to hold it together. About 1945 they stopped putting in the trees and the sidewalks and the isolation of each house became absolutely complete. The continuity was destroyed. One is now astonished to learn of the kind of polemic in the 1930s that people waged against the nineteenth century city—how wicked and inhumane it supposedly was, but there were obviously highly successful nineteenth century cities which were evolved.

DBR: Do you think it is a valid point of departure to start with a formal vision? A vision such as Leon Krier's requires the social and economic order to adapt to the formal order.

CR: So what's new? You can take some of the best areas of London, such as Belgravia. These are formal visions that give quality to the city—a lot of other stuff can occur in the interstices of these pieces.

In the case of Belgravia you had a patron who later became the Duke of Westminster and Thomas Cubitt, who developed it, but the idea that formal visions are contrary to the goals of diversity and popular choice I think is an error.

Surely one must say that the classic American suburb, previous to 1945, is one of the great achievements, e.g., Grosse Pointe Farms, Lake Forest in Chicago, Burlingame, etc. It is an outcropping of the English garden city suburb but it exceeds the quality of the latter, just as the American cemetery exceeds the quality of its English predecent. Both in the English cemetery and the English suburb there are little walls thrown around each individual plot, while the classic American suburb depended on the continuous lawn with orderly planting of elms and so on. The objects placed in it were preferably of an eclectic choice, as were the objects in a good cemetery such as Belle Fontaine in St. Louis, where you got little temples, chapels, obelisks, and so on. The romantic suburb belongs mostly to the English-speaking world and parts of Berlin. This model does not extend to Italy or France. The great charm of Florence in the nineteenth century was that the foreigners from the north could live at Fiesole or Bellosguardo in isolation and privacy, but from time to time they could drop in on the concentrated city for lunch or tea or something.

DBR: Camillo Sitte, Hegemann, or the planners of the City Beautiful offered us form, but often they seemed to be avoiding the "ineluctable" (as Corbu would say) technologies that dominated their times; they were resisting technology. Doesn't one find the same fault with Postmodernist schemes, or with Krierstadt?

CR: You take Edward Bennett's plan for Minneapolis of 1927, a lovely publication that merits a reissue, and in this last fling of the City Beautiful they were able to articulate, whereas later in the 1950s and 1960s they began to build inept traffic interchanges and all that spaghetti stuff. The sixties got all of it wrong, but this 1927 plan has it all right; I don't think cars will go away either. I used to think Leon Krier's idea of a William Morris society with architecture in the style of Ledoux was somewhat insane. But his idea for miniaturizing everything and walking to work and face to face confrontation would be a nice idea that you or I might like. Lately his scheme for very small blocks—he illustrated this by taking me to parts of Pimlico where these tiny blocks exist, actually providing more parking space than most contemporary cities.

DBR: But life in mass society seems more complicated than this revived village; agreed, we might prefer the Italian hill town, but I doubt we would find everybody else in agreement to live that way; who could realistically sustain it? It is even more Utopian than Ebenezer Howard thinking that the Garden City could maintain itself when the prototypes quickly became dormitory suburbs. There are larger economic factors that determine the movements of people.

CR: But, of course, there are large economic factors which determine the movements of people. But may it not be possible to guide and, sometimes, to resist these influences? And, as regards building, surely by themselves the larger economic factors can produce very little. For what are the ingredients which they are able to assemble? For the most part we know them. They are, at best, corrupted versions of less than high style Modernism and the most enfeebled recollections of the later eighteenth century. No, the market place of *laissez-faire* economics is very far from being a void innocent of cultural constructions.

Then, I hate to say it and I am dismayed to say it, but I think that the eclipse of the institutions of monarchy and aristocracy may, unfortunately, have a great deal to do with the problems of the present day city. These were institutions which encouraged parade and magnificence, so that, in London, even the Socialist-dominated London County Council was subject, in some of its undertakings, to their influence. And I think of Kingsway from 1907 onwards, no doubt intended to be an 'imperial' thoroughfare and, certainly, a rival of Regent Street. A composite of memories—Paris,

Berlin, Vienna, and traces of Daniel Burnham's Chicago—a pretty gruesome street, it happens to be; but that is scarcely to the point. *Proposed at the very beginning of this century, it is still the last extensive urbanistic performance to be achieved in London.*

But, after 1945, *on a changé tout cela;* one became concerned with *Existenzminimum* for the masses. And, perhaps all well and good. But, maybe, if you are thus concerned, you can never get great things done. Because it was based upon a sublime vision of equality, the Modern movement assumed that you could start at the bottom and then work up; but it might be that things work in reverse order, that they filter down from the top.

Perhaps a horrible idea? But, perhaps just worth a thought?

Alvin Boyarsky: A Memory

In the last very few years I have been called upon to make obituary eulogies for two beloved friends, both younger than myself, whose demise has diminished my life: in the first case Alvin Boyarsky, obit 1991, and in the second case, Jim Stirling, obit 1992.

And I really can say nothing more than this.

The Alvin eulogy was written at the request of his wife, Elizabeth, and his son, Nicholas, but has not, until now, been published. The two Jim pieces related firstly to an occasion in the Guggenheim Museum organized by Peter Eisenman, and, secondly, to a request from AVISA Madrid.

So there is one eulogy for Alvin and two for Jim; but there could be ever so many more.

Bella macchina! Bella macchina! Brava gente! Brava gente!

These words are uttered in Mantova on a Friday evening of early August 1964; and the voice is that of a little old lady, passionately ap-
plauding and patting my beautiful new and green MGB. Alvin is
about to get out, and I am feeling immensely proud. I have just
driven, mostly on side roads, all the way from Arezzo (Alvin has
been extremely patient); and, at a traffic light in Bibbiena a few
hours before, quite accidentally we have encountered Peter and Elis-
abeth Eisenman. They are *freschissimi sposati.* This is their honey-
moon trip; and it is from hence that there ensues a rather protracted
lunch so that we only arrive in Mantova as darkness is about to descend. We are parked facing the side of Alberti's Sant'Andrea; on
our right is a big, high, and empty wall; and, as the old lady continues to applaud and to pat, I think that both of us feel elated. Macho
instincts have been aroused; and, all in all, it is unfortunate that
Tom Schumacher and Alan Chimacoff have not yet composed their
brilliant little song, or I am sure that we would be singing it:

> Way south of Verona;
> Down Mantova way;
> There's a little old building;
> Called Palazzo del Tè;
> Built by Giulio Romano;
> In a Mannerist style;
> Way south of Verona;
> Down Mantova way.

So Verona/Laredo! With the "young cowboy all dressed in
white linen, all dressed in white linen as cold as the grave" it evokes
Texas. Or does it not? But, for me, and more extensively, it recalls
not only Texas but a certain condition of elegant Jewish wit at Cornell, highly intelligent, highly Italianate, and determined to observe things Italian from an American perspective.

However, though all this—in one way or another—connects with Alvin, at that moment he and I were looking for somewhere to eat dinner and spend the night, which we found, as I

expected we would, at Ai Garibaldini (cheap in those days); and then, after that night, we were planning the usual trip to Giulio Romano's beautiful church of San Benedetto south of the river.

I first met Alvin Boyarsky in September 1957. This was in Ithaca, New York, that town, according to Peter Cook, which with its lavish suburban extensions sometimes looks like a rather sinister version of Surrey.

While I had come there to spend a year as visiting critic at Cornell, Alvin was around as a graduate student in the Department of City and Regional Planning. Apart from England (Liverpool, the Warburg Institute, and Liverpool again), I had come from a variety of immediate experiences: from a year at Yale with Henry-Russell Hitchcock, from a protracted grand tour of North America, impoverished, stimulating, and sometimes traumatic; from a dose of Southern California (Bakersfield of all places); from almost three years in Austin, Texas; and from a number of extended trips to Mexico. In other words, in spite of intervening time in Paris/London, I was exhilarated, intoxicated by American topography, by indescribably fragile and delicate little white-painted towns, by mountains, by deserts, by volcanoes, and by the whole spectacle of a nineteenth-century *Volkwanderung.*

So this was me infatuated with North and Central America and wondering whether certain Italian landscapes would ever more please me—and by this I mean the Val d'Orcia, that mini central Texas landscape south of Siena. And, at this time, how was Alvin? Of course he was younger and his experience was less excessive and picaresque than my own. Alvin was from Montreal, McGill, and from some time working in Montreal and London. In any case distinctly more cool than me. We were introduced by Michael McDougall, long since resident in San Francisco, a fairly devout Catholic (I suppose from a background of Portuguese Jesuits), who had come as another city planner from Hong Kong/Macao and from an immediate background of the Architectural Association in London—an altogether charming guy and, in spite of the name, effectively Chinese.

Alvin Boyarsky: A Memory

At Cornell, the three departments of what later came to be called the College of Architecture, Art and City Planning do not normally communicate. The Department of Art is prone to conceive the other two as crudely technocrat, the Department of Planning to regard the architects as relentless idealists, the Department of Architecture to regard the planners as ruthless positivists. Certainly it was like this in the later 1950s, and like this it continues to be—almost a nineteenth-century philosophical debate, except that nobody, apparently, imagines it to be so. And thus it was entirely by accident and by a breach of institutional taboos that I came to know Michael McDougall and Alvin and Elizabeth Boyarsky.

Michael was living in the Heller House, otherwise known as Morbid Manor; and, since it was reserved for graduate students and people like me, this is where I came to know him and this is where he brought around Alvin and Elizabeth one evening—at a time when this house was still intact. It was an interior of the late nineteenth century with a lot of *en suite* rooms, with a grand piano, an organ, and an Errard harp, with fake and not so fake seventeenth-century furniture, Tiffany lamps, and quite good oriental rugs. With dark walls, during the day it was lugubrious; but at night, with the reflection of mirrors, with *amphorae* hanging in elliptical cutouts, with a miscellany of oils of Dutch ecclesiastical interiors (not so bad) and with a fire burning in the small room, it produced a certain subdued brilliance, like a remote and transatlantic descendant of Sir John Soane's Museum.

Anyway, it was in this house that I first met Alvin and Elizabeth; and I have described this Upstate house in such detail because I think that it left an indelible impression on all three of us. However, as it was, we ordered a pizza, ate it by candlelight; and this is the beginning of whatever story I may have to tell. All the same, from this descends so much. This is because Alvin and Elizabeth turned out to be excessive beyond all the standards of the student group with which they were, necessarily, associated. For instance, living in a dreadful prefabricated hut, Cornell's answer to post–Second World War emergency, they gave sumptuous Sunday breakfasts—bloody Marys, bagels and lox, champagne; and then insisted on taking everybody off to attend odd redneck auctions in Owego, Marathon, Connecticut Hill, or wherever else it might be. But as a friend Alvin also derives from other sources; and as a Canadian he was, perhaps, the ultimate member of a distinguished sequence to whom, at a certain stage, I seem to have enjoyed some access. All of them art historians, these included: Alan Jarvis, later director of the National Gallery of Canada; Sydney Key, whom I knew from attending occasional lectures at the Courtauld; and Syd's friend whom I met in Paris and elsewhere, Juan Boggs, also later director of the National Gallery of Canada. As I see it today, it is into a succession of this sort that, not so unconsciously, I must have placed Alvin.

Indeed, I begin to guess that, contrary to all common sense, to the Canadians I had come to attribute a disarming cultural innocence which, no doubt, they found quite intolerable. But all Canadians, all of them, must be like those I had already known. They must all combine perceptiveness, scholarship, and *disinvoltura;* and, with this predisposition, when it came to meeting Alvin I was patently a pushover. Sydney Key, had he lived, would almost certainly have become yet another director of the National Gallery of Canada; and, since I must have placed Alvin in the same league, I shall now risk a minor parenthesis upon Syd. Way back, he and I made a volatile, sometimes difficult, Italian tour. Looking out of the window of the train, he would say, "Hey, Colin, here's another Benozzo Gozzoli goin' along"; and all this without any trace of English superciliousness and affectation. Nice: but, all the same, Syd's taste and mine were scarcely identical. At that time I drooled over Bronzino, Beccafumi, Parmigiano—as I still do—and Syd's taste was quite otherwise. Nothing *maniera* could he enjoy; and, almost typical of my Canadian sequence, he had been brought up, partly at NYU, as a connoisseur of International Gothic—Taddeo Gaddi, Bernardo Daddi, and all those fabricators of *fondi d'oro* who still mean so little to me. And, hence, our rows. First in Florence, where I simply couldn't stand Italian 'primitives' and where Syd went off to tea with Berenson; and, then, in Ravenna, where, in an argument about the two Venetian columns in the marketplace, I was accused of being a devotee both of Ruskin and Adrian Stokes!

A mixed-up mess no doubt; and what has this to do with Alvin? Simply, I suggest that, in terms of my Canadian partiality, I had made a Freudian transference, that I had resurrected a version of Sydney Key, who had died in 1956, as a version of Alvin Boyarsky in 1957. But were my delusions so very offbeat? Had Alvin been an art historian, I am sure that I would have predicted a directorship of the Canadian National Gallery. But a twenty-year tenure as director of the AA—an unheard of period of time, almost like the reigns of Louis XIV, Queen Victoria, and Franz Josef—is this anything so very different?

During the year 1957–1958, I saw him and Elizabeth pretty incessantly. I proposed names for their hypothetical offspring—I thought that Nicholas and Victoria were appropriate and so, when they were born, they became; in a highly informal fashion, in some way I acted as a sort of tutor; and I also proposed to Alvin his thesis topic. It was to be a group of four essays on Camillo Sitte, Patrick Geddes, Ebenezer Howard, and Daniel Burnham, conceived to be stylistically different representatives of a proto-Modern urbanism. But, of this particular quartet, in the end it was only the Camillo Sitte piece which was written for presentation in 1959.

So much, then, for my year at Cornell with Alvin; but, at the end of this time, when I was leaving for Cambridge, England, he performed, so far as I was concerned, a heroic and an excessively charitable act. In one of those Hertz-do-it-yourself mini-trucks, Adventure in Moving, it was probably called, he drove me and my baggages all the way down to the Cunard pier in New York City to put me on the boat for Southampton—considering the condition of the roads in those days a great act of generosity.

After this, though I met Elizabeth in London in 1959, I was not to see Alvin again until 1962, when he erupted into my apartment in Cambridge just at the time when I had firmly decided to quit, just when I had decided that, though bread alone is scarcely sufficient to sustain life, neither is a daily view of King's College Chapel enough to promote adequate intellectual activity. However, during this four-year interval there had occurred a voluminous correspondence (I had no conception of how garrulous I could be until Nicholas Boyarsky showed me my part of it the other day); and it is partly from this correspondence that I shall now make some reconstruction of Alvin in Oregon, which I think must have been the crucial stage of his earlier career.

So what might have been the position at the University of Oregon, in that remote location, Eugene, when Alvin and Elizabeth arrived there in 1959? There was, I believe, the usual faculty ancien régime, defending its tenure and its privilege, and, uneasily related to this, there was a German emigré presence which was still clinging onto an Expressionist message. Then, into this mishmash of no conviction, there had recently penetrated an ex-AA personality, ex-Yale, a former student of Arthur Korn, who was determined to promote the cause of Russian Constructivism—and, probably, much else. This was Peter Land, well-known to me; and, needless to say, Peter had 'done' quite a job!

An improbable appointment it must have been; and, in what was still almost McCarthyite America, one can only attribute it to the negligence or the ignorance of the 'old guard'. Nevertheless, this appointment was made perhaps as a result of the special pleadings of Christopher Tunnard. So let us try to imagine Peter in action in Eugene. Effectively—or ineffectively—he must have radicalized everything he encountered: the residues of the Beaux-Arts, West Coast regionalism (style of John Yeon), and the recently imported Germanic myth that, after all, the redwoods of Oregon and the Black Forest are very much the same.

As we all know, under pressure even the most degraded of academic institutions will display a surprising resilience; and if Peter was obviously too effervescent for any hope of survival in the Oregon of that period, it must soon have been apparent that he should be 'allowed to go'. It was again, I think, Christopher Tunnard who came to the rescue. Peter was offered a job by the State Department! He was to go to Lima, Peru, and he was forewarned that, though he would be sponsoring programs of social amelioration, by no means should he have anything to do with two dangerous subversives down south. These were 'commies'. They were John Turner and Pat Crook. And, again ex-AA and Peter's classmates, they were doing their own private help the Indios, help the Third World 'thing'.

An interesting commentary upon the State Department and some indication of what Alvin must have encountered when he came to Oregon. All the same, whatever crosses he had to bear must have been decidedly alleviated by the arrival of certain persons from Texas. These were, as a teacher, Lee Hodgden; and as students, they included Michael Dennis and Rick McBride, all of them dismayed by their academic experience in Austin and among the earliest representatives of what came to be a remarkable Texas diaspora.

But apart from these stubborn and disaffected Texans, perhaps a little subversive cell in themselves, with Alvin and Lee, just why did the University of Oregon become so suddenly such a focus of brilliance? And what did Alvin and Lee have to say and teach? A bit of De Stijl, a bit of Corbu, a bit of Alvar Aalto? With a bit of Gestalt stuff, this, I think, it must have been; but, then, how could such innocent material have produced the explosive results it did? I confess myself mystified. For, while the Oregon 'thing' was sustained for a period of only three years, what a galaxy of talent emerged from it! Apart from Michael Dennis and Rick McBride, Don Genasci, Roger Sherwood, Fred Koetter, Barry Borak, Terry Williams, Rick Mather, I could add quite a few others who are not personally known to me.

One may easily understand the heroics, the intrigues, the excitements, the spasms of concentration, the extravagance of the esprit de corps which such an occasion must have engendered; but does one also begin to discern the writing on the wall? For knowing the rabidness of academic politics and knowing the lower slopes of the academic Vesuvius where the lava streams so often engulf the junior faculty, must it not now be apparent that Alvin and Lee were, very shortly, to experience a similar fate as not so long ago was suffered by Peter Land? No, Alvin and Lee were to be encouraged not to stay; and it was hence that, resolved on a career in England, Alvin appeared at my apartment in Cambridge in the late spring of 1962.

It was a visit which I knew was imminent; but when it came, it was still surprising. I don't think he had any fantasies about a job at Cambridge which, he must have known, no influence of mine would have been able to sponsor. Simply he wanted to talk; and I don't think I could have given him any very useful advice, for exactly the same reasons that I am unable to speculate about Alvin's English career, which was not easy going to begin with—a period with Richard Llewellyn-Davies, some teaching at the Bartlett and, later, moving on to the AA. Then, it was in my house in Ithaca (was this in 1967?) that he received the news that, thanks to Bill Allan, he had just been fired from the AA and, according to my advice, accepted that quite respectable job at Chicago Circle, in that city which both the Boyarskys came to hate so much. But after this Chicago interlude, when they perversely persisted in living in a very wrong part of town, and after Alvin's return to Bedford Square and his progressive escalation as an impresario of architectural pedagogics, fundamentally I am too ignorant to know of anything not known to the world in general.

All this scribbling about Alvin has caused me to become aware that my own criteria of recollection are those of a camera rather than of a tape recorder, that I respond mostly to things seen and not so much to things heard. Invariably I recall my very best friends in relation to a landscape, a townscape, an interior, or a table. And so it remains with Alvin. I have extremely vivid mental pictures of him in Skaneateles, N.Y., in Chambéry, at Stupinigi, at Vallinotto, at Caprarola, obviously in Mantova, and at the Cipriani in Asolo.

So my pictures are all early, pictures of a highly intense and engaging Jewish guy making all those characteristic Jewish gestures, the explanatory spreading of the hands, that *I-don't-know, don't-ask-me* shrugging of the shoulder which I have always so much appreciated. But, perhaps, my most perfect picture of Alvin is crossing the Channel on the occasion of the Italian trip, when the following conversation takes place:

Colin: And, Alvin, where do you suppose we shall have our row?

Alvin: Our row? [And there follow a lot of Jewish gestures.] But why should we have a row?

Colin: But, Alvin, I am quite sure that we shall have a row in Ravenna.

And so it was; and so it is that since that day, I have tried never to return to Ravenna and its horrid, shameless oil refineries. But, dearest Alvin, a total charmboat, could from time to time become extremely trying; I am reminded of an evening with him and Dominic Michaelis in 1967. There had been little to drink; but Alvin had become increasingly voluble and had subjected Dominic to a harangue on what he supposed to be his playboy propensities.

So Dominic, when I meet him next day, shrugs his shoulders—almost like Alvin himself—delivers me a *je ne sais quoi* look, and says to me: "ALVEEN this morning, I had too much BOYAR-SKY last night."

Eulogy: Jim Stirling

I was talking with Jim Stirling's mother one night, and she said to me that it was perfectly understandable why Jim was so fascinated with New York. "You see if he wasn't born in New York, at least he was conceived there. And isn't that perhaps the next best thing?" He was conceived, so she said, in a boat off the old Cunard Pier at the end of West 46th Street.

Amusing information: I introduce it as relevant entertainment because it might help to make this particular occasion locally appropriate. But also for another reason.

Jim loathed, as do I, the sanctimonious soft voice, the agonizing verbal massage which is apt to be the predominant tone of obituary eulogia. "He didn't pass away, he didn't pass on. He croaked. And why don't they say it?" He had a Churchillian vehemence about pietistic evasiveness; and I share with him an impatience about the whole sentiment of grief, often a spurious and nearly always a self-indulgent emotion.

So someone has died—kinda tough because you had wanted to say something to them; and now all possibility of communication is forever extinguished. Simply *they* are no longer *there;* in other words, we are denied our pleasure. If this was a predicament which prostrated so many nineteenth-century persons (Tennyson et al.), we had imagined that ourselves (with a twentieth-century sang-froid) might have been able to absorb the situation with comparative ease. But it is not so; and whatever casualness I might attempt to assume, for me death remains a very terrible thing, and over the last few weeks (and apropos of Jim) it has remained constantly in my mind.

This is because Jim was almost my oldest friend, and because for the rest of my life I know that every day I shall be compelled to think or to speak about him.

I first met Jim at the beginning of December 1942 (it now seems to have been an obscenely long time ago) and the place of our meeting was in Scotland at Queen's Barracks, Perth—or rather in a nineteenth-century weaving shed immediately adjacent to it. This was a huge space in which we were all obliged to sleep. About 700 feet long, as I have said about it elsewhere, it might well have been erected in order to demonstrate both the curvature of the earth and the implacable laws of perspective. It was also a space with its own disgusting mini-climate and a propensity to local fogs. It was a strange and unforgettable setting for a first encounter, and it seemed to me a Kafka-like career, a wholly inexplicable destiny to which Jim had been consigned. He was no more than the sweeper up of the floor, and this almost amounted to a labor of Hercules. Beginning almost at first light, he would sweep and sweep, and so protracted was the job that it was scarcely possible for him to approach us (we being Bill Kidd, Denis Owtram, and myself) until the late afternoon when it was almost time for our occasional escape to the Station Hotel, its Gothic corridors lined with vitrines enclosing the amassed displays of Queen Victoria's breakfast service.

Retrospectively (again I semi-quote myself), it was all a bit like an inferior version of Proust's account of the life of St. Loup at Doncières—and all of us knew it. Then, even the hotel itself seemed to belong to a quasi-Proustian category. It was a traditional stop for Victoria en route from Windsor to Balmoral; and there was the charming old waiter. "Oh it's nothing now, sir, but you should see it in the summer, sir. Oh, gentlemen, it's just lovely in the summer." And then there was the room into which he showed us, a Gothic job with a blazing fire and huge hammerbeam roof, and the food which he served—trout, salmon, pheasant, venison, the abundance of Scotland, all of it unrationed and all of it the complete opposite of the weaving shed.

Now, it is for such highly personal reasons as these, the very particular origin of our relationship, that I am unable to think about Jim's architecture very clearly. There is simply too much else which intervenes, including my second exposure to himself. This occurred a little later in Mount Pleasant, Liverpool, when a military apparition came up the hill. Whether it was Black Watch or Argyll and Sutherland I didn't really know; but the profusion and the jingle-jangle with which it was draped was not without a distinct *terribilità*. It was Jim as a sort of military Christmas tree that I was looking at. There was the kilt, the sporran, the skene-dhu, all those pseudo-traditional assists to Scottish machismo, the epaulets and the red beret. All of it was an extreme exhibition of costume jewelry at its most belligerent. And then there was the huge and intimidating mustachio, sparing neither public sentiment nor private expense. Dearest Jim in perhaps his most aggressive phase.

Following this vision, probably in 1944, Jim disappears from my life for quite a time, not to float back into it again until 1949, when I—for some reason or other—had begun to teach at Liverpool and was simultaneously supervising two theses, his own and Robert Maxwell's—an experience from which I learned very much, mostly by way of the contrast between Jim's bravura and Robert's more alembicated fastidiousness. And it was all pretty tempestuous, with Jim standing at the bottom of the stairs and, to the horror of the respectable, positively bellowing for critical attention: "Hey, Rowe, where in Ke-rist's name are YOU?"

Eulogy: Jim Stirling

At this time Jim had just returned from a period in New York where he had lived at International House on Riverside Drive, up near Grant's Tomb, and he was raving about largeness of scale, about Fifth Avenue along Central Park and Eldorado Towers and the Palisades from Riverside Drive and the George Washington Bridge and, what is surprising in that day, the Chrysler Building. But I seem to remember that he was the reverse of crazy about Aalto at MIT.

In any case, something like these were the prevailing images which he advertised, and for me they were extremely interesting. You see, I was led to receive the surely quite erroneous impression that Jim had learned to be simple and easy in New York. At the same time (and so we argued, Jim and Robert and myself), are not the English madly concerned with a suffocating accumulation of visual detail? True. Or don't you think so? But doesn't the evidence of your eyes compel you to think so? In any case, it was the example of Jim that obliged me to come to the United States, where I have spent the greater part of my adult life and where (among the rednecks and the noble savages) I have never been able to find the simplicity for which I was looking.

Beyond the shortest trips—London to Oxford, New Haven to Providence—I never traveled with Jim; but since we shared the same tastes in landscape, I would have greatly enjoyed doing so. For instance, to show him a great American river, I always wanted to drive him down the Susquehanna from Owego to points south; and next year [1993] I had been planning that we should drive down the Adriatic coast of Italy—Osimo, Recanati, Macerata, Ascoli, Trani, Martina Franca, etc.; but, now I fall back upon an excursion which we both made to Paris in 1959.

As I recall we stayed at the Hôtel des Saints-Pères and it was nearby at the Café de Flore that we had arranged to meet David Crowe, who was from our period at Liverpool and had been working for the last eight years in Paris. This was in that phase of Jim's evolution when he was prone to think about Le Corbusier's Maisons Jaoul as almost a revelation from on high. And David said: "Oh,

Jim, you just mustn't rave about the Maisons Jaoul. They are just
not that good, you know. But we can go just around the corner into
the Rue St.-Guillaume and see the glass house which Pierre Chareau did for Dr. Dalsace, almost thirty years ago." Which, accordingly, we did. And Dr. Dalsace, who knew David's uncle, was
charming to us, and Jim went around taking a lot of pictures. And
David said: "Look, Jim, don't go around showing these pictures to
that architectural demimonde which you frequent in London because this is too good for those people."

(But of course Jim did show them; and it was thus there ensued that London *culte* of Pierre Chareau and the Maison de Verre,
which curators of the Centre Pompidou seem to find precocious and
inexplicable and have lately been calling me to ask why and how.)
But this parenthesis anticipates the rest of the story: when we left
the house we took a taxi from St.-Germain des Prés to the Pont de
Neuilly in order to see, in quick succession and to Jim's chagrin,
old-time Pierre Chareau and the latest Corbu.

Probably this was a genuinely important occasion. However, I have mental pictures of Jim in so many other places: in
Venice in the Palazzo Mocenigo at a *ricevimento* given by Vittorio
Gregotti where, sitting next to me, he broke a chair and, in order to
disguise what he had done, tried to remain sitting on it; in Rome at
the Palazzo Taverna at a party for the exhibition "Roma Interrotta";
at Leicester, where he took a fiendish delight in the howlings and
whinings which the wind produced around the spiral stairs and an
even more appalling delight in the reactions of persons on a conducted tour who were pretending not to notice; outside Stuttgart at
Ludwigsburg and Schloss Solitude; and, very significantly, at Has-
lemere where he had gone to look at the Olivetti building. For Has-
lemere was a beautiful case of Jim at his most mischievous.

In a highly proprietary way, rather as though it were a pet
kitten, he had paraded Olivetti; and now it was time for lunch. It
was lunch in a pub, that dreadful, dreary meal, beloved of so many,
which myself detests. And also present were John Miller and Patrick Hodgkinson, when, quite suddenly, I experienced an invincible

need to relieve my bladder. So, to all of them, I said, "Where do I go?" And Jim pointed to a door. And I said, "But it says 'ladies.'" And Jim said, "No matter, no matter. In this country we don't recognize such distinctions anymore. We think that they are completely obsolete." And, while I was still in doubt, there followed what in opera would be an *aria di confusione,* and it must have been provided mostly by Patrick and John: "Oh, you are so retarded, you are so provincial, you have the strangest of American ideas, don't be silly, here we are emancipated and you are still the victim of the most ludicrous repression, go in, go in, go in!"

So grab the scene. I succumbed to the pressure and, still doubting what I was told, I went in, with the horrendous, disastrous results which might have been expected. And then, coming out very, very quickly, I emerged to face the derision rather than the acclamation of the chorus.

To underscore what I have already intimated, dearest Jim, whom I knew in such ways as these, is not exactly a possible subject for morphological analysis on my part; and, as Michael Wilford has observed, he was apparently determined to keep his architecture, or his conceptual struggles, very conspicuously private. The office was the office, and life at home was something very different indeed. So much so, for instance, that my first meeting with Michael did not take place until I was introduced on the Rice University campus in Houston, Texas. But this apart, though I have been delighted by so many of his buildings, I find myself inhibited from talking about them. Could this be because I find myself scarcely possessed of the intellectual *chic* to cope with the choicest of recent critical confections from Paris and Frankfurt which are, to me, so hopelessly arcane?

In other words, I can only continue to be painfully empirical and personal; and, without the benefit of any comprehensive critical and theoretical approach, in effect this means that now I must direct attention to Jim as the collector and the connoisseur, the person whom—in the end—I best knew.

Frequenter of auction rooms where he bought perceptively, paid low, and, since he was not adverse to trade, often sold high. But this is to move too quickly, and one should first direct attention to the lavishness and the largesse, the magnificence and the overwhelming generosity of his domestic arena.

I was privileged to watch this house in Belsize Avenue, not wholly prepossessing, grow from the time he bought it (in 1966?) for rather more than twenty-five years, all the while with the envy that Jim perfectly well knew it would inspire in me. In the beginning it was rather blandly mod. There was the Corbu stuff and the Breuer stuff and the Aalto stuff; but before long, all these pieces had been retired to the wall and the house had become something like a battlefield. Georges Jacob, Thomas Hope, George Bullock, George Smith, and other eminent neo-Classical designers of furniture had come to occupy center floor, and all this was surrounded by glitter, glitter, glitter, by Paris and Berlin porcelain, by Louis Comfort Tiffany, by René Lalique, Waterford, and Baccarat, with candelabra by Thomire upon the dining table, with bits of Puginian Gothic, and whatever else. But after all this laundry list, it must be insisted that everything was monumentally grand and immensely superior; and Jim, like the curator of his own museum, felt incredibly happy within it.

A compulsive collector, he could not let a week go by without buying all sorts of things; and, to a certain extent our judgments concurred. Jim's *château idéal* would, I suppose, have been an Empire villa to which a large Art Nouveau conservatory had been attached. And my own idea was always a small, rather dilapidated sixteenth-century palazzo to which had been added an Empire library. So, on the Empire component we were in complete agreement; and, as do I, Jim liked Schinkel furniture. From time to time, Jim would say, "Got to take you around the junk shops," which meant going to Malletts and Carleton Hobbs and Geoffrey Bennison and all the best shops in London, where a characteristic interchange might be something like this: "Got anything for me today?"; with, on one occasion, the reply: "Well, today I don't think we have anything quite heavy enough for you, Mr. Stirling"; with, as we are about to leave, the further declaration from Jim: "Too much Louis Seize. Too much Louis Seize."

I once spent a week at Belsize Avenue. This must have been in 1978, when Mary and the family were in Normandy. About midday we would go look at antique shops and auction rooms and then, in the evening, we would look over picture books, always furniture picture books. In the morning he would wake me in the most absolutely startling way. He would come into my room at 7:30 with a large glass of what looked like water but which, obviously, was not water, and he would say: "Calvados, it's good for you." Part of his own preparation for Normandy this surely must have been!

About furniture, though I often tried to explain to him that in Upstate New York one could scarcely spend that much money on furniture, Jim remained unconvinced and frequently accused me of unwillingness to buy what he thought I ought to. He was very willing to admit an influence from me in the early formation of his collection (it was a couple of neo-Classical chairs that did it); but before very long, this influence was reversed. However, I know that he remained disappointed with my failure to follow his example. I was almost okay as regards silver; quite good as regards books and engravings; but as for what auction houses call objects of *vertu,* I was sadly deficient. And in this context I am reminded of a conversation which took place only a few months ago. My nephew James Rowe is at Belsize Avenue surrounded by all those trophies of *Existenzmaximum,* the latest of which are a very nice couple of French clocks—Louis Seize as a matter of fact—with superb mechanisms which, patently, are not in working order. So James Rowe says to Jim (rather peremptorily I can't help thinking): "How much did you pay for these clocks?" And what I imagine to be a rather sad and disgruntled Jim replied: "Let me tell you. A lot more than your bloody uncle would be prepared to pay."

I have often wondered why my very dear friend had so little success in England. Was it because in a left-wing profession he was emphatically not left-wing? Was it because he completely disre-

garded the entrenched English tendency to accentuate and embroi-
der every episode and every detail? Could it have been that, for a so-
called Modern architect, he was so guilt-free and without shame?
Could it have been because the English of a certain generation
are still fighting the Spanish Civil War and, in consequence, feel
obliged to wear sackcloth and ashes? Or could it have been the heroic opulence of his general *train de vie,* which even Arthur Drexler
found to be unexpected and astounding?

No doubt all of these questions may be answered in the affirmative; but I produce them in order to make a point: that Jim
the collector must be envisaged quite as seriously as Jim the architect; that his private museum must be regarded as the strict analogue of his more celebrated architectural career.

The last time I spoke to Jim was less than a week before his
fatal operation. I called him up in Berlin. Almost the day before he
had become Sir James Stirling, and to congratulate him, I used a
voice that involved commiseration: "Oh, dear Jim." I knew the ways
in which he could be embarrassed, and I got a slightly malicious
pleasure out of it; but Jim rallied in the most delightful way:
"Well, yeah, it's one of the geegaws, isn't it, from Buckingham Palace and that sort of thing. But, you know, in the end I accepted it
because I thought it might be good for the office in places like Aus-
tralia and Canada."

Although it may sound a little bit sneaky on my part, I
should also say that Jim dissimulated his age. It was Henry-Russell
Hitchcock who once told me that Frank Lloyd Wright had dissimulated his age by three years; and I believe that with Giulio Romano
there may have been a six-year gap somewhere. However, though
Jim was not quite so extreme, he certainly did get away with two
years. Otherwise there is no way of explaining his army career, in
which he fought in Normandy at age eighteen, after having gone
into the Black Watch, received a commission in the Black Watch,
and then gone into paratroops. Simply, the chronology does not fit;
and although—within the bounds of plausibility—everyone may
have the right to be any age that they might wish, it is strange that

Eulogy: Jim Stirling

none of the Stirling obituarists, some of them so highly picayune, seem to have been able to notice this mildly glaring discrepancy.

Now, to me, it is such a grief that one can't read these obituaries to Jim, because I can hear his reactions. He would have been exhilarated, stimulated, outraged; and, if the lousier obituaries were sometimes so vicious and mean spirited, I don't think he would have felt damaged. They were too grotesque: "So that's what those little horrors have been thinking about me, isn't it? And for all those years!"

But by the obituary published in the *Times* (of London), he would have been extremely charmed and diverted. This because the *Times,* allegedly quoting Jim, put words into his mouth; with a bizarre seriousness, it presumed him to have said something like the following, that after "Colin Rowe's *Towards a New Architecture,* the book which most influenced him was Saxl and Wittkower's pictorial survey *British Art and the Mediterranean.*"

To no avail I wrote to the *Times* to disclaim responsibility and to protest their error; but I can both see Jim's charming smile and hear his obstreperous amusement about their mistake: "So it was you, was it, and when you were less than three years old, who ghostwrote that book for Le Corbu? Well, I always had my suspicions. But goddamit, you bastard, why did you never tell me?"

To conclude—or to begin to conclude: I have deliberately attempted to avoid any sentimental adulation of my subject. This because I knew Jim too long and too well, which makes any such approach impossible for me, and also because I know that he would have been utterly revolted by any such performance on my part. Also, I have refrained from any invocation of Jim's architectural career, partly because I presume my disability and, more so, because I don't see how it can be done without visuals and without breaching the purely temporal constraints of such a meeting as this must be. Nor, like Lytton Strachey in his biography of Queen Victoria, have I set out deliberately to disparage my subject. (Although why Strachey felt compelled to cut down Victoria to her very small physical size one can well understand.) The other day, reading about Henry

V, king of England, who died in 1422, I discovered a typical nineteenth-century panegyric which I would have loved to read to Jim. It is Bishop Stubbs's eulogium upon the king: "He was religious, pure in life, temperate, liberal, careful and yet splendid, merciful, truthful, and honourable, discreet in word, provident in counsel, prudent in judgement, modest in look, magnanimous in act, a true Englishman."

Of course, an outrageous, monstrously chauvinist, and willfully romantic statement this is; and, quite properly, the French would never concur. But though Henry V (Agincourt, Shakespeare, the speech at Harfleur, Laurence Olivier, and trips to the Old Vic), though something of a monster, is by way of being a major English hero (after all, he died at almost the same age as Mozart), I can still hear what might have been Jim's reaction to this particular piece of wild hyperbole.

Yes, Jim was brash, gentle, generous, modest, immoderate, splendid, candid, truculent, and talented to excess; but he was no composite of all the Victorian virtues and he would have hated his attributes, positive or negative, to be called out in the manner of Bishop Stubbs—and particularly so since Bishop Stubbs would scarcely have conceived of talent as any virtue which might ever be possessed by "a true Englishman"—"Oh dear no, let's just bumble along and play football."

For his own eulogium upon Stirling in London I am told that Mark Girouard fell back upon what Samuel Johnson had to say about the death of his actor friend David Garrick. Dr. Johnson said that it had "extinguished the gaiety of nations." Exaggerated? But might one apply something like this to Jim? To an extent, I suppose, yes. For the extinction of what has been a fountain of originality, of a complete independence of mind, of an architectural *seriosità* embedded in a wild context of architectural *scherzi* has surely eliminated something very supremely important, a personage to be ranked in the very short list of great English architects, probably to be ranked alongside Hawksmoor, Soane, and Butterfield.

Eulogy: Jim Stirling

But for me, when I think of the death of my friend, and when I contemplate that domestic environment which he so much loved, I can only recall the opening lines of an early edition of Mario Praz's *History of Furnishing*—and he might not only be writing about Jim but also about Thomas Hope or Sir John Soane: "The surroundings become a museum of the soul, an archive of experiences . . . the resonance chamber where [the] strings render their authentic vibration."

And then, even more personally, I can only repeat to myself those lines of Wordsworth from that sonnet, "Desideria," related to the death of a daughter:

> Surprised by joy, impatient as the wind,
> I turned to share my transport, oh with whom
> But thou, long buried in the silent tomb
> That spot which no vicissitude can find.

Jim Stirling (1923–1992)

In England there is no Escorial. There is nothing of such austerity and such rigor. Overwhelming greenness—all those lawns and all those trees—may be scarcely compatible with any display of relentless grandeur; and this is, perhaps, why the late James Stirling (whose pursuit of grandeur was far from excessive) obtained so little work in the country of his domicile.

Bernard Berenson somewhere pronounced that English art has always displayed a tendency to ooze prettiness; and, although this characteristic demureness—Salisbury vs. Orvieto—may often be a virtue and many persons have found it to be so, for others (Matthew Arnold's born lovers of the idea, born haters of the commonplace?), it will certainly come to resemble a stifling cocoon. They want none of it, or little more than the very minimum; and it is no doubt that which Arnold designated as this remnant of English culture which, in a wider and different context, may serve as a partial explanation of both the Declaration of Independence and the existence of the former British Empire. Indeed one can almost hear the clamor for escape voiced by colonialists and imperialists alike. "Don't fence me in" with all those interminable hedges, is what one hears them say; if not Italy, then at least "give me the wide open spaces" of the unknown.

And then, what about *Albion perfide?* And did the French get it right? Or did they get it wrong? Wrong, I think, as regards politics, where—in spite of their many errors of judgement—the English have rarely been malevolent and never possessed that capacity for secrecy which makes conspiracy possible. But about English architecture? And had the French not disdained to direct their attention towards it, they might have discovered a highly rewarding argument. For, as regards architecture, the English—often believing themselves to be so concerned with 'fair play'—seem, almost congenitally, to have been unable to comprehend the rules of *any* game which might *ever* have been imagined. But yes. For, again and again, there seems to have been displayed a willingness to change *every* rule well before *any* game is completed. Let us have no use for undue cerebrality, so declares the alternative version of *la voix d'Angleterre;* and it will be well to listen to it. "We are reasonable empiricists are we not? And if we begin our game as though we were playing football and continue it as though we were playing chess should there be any reason for serious dismay? But are we not captivating and can you not be sure that our results will be ingratiating and charming?" But surely in architecture at least, this almost sublime disregard for any traces of intellectual consistency—and this is London—had the French been able to discern it, had been *le vrai Albion perfide.*

Now Jim was conceived in New York, born in Glasgow (two years before he was willing to admit it), brought up in Liverpool, and didn't arrive in London until he was about twenty-six years old. Then, in his early formation, apart from being a devotee of Le Corbusier, he was a militarist and chauvinist, aboriginally 'British' (attenuated physique and a huge mustachio at this period), sceptical, abrasive, and never completely at ease with the more 'English' presumptions of London. In short, he was almost the provincial hero arrived in the great city from a novel by Stendhal or Balzac—a predicament which can only be French or English, in the end the only two countries where one city supremely prevails.

And did Jim despise London? I scarcely think so, though I have tried to indicate ample reasons for such a possible response. Rather, I can only suggest that my highly talented friend (at that time more talented than capable?) was largely unaware of the intrinsic difficulties which in England must lie ahead for someone of his particular temperament, difficulties of socio-aesthetic consensus which, later, he came to detest.

However, all of this is a very long time ago; and, in a few words, what else to say?

That Stirling, a fountain of originality, breeched the normally garrulous operations of English architecture? That he belongs to the very few who have done so? That these might be: Vanbrugh, Hawksmoor, the icily Scottish Robert Adam (apex of the Edinburgh enlightenment), possibly George Dance, certainly John Soane, and, after him, the fastidious and Frenchified Cockerell and the Gothic Revival tough guy, Butterfield?

But, of course, there is no doubt that Jim belongs to this company who, all of them, must have found the allegedly supreme English architect, Christopher Wren, more than a bit hard to take, a climax of English non sequiturs. "But, isn't it heartrending" (this is Jim on St. Paul's Cathedral), "a very great dome; but, down below and inside out, doesn't it look as though he were a pastry cook determined to use every piece of leftover dough?"

The time was July 1959 and we had just returned from a short trip to Paris where, in quick succession, we had seen Pierre Chareau's Maison de Verre and Le Corbusier's Maisons Jaoul and where Jim's normal astringency had become exacerbated by an inspection of the Val-de-Grace which, back in London, lead to the inevitable comparison of François Mansart's wholly unitary conception with Wren's curiously addictive accumulation of incongruities. And this is to insist upon Jim as an architectural connoisseur.

Jim Stirling (1923–1992)

He knew where all the bits and pieces of St. Paul's had come from: for the west front a combination of the east facade of the Louvre and Sant'Agnese in Piazza Navona; Pietro da Cortona's semi-circular portico of Santa Maria della Pace for the transepts; and for the less eminent areas, the facade from Palazzo Thiene in Vicenza and a casual quote, a false perspective window from the Palazzo Barberini. And he was prone to be appalled by popular taste which acclaims this strangely incompatible, and highly literal, collection. "No, No, never Wren. Just Hawksmoor all the way."

I think that as he grew older, Jim's estrangement from what seem to be the endemic propensities of English architecture, particularly that tendency to articulate and to multiply parts, became all that more profound; and, no doubt, to this one may attribute his growing celebrity in foreign societies—Germany, the United States, Italy—where the standards of Englishness are, possibly, seen less as a norm than as an aberration. And, if you add to this a distress related to what he perceived to be English deterioration, then the increasing forays of Jim into the auction rooms are abundantly explained. He bought what he genuinely admired and he bought obsessively; but was not this delirium of acquisition at least partially a compensation for all those buildings which in the United Kingdom never came his way?

As an architect so he was as a collector. He was addicted to almost everything glittering, and shiny, well made and classically big. At the scale of the *objets* this might mean René Lalique, Louis Comfort Tiffany, post-Napoleonic Paris porcelain, the best of English silver and candelabra by Thomire. But the whole scene was pretty august; and then, alongside this, there was his further passion for the most monumental and the most heavy of Empire and Regency furniture—Georges Jacob, Thomas Hope, George Bullock, George Smith—and it was this brilliant amalgam which came to comprise his own personal theater and museum. With its massive and primarily Empire component and with its many local suggestions of Art Nouveau, one might understand this particular domestic arena to have come into existence as an act of justification, as an *apologia pro vita sua,* as a private analogue for the grand public performance which, in England, was never to be made.

And about Stirling's later buildings?

I have not seen the Wissenschaftzentrum in Berlin, though I greatly admire its accomplished and evocative distributions; and, then, there are the three American buildings.

At Harvard, the Sackler building has made a great bridge between the Fogg Museum and Gund Hall; and, with its representative facade—a vertical presence, and its broad stripes behind—a horizontal support accommodating an eccentric fenestration, it has still barely received the acclaim which it deserves.

At Rice, in that quasi-Byzantine milieu, the extensions to the architecture building are so unassertive that it becomes not easy to discover them.

At Cornell, the Performing Arts Center, the best recent building on the campus, should—perhaps—still be a little better than it is. A very pretty horseshoe theater, based upon the Cuvilliés theater in the Munich Residenz; a very pretty peristyle which owes more than a little to Leon Krier; a great site; potentially a spectacular view; however, a view which remains fatally blocked by a few unimportant, though sacrosanct, trees. Wretched trees! But, short of poisoning them (during the hours of darkness?), there remains nothing to be done.

And, then, the Germanic lands!

So what did Jim find in Germany and what did Germany find in Jim? And I can only confess that I don't know. But, apparently, with German clients he could be completely himself. Apparently they accepted his physical and intellectual largesse, his triumphant magnanimity, in a way the English, inhibitions aroused, could scarcely understand.

But, all the same, just why was the land of Baden-Württemburg so very grand? And just how did so many politicians suspend their disbelief?

Jim insisted that I accompany him to Stuttgart when the Staatsgalerie was still under construction; and I have since been back three times, the last time when Jim was also present and we drove out to Ludwigsburg and up to Schloss Solitude. And, finally, I can only comment upon Stuttgart as a version of the sublime. A work of genius, it has become a memorial to genius, almost like something which ought to belong to the Germanic lands in the age of *Sturm und Drang;* and now, having seen it on four occasions, I can only add that there is no recent building which has so overwhelmed and consumed me since I visited Le Corbusier's La Tourette in 1960 and 1961.

But the Staatsgalerie transcends all of the plausible categories of criticism. It is what it is. It is something beyond dispute; and it is for this reason that I want there to see the ashes of my friend deposited. There is that little semi-crypt which one approaches down a few steps just to the left as one enters the circular courtyard—an episode which still requires explanation; and surely, it is there that one might find a plinth, empty of all inscription and a Roman cinerary—for Jim.

A Postscript on Alvin and Jim

As a conclusion, to the problem of obituary eulogy there is prone to be a sickeningly glucose dimension attached. It is present, at its most revolting, in those lines written about the dead of the First World War:

> *They shall not grow old as we that are left grow old.*
> *Age shall not weary them, nor the years condemn*
> *At the going down of the sun and in the morning*
> *We shall remember them.*

Healing words? Or odious and sanctimonious stuff? But whose was the responsibility? And, not being able to answer the question, I can only indulge myself in a pseudo-obituary from Auden's *The Dog Beneath the Skin* of 1935, a performance which intimates the more than salutary virtues of a true modernity.

He cannot calculate nor dread
The mortifying in the bed,
Powers wasting day by day
While the courage ebbs away.
Ever charming, he will miss
The insulting paralysis,
Ruined intellect's confusion,
Ulcer's patient persecution,
Sciatica's intolerance
And the cancer's sly advance:
Never hear among the dead
The rival's brilliant paper read,
Colleague's deprecating cough
And the praises falling off:
Never know how in the best
Passion loses interest;
Beauty sliding from the bone
Leaves the rigid skeleton.

A *danse macabre* of the twentieth century, with its final exhibition of basic structure—the skeleton's rigidity—this could well
be an epitaph for so much and so many. I remember that both Alvin
and Jim did know these lines. They were of the generation which
had been brought up on W. H. Auden at his most savage.

And, otherwise, what may I say but *almost?* Almost himself
began his career as a student of mine—almost but not quite; and
almost myself will close my career as a student of his—again almost
but not quite. And meanwhile, there remains that brilliance, that
intransigence, that ongoing argument, lots of things looked at together and a ceaseless hospitality such as elsewhere I have never experienced and cannot hope to enjoy again.

Index of Names

Aalto, Alvar, 324, 344
Adam, Robert, 291, 355
Albers, Josef, 24
Albert of Saxe-Coburg-Gotha, Prince, 238
Alberti, Leone Battista, 165, 231
Albright-Knox Art Gallery, 97, 100
Alexandria, 301–317
Allan, Bill, 339
Alphand, Adolphe, 210
Anker, Andrew, 121
Archigram Group, 2
Architettura razionale, 265, 268, 273, 275–276
Arendt, Hannah, 243–245
Arikoglu, Kaya, 32–34
Arnold, Matthew, 353
Auden, W. H., 359–360

Bächer, Max, 221
Baedeker, Karl, 17, 286
Baiter, Richard, 97
Baltimore, 32–34
Baudelaire, Charles, 166
Bell, Matthew, 63, 75, 79, 155, 314
Bellazoug, Myriam, 314
Benevolo, Leonardo, 184
Bennett, Edward, 327
Berdini, Paolo, 57, 60–62, 155
Berenson, Bernard, 219–220, 336, 353
Berlin, 124, 186–187, 188–189, 221–260, 320, 324
Betjeman, John, 166
Binghamton, 6–7
Bofill, Ricardo
    Antigone Project (Montpellier), 320–322

Boggs, Juan, 335
Bohigas, Oriol, 249
Borak, Barry, 338
Bostick, Joel, 47, 48
Boston, 62–67
Boyarsky, Alvin, 331–340, 360
Boyarsky, Elizabeth, 334–335, 336
Bryant, Douglas, 34, 35
Buege, David, 121
Buffalo, 11, 97–119
Burlington, Vermont, 49, 51–55
Burnham, Daniel, 329
Burton, Decimus, 175
Butterfield, William, 351, 355
Byron, George Gordon, Lord, 285–286

Cambridge, Massachusetts, 34–37
Canaletto, Giovanni Antonio, 199,
    200, 297
Candilis, Josic and Woods, 191, 192
Cardwell, Richard, 97
Carl, Peter, 129
Carvalho, Raul de, 222, 253–260
Chan, David, 97
Chareau, Pierre, 345, 355
Charlotte, 286
Chiattone, Mario, 293, 295
Chicago, 81, 84–86
Chimacoff, Alan, 3, 332
Cincinnati, 286
Ciucci, Giorgio, 163
Claire Obscure, 249
Claude Lorrain, 62, 272, 276
Cockerell, Charles Robert, 355
Cohen, Stuart, 2
Congrès Internationaux d'Architecture
    Moderne (CIAM), 264, 269
Cook, Peter, 333
Copper, Wayne, 2, 17–24, 97
Cornell University, 334
    Urban Design Studio, 1–86, 97

Crook, Pat, 338
Crowe, David, 344–345
Cubism, 2
Cubitt, Thomas, 327

Dance, George, 355
De Carlo, Giancarlo, 210
De Chirico, Giorgio, 276
Dennis, Michael, 3, 338
DiMaio, Judith, 121, 129, 314–317
Dimitriu, Livio, 121
Doesburg, Theo van, 181, 183, 216,
    218
Drexler, Arthur, 87, 88, 349
Düsseldorf, 21

Eckbo, Garrett, 49
Edinburgh, 322, 323
Eesteren, Cornelis van, 186, 188
Eisenman, Peter, 87–88, 249, 332
Ellicott, Joseph, 102, 103, 105
Engel, Jaap, 221
Evans, Sir Arthur, 268

Fielding's guides, 286
Florence, 63, 68–75, 234, 324, 327
    Corridoio Vasariano, 288, 289
Fong, Steven, 40–42
Forusz, Harris, 97
Fredericks, Douglas, 48, 260
Furnham, Daniel, 49
Futurism, 156, 162, 292–293

Gehrman, Manfred, 221
Genasci, Don, 338
Gestalt psychology, 24, 245
Giedion, Sigfried, 264
Gilbert, W. S., 263
Gilliland, Sally, 314
Girouard, Mark, 351
Giurgola, Romaldo, 263

Goerner, Werner, 222–223
Goodill, Robert, 75, 80, 155
Graves, Charles, 34
Graves, Michael, 88, 275
Gréber, Jacques, 171
Gregotti, Vittorio, 221, 345
Griffin, David, 34, 36
Gropius, Walter, 264, 322

Hartley, John, 121
Harvey, Sophie, 314
Haussmann, Georges, 210, 253
Hawksmoor, Nicholas, 351, 355
Hegemann, Werner, 171
Herdeg, Klaus, 3
Hilberseimer, Ludwig, 2, 150, 186–
    187, 188, 208, 209, 246, 324
Hildebrand, Adolf von, 220
Hinders, Kevin, 155
Hitchcock, Henry-Russell, 349
Hitler, Adolf, 253
Hodgden, Lee, 48, 49, 338
Hofman, Thomas, 63
Hope, Thomas, 352
Hord, Carter, 63, 81, 82–83
Houston, 8–10
Howard, Ebenezer, 328
Hurtt, Steven, 4, 14, 24

Ingersoll, Richard, 319
Internationale Bauausstellung, Berlin,
    14, 221–242, 320
Itten, Johannes, 24

Jahn, Edward, 221
Jarvis, Alan, 335
Jefferson, Thomas, 57, 262, 281
Jellicoe, Geoffrey, 213
Johnson, Samuel, 250, 313, 351

Kahn, Louis, 90, 123, 232
    Jewish Community Center (Tren-
    ton), Bath House, 278, 280
Kaufmann, Emil, 262
Kelly, Brian, 155
Key, Sydney, 335–336
Kim Tan, 63
King, Moses, 293, 294
Klamon, Andrew, 63
Kleinman, Martin, 121
Klug, Jeffery, 57–59
Koetter, Fred, 3, 88, 97, 273, 338
Korn, Arthur, 337
Kossack, Egbert, 221, 224
Krier, Leon, 129, 248, 261–262, 271–
    281, 326, 328, 357
Krier, Robert, 129, 230, 261, 268–270

Land, Peter, 337
Laugier, Marc-Antoine, 233, 273
Lawler, Daniel, 314
Le Corbusier, 2, 14, 17, 90, 181, 184,
    194, 202, 219, 244–245, 264,
    267, 271–272, 324, 354
    La Tourette, monastery of Sainte-
    Marie de, 358
    Maisons à Redents, 208, 209
    Maisons Jaoul, 344, 355
    Plan Voisin, 187, 190, 191, 246
    St.-Dié, proposal for, 202, 204–205
    Unité d'Habitation (Marseilles),
    204–208, 210
Ledoux, Claude-Nicolas, 276, 328
Lelyveld, Amy, 314
Le Nôtre, André, 213
Leonardo da Vinci, 291, 292
Littenberg, Barbara, 129
Llewellyn-Davies, Richard, 339
London, 40–42, 173–179, 199, 238,
    326, 355
    Kingsway, 328–329

Loudon, John Claudius, 173
Lutyens, Edwin, 171, 186, 187
   Grey Walls (Gullane), 171–173
   Hyde Park Corner, proposal for,
      173–175, 176
   Piccadilly Circus, proposal for, 175,
      176

MacDonald, Kent, 314
Machado, Rodolfo, 273
Magnago Lampugnani, Vittorio, 222
Maki, Fumihiko, 305, 308
Manfredi, Michael, 37–40
Mansart, François, 355
Marinetti, Filippo Tommaso, 156
Massachusetts Institute of Technology,
   88, 324
Mather, Rick, 338
Maxwell, Robert, 343, 344
May, Ernst, 322
McBride, Rick, 338
McDonald, Arthur, 26, 30–32
McDougall, Michael, 333–334
Medici, Cosimo de', 288
Michaelis, Dominic, 340
Michelucci, Giovanni, 69, 74–75
Middleton, D. Blake, 4, 5–51
Mies van der Rohe, Ludwig, 169, 170
   Nationalgalerie (Berlin), 250
Miki, Makoto, 97
Milan, 191, 192, 324
Milwaukee, 48–51
Minneapolis, 121, 285–286, 293, 296,
   299, 327
Mitterand, François, 302, 308
Mondrian, Piet, 216, 217
Montreal
   Place Bonaventure, 293
Morris, William, 276, 328
Mortensen, Paul, 62–67
Mubarak, Suzanne, 302, 308, 311

Mumford, Lewis, 181
Munich, 3, 20, 108, 109, 208, 211
Museum of Modern Art, 87–88
Mussolini, Benito, 156, 162

Nash, John, 40
   Chester Terrace (London), 185
Nealy, Craig, 49, 51–55
New York City, 24–32, 37–40, 81, 82–
   83, 87–96, 200, 341, 344
   Chrysler Building, 200, 203
   Grand Central Station, 291–293
   Lincoln Center, 247
   Rockefeller Center, 153, 179–181,
      325
Nigg, Erwin P., 6–7
Nolli, Giambattista, 17, 127, 129

Okomoto, Rai, 49
Olmsted, Frederick Law, 49, 233, 236
Olympio, Elpidio, 97
O'Neil, Cheryl, 75–78, 155, 314
Oswald, Franz, 3, 11–14, 97

Palladio, Andrea, 296, 297
Palmore, William, 314–317
Paris, 19, 106, 107, 124, 191, 192,
   237, 246, 248, 344–345
   Louvre, 208, 211, 288, 290
   Palais Royal, 19, 210, 213, 248
Peterson, Steven, 26, 28–29, 129
Pevsner, Nikolaus, 264
Phillips, Irving, 8–10
Platt, Charles, 171
Poggi, Giuseppe, 69, 73, 234
Pope, Alexander, 281
Posener, Julius, 222
Potters, Steven, 88, 121
Poussin, Nicolas, 57, 62, 276, 281,
   282
Praz, Mario, 352

Proust, Marcel, 72, 342
Providence, Rhode Island, 43–48
Purini, Franco, 155

Reps, John, 1
Rietveld, Gerrit
    Schroeder House (Utrecht), 173, 174
Robertson, Jacquelin, 88
Rome, 4, 75–80, 124, 127–153, 155–
    164, 196–199, 248, 322, 325
    Palazzo del Quirinale, 3, 210, 212
    Sant'Agnese, 199, 200, 203
    Vatican, 288
Rossi, Aldo, 129, 249, 275
Rousseau, Jean Jacques, 266
Russell, Bertrand, 277

Saarinen, Eero, 324
St. Petersburg, 124
St.-Dié, 23
Scharoun, Hans
    Kulturforum (Berlin), 231, 234,
        240, 245–246, 247
    Siemenstadt, 322
    Staatsbibliothek (Berlin), 254
Schinkel, Karl Friedrich, 276, 280
Schmarsow, August, 220
Schumacher, Thomas, 2, 14–16, 88,
    332
Schwarting, Jon Michael, 24–27, 88
Schwerin, 22
Scott, Geoffrey, 220
Scott, M. H. Baillie, 171
Scott Brown, Denise, 168, 275
Seligmann, Werner, 97
Senney, Esteban, 260
Serlio, Sebastiano, 281
Sherwood, Roger, 3, 338
Silvetti, Jorge, 274
Simson, Otto von, 222
Sitte, Camillo, 17, 270

Slutzky, Robert, 24
Smith, William, 314
Soane, Sir John, 351, 352, 355
South Amboy, New Jersey, 14–16
Speer, Albert, 253
Stearns, Carl, 88
Stirling, James, 230, 275, 301, 305,
    314, 341–358, 360
    Sackler Museum, 296–299, 357
    Staatsgalerie (Stuttgart), 357–358
Strawbridge, Bill, 121
Stübben, J., 270

Taut, Bruno, 320, 322
Texas, 326
Todi
    Santa Maria della Consolazione, 182
Tunnard, Christopher, 337
Turin, 56–59
Turner, John, 338
Tynan, Derek, 48

UNESCO, 301, 306
Ungers, Matthias, 14, 221, 230, 260,
    270
University of Virginia, 262, 281

Valadier, Giuseppe, 127
Valk, Arthur, 24–27
Vanbrugh, Sir John, 355
Vasari, Giorgio
    Uffizi (Florence), 207–208
Venturi, Robert, 49, 129, 179, 275
Versailles, 213–215
Victoria, Queen, 238
Vigevano, 191, 193
Vittoria, Spain, 204, 205

Walker Art Center, 121, 285
Warburg Institute, 57
Warnecke, John Carl, 306, 308

Index

Watkin, David, 168, 275
Weintraub, Mark, 81, 84–86
Wells, Jerry Alan, 3, 88, 97
Wiesbaden, 18, 24, 194, 195
Wilford, Michael, 346
Williams, Terry, 338
Wittgenstein, Ludwig, 277
Wolff, Rita, 281, 283
Wordsworth, William, 352
Wren, Christopher, 199
    St. Paul's, 355–356
    St. Paul's Churchyard, proposal for,
        177–178
Wright, Frank Lloyd, 171, 220, 349

Yale University, 199, 201

Zagari, Franco, 310
Zurich, 11–14